GOD,
He Don't
Live In No *Box*

By

JACK WESTMORELAND

PublishAmerica
Baltimore

First printing

ISBN: 1-59129-736-2
PUBLISHED BY PUBLISHAMERICA BOOK PUBLISHERS
www.publishamerica.com
Baltimore

Printed in the United States of America

Dedicated to

Helen

Read, "The Unity of God"

ACKNOWLEDGMENTS

I proudly, gladly and humbly acknowledge Mary Cooley, a gentle sweet person, who is way above remarkable, actually read, deciphered, and survived my left-handed writings. This work was written with pen and paper. Amazing. You can easily imagine the torment Mary (cheerfully) endured. I also greatly benefited from her judgment, advice, and patience.

To my wife, Helen, who diligently proofread every word. Often times, it is great to have a "Martha" in the family.

Thanks be unto God for the fond remembrances of: The "Big Three" spiritual influences in my life: My Grandmother, Mother and "Pop."

With multi and individual appreciation to those living and *in Heaven*: the many advisors, supporters, helpers, friends, readers, role models, critiquers, family and dear ones listed below, in no particular order, except as they came to me, forever etched with lasting appreciation and memory in the aging lobes of my mind, and wherein they are fondly filed.

Gary Fogus, Jayme Douglas, Lauren Long, Alek Harwell, Timmy Distell, Steve Hallford, Renee Douglas, Doris Hallford, Bob and Helen, Jimmy and Deena, Charles and Carol, Howard and Betsy, Ann and Dale and Doris "Howard", Drew Case, Walt Peterson, Christie Distell, Tiffany Alverson, Pam Browning, Angelia Cline, Sissy Spann and Charlie, Joanne and Eva Merck, Stephanie and Laverne, Katherine and Watson, Steve and Ginger, Judy Preuter, Les Jacobs, Tony Oxley, Jack Josey, Hal Gaymon, Robert Bob Pierce, J. H. Shelley. And Dick Puffer.

Pastors Dora and Ben Gafford, Gwen and Rev. Darryl Bogatay, Gloria and Rev. Bill Bouknight, Peny and Gale Roller

Uncles: *Dwight, Broughton, Clyde, Ondie, Lloyd, Thomas* and *Hoyt*. Special Teachers: *Miss Norma, Miss Sara, Miss McBath,* Miss Patterson, *Mrs. Dewolf, Mrs. Eleanor Farmer,* Mrs. Barnett, Dr. Barnett, Dr. Aiken, *Dr. Fuller*

Finally, a listing of unique individuals, with *italics* indicating the ultimate "promotion":

Glenda and the late *Paul Anderson,* The late *Dr. James Allen*, the Beloved, Ruth and the late *William "Nick" Nickelson,* Evelyn and the late *Rev. Ray Rumsey,* Dottie and the late *Rev. Harry Poland,* Wanda and *Bernice Julian Ollis,* Betty Wiggins and the late *Joe Wiggins*, and *Rex Parrott, a*nd to, per chance, any dear ones that were unintentionally omitted, let us use these omissions for *benefit,* thus allowing these dear ones an opportunity to practice the forgiveness our Lord taught us and which I certainly do not deserve.

And finally, a most dear and important wonderful friend and a great agent, **Brenda Bailey,** who allowed the Lord to use her to "answer" a prayer, that I had prayed approximately 2784 times, thus allowing "God, He Don't Live In No Box" to be published.

What a magnificent list of people the Lord has placed across my path.

FROM THE AUTHOR

Strange, but I never thought of myself as an "author." I just try to write sort of like I talk; and that, even I know, is not necessarily *good*. Nonetheless, the title of this book "God, He Don't Live In No Box" was my own clever (??) idea of a marketing strategy to entice the hurried and haggard browser-shopper to pick the book up (out of forty dozen attractive interesting choices) and buy it because "something" caught their eye and this: For your information, the original title is "The Many, Many, Names, Titles and Attributes of Our Glorious and Wonderful Lord and Savior Jesus Christ, The Holy and Only Begotten Son of the Almighty God, Creator and Majesty, who reigns now and forever more, and who is Holy, Holy, Holy, but loved us enough to become a dying lamb serves us as a gentle shepherd and feed us and care for us and love us..." (I'm just kidding). But the titles and names go on and on, world without end and even the world itself (said John) could not contain the books if... But, to my utter amazement, I (the author) learned that this title, "God, He Don't Live in No Box" was indeed THE title that really described the messages God was delivering in this book.

Fact is: We need all of these "names" (and I've collected over ten hundred) to even begin to begin to try and describe "Him" the Lord of All.

In case you are interested, my favorite is **"Jesus."**

As you might suspect, my agent, editor, publisher and several others thought the title could perhaps be a mite long...and suggested I shorten it, or else! I really and genuinely like the revised title, "God, He Don't Live In No Box" because it certainly is a "neat" and appropriate way of describing what all of these multi-names and titles are showing us, i.e. believers and non-believers. Often this message is relayed in subtle ways, or, not at all, and just left to the Holy Spirit to handle the "unsaid" and beyond. After and only after, you finish reading this book, I have a strong feeling you will agree with this point. And you will also hopefully see where we all have been "guilty" of wanting to put God in a box, or worse yet, put God in our box.

And now, the long hours and wonderful agony of writing this book are over and it is time to type "The End." Only it is not The End! For with this book, goes my sincere and continuing prayers that the messages relayed herein, will spread, warm, illuminate, illustrate and activate the love of God and how very real He can be to us all, if we let Him out of the Box and into our hearts and lives. *Now and beyond forever.*

Love & Prayers,
Jack

ABOUT THE BOOK

What a strange feeling to write this "preface" to my book, or perhaps it is a "forward." Frankly, I don't know the difference. What I will try to do is tell you how this book came into "being" and then how it evolved by steps until finally being published. I'll also try to describe some of the "hows" and "whys" and "when's" and "whatever's." As I begin this process, I come to a long *pause* and wonder if very many people actually ever read these early sections of any book??

Don't worry if you happen to <u>not</u> read this (bit of humor), for some of this history is mentioned in a few of the devotional "chapters," e.g., Alpha to Omega, etc.

This book actually has a "non-beginning" of sorts because I did <u>not</u> plan, nor think of a book. About 20 years ago when I was in the midst of a very demanding job in the corporate world (a job which I enjoyed very much) as Director of Human Resources, the hours, demands and stress were very high. (I once told the Chief of our company that I had <u>the</u> toughest job of any one in the company, to my dismay he heartily agreed and sympathized with me). The stress was high. Perhaps this is the source of another book. Nonetheless...

Nonetheless, after one day at work that was especially stressful having to review a gruesome autopsy report with a family about the tragic death of their husband and father, an event which I had also witnessed the "aftermath." Or having to interrupt a beautiful young wife and mother, happily and busily at work in her flower garden on a lovely spring morning, and break the unbelievable news she was now a widow; but desperately trying to keep my own composure and search for kind and gentle words to non-describe the harshness and ugliness of an accidental death, or, sitting across my desk from a long-term 44 year employee, who had to be "let-go." A nicer word than "terminated" but actually meant he was being fired in the midst of a recession because in a rare burst of anger he had hit another employee, hard in the face. Certain things are unpardonable sins in the workplace world. At times I cried with the man, really empathized and "let-him-go." And sometimes, what sounds like "easy stuff" could break your heart and can bring extreme stress having to communicate to a long, long term, loyal, dedicated grandfather-employee, that you are unable to fulfill his long time dream of having his grandson join the company working as he had done and where he had worked and sweated for 49 years; and for the feeble reason that this young man had spent 6 years on a four year degree, barely a 2.0 grade point average and majored in "partying and frivolity..." and we, a huge corporation, just didn't have a need for a "sociology" major. The loving grandfather simply did not understand and I, became the bad guy. That's what I got paid for.

Now, the evening of the day of the gruesome "autopsy death," and I was even honored, (and humbled) to be asked to speak at the employee's funeral. Finally at bedtime, how do I possibly sleep after what I'd seen and experienced...and still can "see."

Answer: A very simple plan: We pray and ask for a night of sound sleep. And He gives it.

But then there are those other times when I would awaken at 3:00 a.m. and not be able to get back to sleep. So I would use the time to pray. And pray and pray. But no sleep. Now; finally cometh the non-beginning of this book. I began (silently, of course) to *think* of names of my Lord, e.g., Shepherd, Prince of Peace, Messiah, Christ, Lord, Savior and on and on. This little simple exercise was marvelous, effective, enjoyable, and did-not-disturb my wife. When I fell asleep (sooner or later) it did not matter. Either way I had used the time not just let it use me, and I did not miss the sleep. The technique was

> simple
> practical
> worthwhile
> enjoyable
> beneficial, and
> spiritual

These are bulletized for your benefit because these became some of **my major objectives** when I began to write the first draft.

Unfortunately, (but who really cares and what does it matter) I never kept a journal. After weeks or months, and I reckon, being a slow learner I had the brilliant idea of putting them in alphabetical order, i.e. Abba, Almighty, Author, Bread of Life, Master, Teacher,

9

and all the way to Omega or Z, to My Zeal.

Then, you guessed it. There got to be so many that I needed to write them on a lined pad. That was evolutionary step three. (Note use of non-Biblical term).

Step number four: One Sunday morning after being asked to sub for a Sunday School Class, the Ladies Class comprised of dear saints, I collected a list in alphabetical order of 40 names and titles. I tried to keep it at "26" but *failed*! The "List was a BIG hit and the summary was obvious and effective. These women had never seen or thought of the Lord in this particular way. My ending sentence which mirrored their thoughts and meshed with our combined spirits, unctioned by the Spirit, was something to the affect that we needed all these 40 names and titles, **and many, many more** to even begin to describe our Wonderful, Amazing Lord. It was on this day, I had the idea of a Daily Devotional of Names and Titles of Our Lord. So the collection process continued. Without having to try very hard, I gathered more "names." Today the list has expanded and includes "Attributes" so that I have over 1,000 on my list and still increasing. Thus, the working title became "The Many Names, Titles And Attributes Of Our Wonderful Lord."

For a long time I have used and loved Devotional books. Oswald Chambers, in my opinion, is the dean and granddaddy of this type of publication. And I had no thought that I could ever, ever match this "Master" of Devotionals. I haven't even tried. (After all, I am not stupid, per se.)

The only possible "negative" I have on most devotions is that the format and style seem to be "basically the same" and you usually know about what to expect each morning when you turn the page to begin your devotional reading. **But I quickly point out that there isabsolutely nothing wrong with this.**

My boss once called me a "maverick." I let my chest swell almost sinfully. Then, I learned he did not necessarily mean it the way my ego intended. My literary philosophy is that "if you are not really good, or great, then you need to be different to a point. Certainly, I do not consider myself good or great so I needed to use a different approach.

My favorite Chinese proverb is "what are the right answers?"

Early on, I knew that the book should be different, easy, casual, so that there was a natural feeling and a constant blending of thoughts and inputs of the Holy Spirit. This meant that the Holy Spirit had to be **first, in control and last**. In my humble faulty opinion, I have really tried to do this. I'll give an example of why I can make this statement. Recently, when I had a need to re-read some devotional I wrote two years ago, I began to weep and was reading touching material that felt heavenly foreign to me, as though I had absolutely nothing to do with the writing of what I had just read. Can you imagine the awe and the blessing and the humbling of such a private, personal, spiritual moment? And the excitement of deeply wanting to share what God and His Holy Spirit had done and was about to do with these devotionals. If I had to write the "sum total" of this in one sentence, It would be: *I want Jesus to be real to others as He is real to me.*

At some point in reading this book, you will begin to see others (and yourself) which is exactly what happened to me–and then you will understand **why** the "new" title, "God, He Don't Live In No Box" is actually a very suitable and fitting title.

Finally, the Lord has been very real to me in writing this book. May each and every reader have the same experience and feel closeness from A to Z.

A FRIEND OF SINNERS
(NO MATTER WHAT THEY'VE DONE)

I occasionally hear remarks from people who wonder if God has a sense of humor. There are many debates and opinions on this subject. I use to wonder about it myself. Then, when I was fifty years old the answer came. At least I think it came???

In fact, I was exactly "fifty." My birthday. It was early morning and I awoke feeling great. I sat down with my Bible and began to meditate. There was not a tinge of a complex about being "fifty years old." To be candid, I had crossed that psychological hurdle twenty years earlier when I reluctantly became 30. Another birthday, the big "four-Oh" milestone, didn't even faze me.

Now, proudly I was fifty, and alone with God. Talking to myself (some people call it meditating) I prefer to call it "talking." Feeling alive and 200 percent "charged," I was thankful to be healthy and full of vigor. I must confess that ordinarily I am usually not a morning person. My wife would insert "*definitely*" on that statement.

The Lord has really blessed me and I then recalled five times in those fifty years that I had almost been killed in various types of accidents. (1) a head-on collision of two cars meeting at 60 mph; (2) a 1939 Ford spinning two 360 degrees out of control that rapidly rotated between a huge oak tree inches from the front bumper and one-half second later a gasoline pump inches from the front bumper; (3) a falling helicopter with a very quiet engine; and (4) a decayed 18 foot treetop falling from a tall pine tree, scraping my right shoulder and missing my head by a few inches, (An inch may be as good as a mile but I would have preferred a mile.) and (5) being rammed from behind by a hydroplaning automobile as I sat helplessly in stilled traffic.

So after that quick review with the Lord, I began to rejoice and be glad. My cup was running over at the brim. How wonderful to be 50 years old! In fact, I recall saying to the Lord, "Wow, that's half a century Lord there really needs to be   some sort of celebration, with a marching band of approximately 76 trombones and at least a few brass cymbals clanging.

Beginning to open my Bible (and I do recall, that, quite

appropriately, I was using the Living Bible on this particular momentous occasion), I meekly, or not so meekly, suggested to the Lord, that in honor of my half-century accomplishments (most of the years spent attending church twice on Sunday and almost every Wednesday night for Prayer Meeting and too numerous to count, Revival Meetings), perhaps, if I might be presumptuous (holy boldness), that the Lord would graciously allow the Holy Book to divinely fall open to an appropriate page and the very first verse my eyes fell upon, amidst all the holy scriptures, would be divinely placed in order to pay personal homage to this wonderful occasion of my 50th birthday. And as I let the blessed pages of Holy writ fall gently apart, my eyes did behold verse five of Psalm 69, i.e. "Oh God, you know so well how stupid I am, and you know all my sins."

POSTSCRIPT: This incident somewhat reminded me of the joke about the preacher who desperately needed to hear from God about an important matter he was facing, so he went through the exercise of allowing his Bible to randomly fall open as though speaking, directly to his question. But not liking the first answer "Judas went and hung himself." He tried again and next read, "go thou and do likewise." As to my own experience, I never did really decide why this happened to me and after a lot of thought was able to boil it down to three possibilities:

1.   It was just a statistical probability of "coincidence," or
2.   God really does have a sense of humor, or
3.   God was trying to tell me something!

I think I prefer either one of the first two answers. Nevertheless, I went back to reading the good old King James Version, albeit a mite more difficult to understand. Amen.

A FRIEND
(WE NEED)

Jesus, if you want him to be, meets all the criteria for being a friend, a very good friend. What do you look for when you describe a good friend?

One that is there when you need him/her.
One that cares.
One that listens.
One that can forgive (when necessary) and keep on being a friend.
One that is gentle; and one that occasionally can be "tough" when called for.
One that sets an example for you (and others).
One that is your role model.
One you like and love.
One you hold in high respect and high regard.
Someone that you feel "close" to, even when he might be far away.
Someone that is reachable.
One that you can talk to at anytime.
Someone that you have rapport with.
Someone that has never asked you to do anything they haven't done.
One that you know where they stand on important (and minor) issues.
Someone that will sacrifice for you.
Someone that seems to be able to read your mind, i.e., knows your thoughts from afar.
Someone that has proved himself/herself (without being asked).
Someone that is never too busy for you.
Someone that you feel loves you back and seems to want your love.
Someone very hard to find. One that gives unconditional love. WOW!

Someone that is dependable, available, genuine, sincere, consistent, and any other nice words you can include.

"No one ever cared for me like Jesus"

A PERSONAL FRIEND
(NO MATTER WHAT)

To me one of the absolute most wonderful things about my "faith" is that I have a personal relationship with my Lord. (Note the personal pronouns in this one sentence.) There are numerous other benefits that could be listed, i.e.

the value of an eternal (forever) relationship. Otherwise, when I die   *that's it!* As it is I have a strong blessed assurance that there is indeed something other than and beyond this earthly life.

the joy and satisfaction I have day-by-day just in knowing Jesus. This is a "current" useable now readily accessible benefit.

A "resource" (for lack of a better word) that I have at my instant fingertips when I need help, comfort, guidance, and wisdom. This "resource" is suddenly and always with me, virtually instantaneous, a millisecond away by starting to call, *or even think* the name of Jesus.

Put another way, The Holy Spirit, which Jesus sent to me (note personal attention and application) when He went away. It's impossible to find a better name than "Comforter," And while I can't see the Comforter, I really don't need to. This Holy Spirit *envelops* me outside inward **and** inside outward. What a presence!

A confidence factor I have because of the strength and assurance He provides. Otherwise, I would be a limp wimp, totally useless and incompetent, and most miserable. Instead, I can do all things and His   joy is my strength.

Now back to my initial point, which is also the most significant, is that the mighty God, awesome Creator and Holy, Holy, Holy Divine Being is <u>personal</u> to me. Where can I go to flee from Him, (even if I wanted to) because He is always with me? In fact, one of the last things He said on this earth, "I am with you always" continues to this very day to be preciously true.

When I sit in a church surrounded by others in *corporate worship*, which I certainly need and enjoy, the personal contact and communion

17

I have with him is still there. When I awake all alone in the middle of the night, He is with me so very close. When I am occupied with family or business associates and engrossed in activities and cares of this life, and, then I need to escape to even a few moments of solitude. We are once again in direct, personal communion. My Lord has many, many names and titles and attributes, but what a friend! What a Friend!

A TENDER GOD
(A SOFT TOUCH OF LOVE)

The following is a list of **hard** questions you may need to ask yourself. These are not meant for personal enjoyment.

Does God ever seem far away?
Do you feel the distance between you and God widening?
Has the excitement you once felt diminished?
Has the Love of God and Love for God lessened in intensity?
Do you ever feel the Bible is "old stuff"?
Has your prayer life faltered, until you feel a coolness, from God when you begin Our Father ?
When you awaken in the middle of the night is His presence near? (As it once was.)
Do you perhaps wonder if God measures your spiritual temperature and thinks   something is wrong?
Do you ever wonder if the living waters flowing out of you are becoming stagnant?
Do you ever remember what the Lord said he would do with "lukewarm" followers?
Would you think that perhaps you are spending less time reading your Bible?

Obvious fact: God has not moved. Nor is He less interested in *you* or less interested in your spiritual welfare. As far as the middle-of-the-night question, "I am with you always" still applies. The prayer time and Bible reading time questions are easy to measure and assign a quantified, numerical specific number. To re-coin a phrase: the answer was as obvious as the pronounced nose on my face. And I really did not enjoy the "lukewarm" and "stagnant water" questions.

Now, at this point, it would seem to be the appropriate place to include a nice (and obvious) list of suggestions for improvement; corrective action plans. Right? I would *bet* ("bet" is just a figure-of-speech term) that we could each develop a nice long impressive list of things we need to do, or improvements we need to make. Right?

But, what do you say: How about, if we put this off until later, maybe tomorrow, or one day next week. Right?

Wrong!

P.S.   For some reason, lately a familiar painting that I've seen all my life keeps coming to mind. You know. The one, where Jesus is standing *outside* at the door, knocking.

Do I have to keep letting him in?

A WONDERFUL GOD
(AND HE "BELONGS" TO US)

Suppose we played a mental-spiritual "game" and listed the ten most important biblical sections in the Bible: **surely** John 14:15-20 would have to be one of the highly select scriptures. For in this short "gold mine" of approximately 100 words, Jesus outlines the supreme correlation between divine love and obedience, announces the arrival of His "replacement," purpose, duration and operatives of the Holy Spirit, His own departure from the earth, assurances, His post-resurrection, promises; *unions* between Jesus and God and Jesus and his followers and Eternal Life. Wow! What an encompassing listing!!!

It may be difficult to find as many vital topics mentioned in so few verses of scripture. This "treasure" may be due to the concise method John uses in penning these final teachings of Jesus, or it is possible that these verses are verbatim for after all time was running out for Him and these very crucial subjects needed to be covered. Perhaps, they had been taught/discussed before. If so, their importance required one final review.

How many of us have spent what we knew were the *final hours* with a close relative, or friend, knowing that certain thoughts needed to be expressed. Maybe they did not *need* to be expressed but you wanted to be able to communicate *deep* thoughts of love or appreciation or admiration or thanks (especially THANKS?) one final time, well knowing you would carry the memory to your own death.

I was fortunate "fortunate" is not the most appropriate wor d: I was BLESSED, BLESSED, BLESSED to have had such an opportunity ("Gift" is a more accurate word). I had the "gift" presented to me, in a very private, quiet and personal way. Fortunately, I recognized "it" at the moment the gift was presented. It was a *divine* moment and the Holy Spirit spoke to me without words per se; but I "heard" the sentence, every syllable of the twelve word sentence, including the comforting question mark at the end of the unspoken statement: "Jack, is there anything else you need to tell your Mother?"

I only had need to carefully ponder for a few pensive, precious moments before I gave my final answer:

"No Lord, nothing else."

ABUNDANT WEALTH
"YOU CAN NEVER USE IT UP"

Having somewhat of a marketing background and having once been told that I was creative (which I've always remembered), I enjoy trying to think out-of-the-box which means I try to think of something no one else has "thunk" which is past tense for "thinked." Who knows, perhaps someday I will succeed. One of my bosses (and I've had many) once told me, "you are a maverick" and my chest immediately swelled with pride (the kind that goeth before a great fall) and sure enough, when he saw my chest continuing to swell, he explained that being called a "maverick" was not necessarily a compliment. So I immediately fell back into my humble mode and stayed humble for nigh onto thirty minutes.

After providing the aforementioned background, I enjoy trying to think up new and different ways, or at least a new *slant* on ordinary things, like for example: morning devotions. Here are some examples within an example: instead of reading the Bible, choose some of your favorite selections from the Bible and hand write them (hand print is even better). Another thought: hand print your favorite top seven selections. This simple but highly effective technique forces you to slow your thought process down. Hence, you glean more from the scriptures.

The list goes on: If you really want to impress your friends (like for example) at a church social, Sunday School class party, a family reunion or high school class reunion, stand up and recite from memory the first chapter of I Chronicles, verses 1   54. I can promise and guarantee you very few things in life will impress a group as hearing you recite from memory (Note, no notes or peeking at the Book.) a whole bunch of "begats." They will talk about you for days, maybe weeks.

Obviously, this is an attention-getting technique but it is a great way of warming a group or class up and effectively sets the stage for you to make a number of serious comments about the word of God, weave in your testimony or establish any number of spiritual points.

Now here is another "jewel." And with this one, it is "open book," so relax and do it. Go through the entire Bible, quick scanning and then hand print **one** favorite verse from each of the sixty-six books. This collection then becomes *your own* "sixty-six gems" or you can publish it as "Sam's Favorite "Nuggets from God's Holy Word." Only remember insert your own name instead of Sam's, since that was just an example within an example. Besides, you do not want "Sam" to get the credit for something you did.

Another promise I can absolutely guarantee: Immediately after your "demise" (sounds "nicer" doesn't it), than die or death, your children and grandchildren and many others will want their own copy of "Sam's Favorite Sixty-Six, et al." Their fever will cool down as you grow colder, but the very thought of your offspring "fighting over your religious book" kind of warms your heart and makes the goose bumps start moving around like a bunch of bumper cars at a carnival. Does it not?

To make it easy, I'll list a few of my picks from my own sixty-six, elsewhere in this book. After a bit of jesting, I can assure you that the process of "finding" your own sixty-six will be rewarding and worthwhile in numerous ways. And besides, the book of Jude is a piece of cake. Plus, Obadiah is not so tough, either. You will be pleasantly surprised at the "gems" you find in some of the lesser-used books. In almost each of the 66 books of the Bible you can find, what I term a *classic verse*. Most likely, it is one you've heard before, oft repeated, impactful ("meaty") content that really hits home. Or, perhaps it is just *one* that you happen to like because it grabs your fancy or hits home with you. That's what matters. And don't ever sell God short. He can spiritually individualize a phrase that speaks universally to everyone or speaks specifically (privately) to you. If you've never done a study like this before, you are in for a delightful time.

I will personally guarantee the "worthwhileness" of doing this exercise. Better still, God has already guaranteed it.

II Peter 3:8	**III John 1:11**
I John 4:7	**Jude 24-25**
II John 1:8	**Obadiah 1:4**

ADVOCATE
(OUR PERSONAL DEFENDER)

It was one of those middle-of-the-night wake-up experiences. We all have them. Couldn't go back to sleep. So I thought I used the time to pray. Something I've done many times. Quite successfully, I might proudly add. Only this time I could not get the prayer "started."

Middle-of-the-night thoughts, slow to form at first, then moved faster by fear for whatever the reason, I could not imagine that I could suddenly, so easily and so casually "talk" to God. What right did I have? How dare I be so casual and so bold to enter into the presence of the Holy Lord God of the Universe?

It didn't seem to matter that I, a seasoned Christian of many years most certainly someone who had prayed hundreds of times before in all type of conditions and circumstances, including many times in the middle of dark nights and now I couldn't get my prayer started. Had I lost my senses or worse yet, had I lost my cherished and close relationship with God?

By now I was wide-awake and shocked by my predicament. I began to review the basics. Suddenly the stark truth smote me. No, I wasn't losing "it" after all. In fact, my reasoning wasn't really that far afield. I didn't have any right certainly none that I had earned to enter before God's Holy Presence, but, because of Jesus and what he had done, and because he was my Advocate, I could indeed come into the Holy of Holies, and it was as simple and straight–even easy to do so, because God's Son, Jesus, had become my personal advocate.

What an amazing statement to summarize such power and privilege. How beautiful the simplicity of the methodology and how awesome the reality of it all.

AGAPE LOVE
(UNCONDITIONAL LOVE)

We don't understand this subject. We humans, mortal, people, sinners, whatever we are called, don't really understand Agape Love. In fact, we do well if we just grasp temporarily the concept of Agape. Maybe we weren't meant to *understand* it. It is hard to define. Agape Love is much like a foreign language to us. Actually, it is indeed *foreign*, i.e. heavenly and/or divine, versus earthly/human.

Many times I have read the definition and expository explanations. To best describe my own quandary with Agape, I feel like I do understand it, while I'm reading the definition. But soon, and maybe it's the "tares and cares" of my busy life that choke out the clarity, confusion sets in; that is the reason I need to start the process all over again–and wrestle with the concept all over again.

Any study of Agape Love will most certainly use the terms sacrificial love, unselfish love. Dr. Kenneth S. Wurst, as quoted in George Sweeting's, "Love Is The Greatest" states that "Agape Love has the idea of *prizing*   and that it is the noblest word for love in the Greek language." (italics mine)

Moody Press 1974 Page 27

AGONIZING SAVIOR
(HORROR BEYOND DESCRIPTION)

The man was suffering. Deep suffering and horror beyond description. Even though he was beginning to sink into unconsciousness, the pain was so severe that it would bring him back to the reality he sought to escape: that he was dying. And that he had only a few minutes left to live. Oh, how he wanted to escape from the pain. At times the brief respite of unconsciousness seemed to offer the only way out. But then, he couldn't breathe. At least he could exhale. Then a panic fear would take over. For seconds, the "fear" was actually worse than the excruciating pain. He had to breathe. And the only way he could exhale was to shift his weight away from his arms and shoulders onto his feet in order to lift the weight from the diaphragm so he could breathe out one more time. But then the unbearable cycle of pain began all over again.

In spite of the never-ending cycle of pain, his thoughts could be strangely clear. And he knew his mother was just a short distance away, having to witness the horror of his suffering. This hurt him almost as much as the physical pain. He knew that in spite of the hurt and the thirst he still had a last detail to handle. What was he to do? Then he saw John, beloved John, standing nearby. Just a little earlier all of the others had deserted him. But there stood his beloved John. He understood the other disciples' actions and had already forgiven them. But it still hurt!

With all the final effort he could muster, and it meant shifting the weight again in order to have the air to speak, using only the fewest of words in a seared throat, looking briefly into the eyes of his mother and then at John, he gave each of them to the other with two short sentences that conveyed all that needed to be said.

Jesus never, never, forgets a detail. But quite often, uses one of his followers. I am hit with the thought; am I going to be standing *where* I should be *when* the Lord needs me??

Note: Many of my own thoughts (especially in the first paragraph were certainly influenced by my reading Jim Bishop's "The Day Christ Died." It should be required reading for *every* Christian. And it sure wouldn't do any harm if sinners read it also.

ALL POWER
(BEYONDEST AWESOME)

In one of the very best recorded sentences that Jesus ever spoke, He makes a very concise statement that in many ways says it all. **"All power (authority) has been given to me in Heaven and on earth… and lo, I am with you always, even to the end of the age."** Matthew 28: 18b, 20b

The "red-lettered" words of Jesus are always precious. They are beyond value. I always wish he had said more, elaborated, expanded, given more examples, more details, etc. etc. Jesus did not need to. Verbosity was not necessary. For each and every word he spoke was *weighty* and *complete*. "Every word of God is pure (flawless) like silver refined in a furnace, purified, seven times." So when Jesus said, "*all* power is given unto me in Heaven and earth." There is justification for italicizing the word "*all…*"

This all-encompassing statement, I think, is one of the most blessed and wonderful aspects of our Lord and God. As written earlier, we need **all** these names and titles and attributes to even *begin* to describe Him. Personally, I became spiritually and intellectually and empirically frustrated in my own limitations in finding the right (exact) word so that it expresses both content and intensity, i.e. quality and quantity, of the thought that seems to be *begging* for expression. For after all, in almost every case the point I am constantly trying to make is always at the extreme point of "beyondest."

The word "beyondest" is a case in point. I don't think it is in the dictionary. At least I've never seen, nor heard it. I was at a helpless futile point in trying to express the splendor and power and might and glory and wonderment of God's power. I was gloriously stuck in the midst of doing the impossible of trying to describe *our* God, who in the middle of the Divine rapids became <u>my</u> God. I was struggling and lost somewhere in the fringes of heavenly bewilderment reaching to the extreme right of the plus side of an insufficient scale, when I gladly surrendered to allowing "beyondest" to suffice for the moment. Somewhere in the midst of the exhaustive turmoil of trying to do the impossible to describe **my** God and **our** God because He neither has

28

nor knows of impossibilities. So all I am left to do in such moments-of-thought is to say "AMEN."

EXERCISE: As you read this book and you too sense my many "failures" at finding the "right" word, allow yourself, with the Spirit's individualized and personally unique assistance to **you** to discover the word, or words, that better fit. And one thing I am sure of, there are many!

ADDENDUM: Early on in writing this book, I often became frustrated at myself because of the redundancy, as I saw myself using one word over and over again. I frequently used the noun-adjective "awesome" in trying to describe God and/or one of His many traits, characteristics, names, titles etc. For most of the years of my lifetime the word "awesome" had been infrequently used (properly, so I thought) to preface extraordinary people, places and things. Then the teenage population "stole" it and began to describe hamburgers, hot cars, weird hair colors and hair styles, rock stars, ankle bracelets and a zillion other "awesome" weirdoes, fads and stupid things and happenings. Then, without regard for whatever and in my own desperation search, I began to *take back* the word and put it back in its proper place, i.e. in union with God, who is after all, the first and the last Awesome Being and He certainly is Awesome and does awesome things, in awesome ways, on a routine basis. In fact, think about it! He is "Beyondest Awesome."

AMEN AND AMEN!

THE ALL TIME "DONOR"
(AT A PLACE CALLED THE SKULL)

Visiting a church while on an out-of-town trip, the choir and congregation sang a selection of hymns with a common theme, i.e. the blood of Jesus. A lot of memories were stirred, since my oldest sister and I learned these songs many years ago from our grandmother who taught them to us as she played her old-fashion pump organ and we absorbed words and tunes that were never to be erased. "There Is Power In The Blood;" "Nothing But The Blood Of Jesus" and "Are You Washed In The Blood." And even though they didn't sing it that Sunday morning, "The Blood Has Never Lost Its Power" would have been appropriate.

I further remembered some "theology" my Mother taught us about the "blood of Jesus." She explained that there was more than enough *power* in one drop of our Savior's blood, even one tiny drop, to supply our greatest need. She strongly felt that in times of our dire needs we should "plead the blood of Jesus." I was not specifically taught this as a rigid policy but I grew up *reserving* that phrase for my most *desperate* needs. I never felt the necessity to keep a record of answered versus unanswered prayers, but my faith did not need convincing on this particular point in my Mother's biblically based depression days theology.

That morning as we sang these old familiar hymns from long ago, our words and music became more than sprightly melodies and inspiring moments. Only God knew all that was felt in these acts of worship by the varying individuals. Included, I am sure was praise for what our Lord had done, was doing and would do. Thanksgiving and pleas and acknowledgment and joys and cries were intermingled in praise and prayer of both individual and group expressions. Gloriously, God heard them all. Above all, His love and presence were experienced and reassured by the Holy Spirit.

Thanks be unto God for Mothers and Grandmothers (and Fathers and Grandpas), who taught and influenced us by word and by example, reinforcing our faith in Jesus who gave His blood to each and everyone (whomsoever). Thus, Jesus is indeed the ALL-TIME DONOR of divine blood for all of humanities' needs.

Then, now and forever! AMEN.

ADDENDUM: Driving away from church that day, I thought back to several years ago when there was considerable discussion underway by some of the more progressive (ugh) denominations that wanted to modernize (ugh, ugh) their church hymnals so as to eliminate, delete and obliterate any references to **blood.** My grandfather would reply (after he stops "turning") that such stupidity would be identical to saying, "let's have toast for breakfast, but not use any bread." The modernist viewpoint was that all the references to "blood" were in poor taste and too *gruesome* for today's culture. Well, talk about "gruesome," how gruesome do they think it was for Jesus to die on a cross but only after He had suffered intense agony and pain and moaned and cried and thirsted and writhed and gasped for breath and cramped and bled, and smothered and sweated and bled, until Indeed it was gruesome when blood and tears flowed mingled down. "What a paradox and what a graphic way to illustrate Divine Love. That is what it took for Jesus to pay the price and sacrifice His life and give all His blood.

ALPHA TO OMEGA
(A TO Z)

You may find this interesting, strange and even a bit amusing. On any number of occasions, I have tried, without success, to condense these many, many "names" of the Lord to the logical summary of twenty-six. The obvious reason being that there are twenty-six (26) letters in our English alphabet. On every occasion I have "failed" and used more than the legal limit.

Over a period of time, I have collected around one thousand names, titles, attributes, etc. This "gathering process" has in and of itself been a tremendous personal blessing to me. I recommend that everyone (even atheist) do the same thing. Ignore my list and file it away. Then, do your own "gathering."

The first time I needed to condense the list to "26" was for a Sunday school class that I was preparing to teach. Twenty-six would be enough and would illustrate the point I wanted to make. But I "failed" and entered the class with a list of "forty." No one criticized me for this failure, as you can easily understand.

My best ever attempt is shown below and appears on twenty-six lines. But note the clever way I have used to *almost* make it.

Almighty God
Blessed One, Bread of Life
Christ, Counselor and Comforter
Divine of All
Everlasting God
Faithful Father
Gracious God of Grace
Holy, Holy, Holy One
I Am   Immanuel
Jesus the Christ
King of Kings
Lord of Lords
Messiah and Master
Never Failing God
Only Begotten Son of God

Prince of Peace
Quickner/Quietner
Risen Resurrected Redeemer
Shepherd and Savior
Truth, The
Unity Three-In-One
Vine, The Victory
Way, The
X Christ of the Cross
Yoke of Christ
Zeal   My Zeal K   ing of Zion

Here are some practical, down-to-earth, common sense uses for this listing. Note that this is a partial listing, which means that **you** can forevermore add to the way for using these names for your own spiritual development and edification. You do not have to memorize the list. You only need to become somewhat familiar with it, and the format itself will aid you in capturing and recalling the names, once this initial easy step is done.

1. You will never again have to be bored.
2. You will have at your "beck and call" a convenient mode for entering into worship and or prayer.
3. You will have one of the most perfect and natural ways of entering into a peaceful night's sleep. Recite the names until zzzzzz
4. You will have an ideal spiritual-mental method for better utilizing your idle time, e.g., driving down the interstate, waiting in a doctor's office, or "stewing" in stalled traffic.
5. You can choose any name or attribute on the list and then customize how God has blessed you in that specific area.
6. You can choose some area of your spiritual life that needs development or strengthening and then use attributes of our Lord to gain improvements. Example: problem with depression, fear, need for peace.

7. Preface each "name" on the listing with "you are **my** Almighty God and you have always been there for me; you are my Bread of Life and I ask for forgiveness for all the times I have taken you for granted; you are King of Kings and my Lord of Lords and I gladly acknowledge you now, as my King of Kings and my Lord of Lords; you are my Vine and I desperately need and want to be attached to you

Lord, I am a lowly branch and I need to be attached to you; I can only get the nourishment I need from you and you alone; Lord, you are the way, the one and only way, and I want no other way. You, Lord are the way I   live move and have my being in You!

PRAYER: Precious Lord Jesus, you are my personal "Alpha" and "Omega," my A to Z. You are all and everything in the middle, to the very end. I have no other source; I need no other Source. In this busy life I live, may I never, never, forget you for I am blessed to know that you will never forget me. You have promised that you will be with me always. And when I come to the end of my rope, or even to the end of my life, my Omega will be there. **Amen.**

ALPHA, OMEGA AND BETWEEN
(ALL ENCOMPASSING)

For me it began slowly, with no forethought or plans or objectives or goals in mind. It began in the middle of a dark night, somewhere between 3 or 4 a.m., when I could not get back to sleep after a long stressful day in the non-ending mire of serving another day's sentence in the corporate world. And the punishment of non-sleep only served to remind me that the next day's sentence was only four quickly vanishing hours away.

I had already counted a massive number of sheep, gray sheep, that jumped one by one, silently and endlessly, one after the other, one by one, over a monotonous fence, barely high enough to provide only boredom fatigue. None hit the top rail. They jumped endlessly and effortlessly. Where they went after the jump, no one knew or cared. Where they came from wasn't a concern. All that was known was that there was a non-ending number waiting to jump and add to the count that went nowhere. But sleep, was still nowhere around.

So I began a middle of the night prayer. Still not sleepy, it seemed like a good thing. After a leisurely time of prayer and I had prayed for everyone I knew (and the missionaries), I began to think of all the many names of Jesus. There were a lot of them. I know not when, I fell asleep. I awoke only after the clock had been shaking and making a racket for who knows how long. But this I do know. I awoke refreshed and ready to become part of a new day.

In the middle of the night, I continued to practice reciting names of the Lord. It was not a vigil. It was rewarding and refreshing. If I fell asleep early on, so be it. If I stayed awake and did my prayer-meditation, even better. I never once felt I had "missed any needed sleep." Instead, I felt that I had acquired some *new time* and better still, time with the Lord. In the quietness and darkness, I was alone with my Father, my Savior, my Friend, my personal Emmanuel, my King, my Shepherd, Jesus, Lord and Eternal God. So many beautiful names and they all had individual and collective meaning. And then one night after several weeks of this, (perhaps I'm a slow thinker), I thought about putting them in alphabetical order, i.e. Abba Father, Bread of

35

Life, Christ, Deliverer, Eternal God, Heavenly Father, I Am, Jesus, King, Lord of Lord, Master, Lamb of God and   on and on to Omega.

Between Alpha and Omega, there are at least one thousand "names" and even more waiting to be discovered, coined and expressed–and when **all** of them have been prayed, praised, thought or uttered, they only scratch at the unending Divine surface of our God, who is far too great to describe or imagine.

AMAZING GRACE
(WHAT ELSE COULD WE DESIRE)

There is a consensus among recovering alcoholics that it is nigh unto impossible for an alcoholic to *begin* to recover, until things have gotten so bad that they seemingly can't get any worse. Described another way, the drunk has to hit what is called "rock bottom." Not just another rock bottom, but absolute rock bottom is one that even the "drunk," who has already experienced numerous "bottoms" now, someway and somehow recognizes that this time he or she has indeed reached *the* bottom.

A very close friend and former work associate had experienced a number of rock bottoms. Alcohol and drugs had joined into a seemingly unbeatable team to almost rob him of his lovely and devoted wife, several children, young and very young, loss of a good paying career, talents and creative skills, once sought after, now were not worth even minimum wage. A flunked graduate of an expensive Addiction Program that did not even come close to working, wrecked automobiles, integrity and character that were no more. Huge credit card debts and unauthorized expenditures from an unforgiving big corporation that once prized him. All was lost. Failure and disgrace piled on top of miserable attempts that went nowhere up. He was underneath the bottomless pit and no hope of hope. All was lost. There was absolutely no hope. At this utter point when there is no hope and no need to even try again: there is only one thing left

Jeff (not his real name) told me about the absolute and final rock bottom point. It may not sound like the worst rock bottom experience you've ever heard of, but for Jeff, *it was!* And it *was the one* that began the turnaround to humanity.

Picture this: This one time football hero turned successful corporate manager, once a model husband and father, had finally at age 39 landed a temporary job. He was being paid minimum wage on a second shift job sweeping out nasty foul-smelling slush and sludge in a hot humid basement. He recognized this particular rock bottom and started to tell the Lord how bad it was. When across the basement work pit he saw his nineteen-year-old supervisor whistle at him and motion for him to come to him, with about as much dignity, as one would call a stray mange-eaten mutt of a dog. Bingo: the bottom had finally hit, like a ton of rocks.

That was one miserable night about 15 years ago. Jeff did, after a long tough struggle, make it back to the land of the living and decent. Jeff will now gladly (not proudly) tell you the entire story of agony and anguish and disgrace and defeat and shame and guilt. He jumps at the chance to tell one person, or a large church congregation on Sunday morning, the story of his sin and shame. How this particular rock bottom got his attention and how he found the "Grace" to make the long rough climb back toward glimmers of daylight, forgiveness and restoration. And Jeff will tell you his real name. Because, at rock bottom, when there is no hope for hope, there is only one thing left. God's grace. God's amazing, marvelous, wonderful, saving, redeeming *grace*. God's Grace! The Lord did indeed, after a tough time, restore Jeff's life, family, job, finances and on and on. The mercy and grace of God was absolutely real and active. All the King's horses and all the King's men and all the magic wands could not have put Jeff's life back together, but Jeff's amazing God did. It was indeed a most beautiful example of God's Amazing Grace.

AMAZING GRACE II
A SAD, SAD ADDENDUM
(BUT READ ON...)

Every word and sentence in this book is true. The life experience stories are also true, with only two explainable exceptions, e.g., to protect identity. Just before the draft of the book was to be sent to the publisher, I received a call from Jeff. That, that Job (Jack in this case) feared most had happened. After nearly 15 years of being squeaky clean, Jeff had "fallen" with exclamation marks!!! In Jeff's own words of summarizing his most pathetic and miserable condition, "Is worse off now, in all respects, than it was the first time."

Having personally lived (vicariously and in real time) through the earlier shame, guilt, disgrace, financial mires, family destruction, career completely smashed, etc., this relapse (what a kind, under stated word) ...this "disaster" had ended this beautiful turn around success story, due to God's amazing grace, this story with such a fairy tale perfect ending. I selfishly wanted it to be printed in the book and momentarily considered just "letting it go." After all, it was a 100 percent factual account. However, and this is an important "however," I had also written the devotional on "The Truth." You'll find it in the "T" section.

There is no such thing as "pretty good integrity" or "fairly good integrity." It is, or it ain't. (sic) Thus, the sad addendum **had** to be included.

As I began to write, I suddenly had a painful personal revelation. And I "betcha" a lot of other people was as guilty as I. It goes like this: upon learning of Jeff's second downfall, **and after all** God had done for him and his poor family, there was no way, absolutely no way, that Jeff deserved even another smidgen of forgiveness and love. Jeff had done it! Big time! He had blown it! And this time, mind you, this time it came close to being the unpardonable sin.

But to be very candid, this was tough on me and I well knew I was not the one doing the real suffering. But do you know what I did: *I tried to put God in a box.* God had already given Jeff and his family a bunch of miracles and poured forgiveness and mercy all over them.

Jeff flat out did not deserve another chance to blow it. And I watched as a lot of good Christians reacted and there was a bunch on my side reacting the same way I was about to do. We virtually had God captured and in a box, (so we thought.). But God, hallelujah, *He don't live in no box*! Fortunately, I was able to let God out of that box (bit of humor), during that devastating phone call and only near the end of the conversation came to my senses. What right did I have to tell God how many times he should forgive, or pour out his amazing grace. Answer: none.

As of this writing, the battle still is not over and some of the good Christians are still building their boxes. They've given up on Jeff–and with good cause. However, and this is a good "however" there is absolutely no doubt: God is not in any sort of box and that His mercy is still actively working in undeserving lives and His beautiful 7 x 70 Amazing Grace is still just that ? Amazing Grace!

And it can be wonderfully added that this Grace has been and is being manifested in a myriad of ways while another camp of Christians (with no boxes in sight) are busily going about their daily routines and still interested in Jeff. And it is very easy to recognize them, **because of their love for one another** (including Jeff).

P.S. I love and admire Jeff so much. It hurts to the core to see his grief, shame, and nigh onto impossible, against-the-odds struggle. Jeff is determined to make it and is very strong in his faith. Seeing all this, I had a burning need to express my gut feeling to him, so I said, bluntly and lovingly,

"Jeff you are my hero.
Jeff, you are a crummy hero,
But Jeff you are my hero!"

Jeff and I had often prayed together. This time, without saying it, we both knew God was still merciful and was still in control so we laughed together.

Please, dear readers, pray for Jeff and his beautiful family.

AMAZING LOVE
(WE DO NOT DESERVE)

Why does God love us? Why does He care about us? Certainly, with all His power and God-sufficiency, He doesn't need us or have to have us.

I don't know that any mortal really has the answer to this question, even though the topic has been expounded in a trillion ways. Does He love us because He is lonely? Does He care about us because He made us on such a personal, i.e. hands-on basis and looked into Adam's eyes, mere inches away from His own eyes? Do our eyes really mirror the soul? Does He love us because He made us in his own image? I would suppose that we are the <u>only</u> things He made in His *own* image.

Or does He love us because we are so small and pathetic and helpless? After all, the stars and mountains, oceans, and rivers were so huge and majestic that when he created them, it wasn't necessary that he be so close, i.e. eyeball-to-eyeball. There must be a difference in creative contact and personal contact. Ours was personal, in-his-image soul never-dying contact.

As a comparative example, once God made a mountain and the forces of nature were set in motion, the mountain didn't need a lot of care and attention. Set a mountain on fire and it will grow back. It is very difficult to kill a large redwood tree. Erosion is about the worst thing that happens to a mountain and after several trillion years of erosion it still stands. A few mountains blow their top–and still remain.

Everything God ever made had energy in it, but perhaps the best answer is that He *breathed spirit* into us.

Whatever the correct answer, or answers, might be, it just makes His love all the more *amazing*.

AMAZING LOVE II
(CONTINUES AND CONTINUES)

Years ago, there was a deacon in our church, who when called upon to pray, would usually begin each prayer with "Lord, it amazes us that."

I never grew tired of hearing this "preamble" because it had a ring of bewilderment and sincerity that said so much.

"Lord it amazes us that we can even come into your presence."

"Lord it amazes us that we can give anything to you (offertory prayer)."

"Lord it amazes us that you know, even before we pray, what we are about to ask for "

"Lord it amazes us that you, the High and Holy Lord God, sitting on a Heavenly throne, are also right here in our midst as we begin to pray "

"Lord it amazes us that you know our names, you know our thoughts from afar off and you know the number of hairs on our head "

THE AMEN
(BUT NOT THE END)

These are the words of the Amen, the faithful and true witness, the ruler of God's creation. Rev. 3:14

Isn't it interesting how frequently we use the word "Amen," without ever realizing its full significance? Truly it has to be a descriptive title for Jesus. And without any doubt whatsoever, it is a fitting closure for our prayers.

The word is shown 73 times in Strong's Concordance but only once as a name or title for our Lord. Webster's dictionary (I actually looked it up!) uses such phrases as "used to express solemn ratification expression of faith hearty approval as an assertion."

There is nothing "new" that can be said, or needs to be said, about this familiar word of our faith, so I thought (to myself) why not try closing out some prayers <u>without</u> using this term.

If nothing else, this little exercise does cause us to actually **think** about what we are saying, rather than continuing to use it as a rote, mundane, automatic, no-brainer expression when it is actually anything but that, i.e. read again the 14th Verse and note the capital "A." Aren't we in effect saying as our closing statement of prayer that we offer this prayer to God as His Son taught us to, i.e. "Our Father?" That we are asking in the name of His Son (as He taught us to) "whatsoever you ask in my name" and that contained in the name of Jesus, the Great I Am and the Great Amen, and the faithful and true witness, the ruler of God's creation.

Think about it: we certainly don't have any power or any authority of our own we don't have any "holiness" to make us comfortable in The Holy Presence and we have hardly any "righteousness" (perhaps a filthy-rag's worth) so it would certainly behoove us to end our prayer request, respectfully, with the authority bestowed upon us (freely given to us) so that we have some "credentials" for even entering into **HIS** presence, much less having the audacity (nerve/guts) to ask for anything.

Nevertheless, here are some options to using the word "Amen" in

43

your prayer-endings.

Lord, we end this prayer, as we began it, totally unworthy, but by your mercy, which allows us to ask in the name of Jesus.

Lord, you are the one and only Great Amen, so it is with a mixture of boldness and humility that we have prayed to Our Father.

Lord, your goodness and your mercy and your patience and your long-suffering amaze us beyond words and comprehension and the best we can ever do in trying to know *why* you love us is <u>that</u> you love us!

ANCIENT OF DAYS
(BUT HE NEVER GROWS OLD)

This may be one of God's "better" titles, if there is such a thing. Perhaps this noun-adjective is exactly what we mortals need, if we are ever to begin to understand God's immortality *everlastingness*.

This title always struck me as one of the more "odd" names of God. I easily understood the significance for God is as "ancient" as you can get. He was pre-omega, prior-beginning. God is, was, and forever will be "always." We need each and every name in this book (and more) to just begin to describe our mighty God. And we need "Ancient of Days" to help tell of his eternal nature and help us grasp the timeliness of God. If by faith, we can begin to understand his "ancientness" then it will be easier to understand and accept his "foreverness." And this may be one of the ways to understand the two (2) *"ends"* of eternity, which really means there never were ends or beginnings, even though we think of the beginning as being the starting point and eternity as being the ending point. That is totally wrong because eternity is just the beginning of something that will never end and the so called "beginning" always was, so it never really began, even though the Bible begins by saying "in the beginning" was God. Note that it did not say in the beginning God began, but it says, He *was*.

I'm not doing very well at explaining this, am I? Perhaps I should explain it like my grandmother did when I was 6 or 7 years old. I asked her "Where did God come from?" She never batted an eye or missed a beat. She took her big Bible down and showed it to me. She carefully pointed out the opening cover of black leather and held it between her two knurled fingers. Then she explained, "God has given us enough to try and understand. All we need to know is on the inside between these two black covers. Therefore, we shouldn't trouble ourselves with what's on the front side of the cover."

Don't you suppose we aren't supposed to have all the answers and that our human limitations are already stretched beyond mortal capacity.

P.S. Sometimes my grandmother's explanation needed a little time
to pass, so I could think them through but w   ith a little time, I
never once felt that my grandmother was wrong.

AUTHOR
(OF OUR FAITH)

To say that Jesus is the "author" of our faith is one of the most important and profound statements ever made. And while it is indeed profound, it is especially impressive because of the simplicity. "Profound" and "simplistic" do not normally go together. In this case, each factor of the structure is perfectly meshed, as only the author of authors could do. And each component of the plan is unique!

Here is a listing that illustrates the divine masterpiece.

He thought of it first (from the foundation of time) which is as it should be, since He is the Creator.

He designed it, so who better to be the author.

He has the starring role and only He could assume such awesome responsibility.

He allowed each of us to play the "supporting" role.

He created the perfect plan and one that would be applicable for all ages.

He designed it so that any and all could participate (whosoever will).

He designed it so that it would never have to be revised; neither would it ever become obsolete.

At the very heart of the plan are two key features: unconditional love and faith.

The plan cannot be bought or earned.

The greatest benefit of the plan is "priceless." Beyond price and priceless because it cannot be purchased. It is a "gift." Note how profound and simple. Heavenly profound and yet totally simple, i.e. "free."

He lovingly and creatively designed the plan for the "masses," i.e. all of humanity. And yet, each time the plan is executed, it must be done on a one on one individual basis. It is **not** sold and/or accepted on a family, group, regional, denominational, or national basis. NEVER, NEVER. It cannot be inherited or bargained, for it is always a personal plan, personally accepted.

He illustrated the priceless value of the plan by paying in advance the ultimate price, which was His only Son and the contract was signed and sealed with the blood of the innocent "Lamb."

The half has not been told, but to conclude the most unusual feature of the plan is that it is up to me to decide as to whether I want to accept it! Or, reject it??

The plan was offered and authored in Divine Love.

AWESOME
(THE BIG, BIG ADJECTIVE)

There was a time when our teenagers discovered this word and did a pretty good job of monopolizing it. Overnight almost everything became "awesome" be it a concert, or a milk shake, or a movie, or a car, or a new blouse, or whatever moved and/or stood still. Better described, the word is capitalized, put in bold letters, underlined and followed by several exclamation marks.

This is not to be critical. When an emotional experience overwhelms us to the point that our vocabulary is not sufficient to express the explosion inside our innards and to keep from erupting physically, or having a need to run in rapid circles, so as to properly release joyful pent-up emotions–then the word "awesome" served a worthwhile purpose and kept bodies intact all over America. Awesome became a release valve. Hot water heaters have them. They are called "pop-off" valves.

For a turned-on, excited and unashamed *believer*, a similar situation could or should apply. Only in most churches, such behavior is taboo. This makes it tough at times, considering that some psychologists have indicated that seventy-five percent of our actions and thought processes are based on, or attributed to emotions. What this boils down to is that we average American citizens can go about our daily lives and properly express excitement and appreciation. This is especially true, while attending sports events and other secular meetings where we can go absolutely wild and berserk. It's called being a "fan" which is where the word fanatic comes from. We can jump up and down, shriek wildly and noisily, yell and dance or throw beer cans and even pass live bodies of fellow fans over our heads from the stage to the balcony. All of which must be acceptable behavior, since they often hire policemen to monitor such stupid happiness.

Conversely, if as we are sitting in church one Sunday morning and suddenly one amongst us should have a realization that the God we serve has been so gracious and kind to us, kept us from danger, run our cups over and blessed us, time and time again, until we are nigh onto overcome with joy, unspeakable and full of glory. Now, if we were in any other place other than church, (most churches that is) then we could feel the freedom to orally erupt with some Biblical term of praise or thanksgiving. "Hallelujah" or "Praise the Lord" used to be appropriate in most churches, but unfortunately we have now grown dignified and dull in our worship, whereas, years ago such expressions were in common usage. Around the turn of the Twentieth Century there were reports of "shouting" in Methodist churches. My grandparents also referred to groups known as "shouting Baptists." Mercy, Mercy!

In the typical mainline church, members, who have been warming the same pews for years, would probably faint, or have a hissy, if God was given a spontaneous (out-loud) expression of praise. At the least, there would be no place on the program of worship for such behavior. Deacons and elders would need to take a six-week sabbatical for rest and recovery.

There must be an appropriate scripture verse somewhere in the Bible that describes the holy stagnancy that exists in most mainline churches, whereby members sit Sunday after Sunday in staid dignity with no signs of life or joy. All the while, these same non-exciting churches have lost and are still losing members by the millions, all because they have a form of godliness but don't want anything to do with the power of God.

II Timothy 3: 5

THE ALL-CARING GOD
(THE GOD OF DETAILS)

Our almighty, all-powerful God, God, who was creator of all, great and small, including galaxies that cannot be measured. Also, tiny invisible atoms, yet majestic and glorious, indescribable and also immeasurable.

Pause in your wonder and amazement to note the attention and concern of our God as it reaches down to the least and the seemingly insignificant.

Divine focus that centers on one lone sheep who gets lost even when He already owns all the others on a thousand hills.

Knowing the tiny coin given by a nameless widow. (He also knew her by name)

Caring about a single bird's injury. And the bird doesn't even have to be beautiful.

Concern for a short little fellow up in a tree.

Willing to be seen having dinner with a tax agent.

Special concern about the poor (also the meek and humble).

Care for an outcast; someone ostracized by others because of a bad reputation.

Those forgotten by others and considered worthless (like orphans and widows).

Knowing the number of hairs on our head (and the same concern for baldheads).

THE ALL-SEEING EYE
(ALWAYS ON THE WATCH)

When I was a small boy, my dear wonderful saintly grandmother that I loved dearly had a highly effective way (albeit, somewhat "devilish") of correcting me when she caught me in some mischief: she would begin to sing a refrain from an old hymn:

> **"There is an all-seeing eye watching you ...**
> **every step that you take,**
> **every mile that you make ...**
> **there is an eye watching you."**

To a small lad this can be somewhat disquieting and discomforting to know that God sees any and everything. But with just a little maturity, one quickly recognized the advantages of having a God that knows you personally (and you can also know him personally too) God cares enough about you to watch your every step. Later on, we call it "Divine Intervention" but almost everyone can cite instances of where, but for the grace of God, great harm or death would have come. At age 8, or 9, I almost ran into the house where we lived (no family member was there at the time) as I had many times before, only, "something" instantly stopped me and for no apparent reason, I halted frozen, like a stature on the front steps. I *knew* to not enter my house. Soon after, we learned that two burglars were in the house. Why did I, in the bright sunlight on a beautiful day and in the midst of a carefree playful mood of an 8 year-old, without a care in the world, suddenly stop?

THE AVENGER
(EVENTUALLY)

This is perhaps one of the most difficult "names" of God that we have to accept. Certainly it is one of the hardest ones that we as Christians have to *implement* into our daily lives. This could possibly be listed as one of the "love principles" of the Bible: when someone has "done us wrong" and there is no fairness, no justice, no right, only downright ugly evil, seemingly no way to forgive, no more cheek-turning possible, no way to undo the damage, etc. etc. etc. When every ligament in your body has been stretched through agony and deep hurt and there is no elasticity left to return from the bitterness and resentment. When every thinking cell in your body cries twenty-five hours a day for REVENGE!!

Then, the love principle begins to speak in the silent voice of the Holy Spirit. You can hear it in the midst of the constant noise and turmoil of internal word storms and unending winds of bitterness. You try not to hear it. But amazingly nothing can subdue the quiet voice of God's spirit; not even years of trying to ignore it. And often, all this quiet voice does is repeat a single verse over and over,

"Vengeance is mine I will repay, thus saith the Lord."

THE AWESOME GOD AND YOU
(WE DON'T DESERVE SUCH)

Haven't I told you before that our God is so very awesome that we need a lot of names or titles or words to even come close to trying to describe the Awesome Wonderful Mighty Eternal God. (Get the picture??)

Like you need *nouns* because God is a person. Ah, yes, not only is He a person but He is three persons in one, so now we need another noun, like Trinity or Triune God.

Remember, dear reader, a noun is a person, place or thing. God is also a noun-place because He is a place of Refuge, or a place of Rest.

But let's not leave out *thing*. Because God is also peace and peace is a wonderful "thing" to have. In fact, I suppose many of God's intangible facets are like things. You can't always touch a thing, like joy or hope or strength, but these are nevertheless some of the things we cherish most about God.

I could go on and on with these wonderful thoughts, but perhaps it would be a good time for me to stop and let both of us meditate on this one little facet of our Lord and our God. Otherwise with all the zillions of facets yet to be uncovered, we could overload our puny circuits.

And besides, on another day and on another occasion, we have to discuss and write about the scriptural fact that our Father is invisible. Now that, dear reader, is going to present some more challenge as we *look* into and try to *see* the *invisible* side of our God. Do you *see* what I mean?

Wow, isn't our God awesome!

THE AWESOME GOD
(BUT THE DECISION IS OURS)

Isn't this an awesome, overwhelming load our Creator, our Lord, the most Holy God has handed us? Yes, yes, admittedly yes indeed! However, our all-wise Lord has handed to each of us the balancing segment to this eternal equation that suddenly makes the quandary totally fair. He never forces the discipleship role upon us. The ultimate decision is ours: to accept, or reject. Try to imagine that? It is left up to us to reject this awesome God. It is our responsibility to reject (or accept) God's Holy Son.

God has willingly offered to give us His Son; His only Son. But in the final analysis we must make the decision. What an awesome decision? How awesome that an awesome God, who not so coincidentally created us, would allow us such an awesome responsibility.

An eternal responsibility.

BABE OF BETHLEHEM
(A TOUCHING BEGINNING)

The baby Jesus is more than a wonderful Christmas story. I suppose that is about the only time we give this aspect of the Divine very much thought. But when you stop to think about it, this is the very heart of what our faith is about. The masterful writer Oswald Chambers said so well and succinctly with only four words. In the middle of a page of beautiful, lengthy words, the sentence literally jumps up and exclaims, **"God became a baby."**

Speculate for a moment: What if Jesus had suddenly appeared one day as an adult in Jerusalem, announced that he had arrived to put us in a right relationship with God the Father? Could our minds have handled it? By appearing as a baby, He gave us more time to become accustomed to the advent of his arrival. After all, a mere baby is so non-threatening to mankind and that gave us time to accept the idea and the man. And what better way for Jesus to *relate* to us, (which is after all, why he came in the first place, i.e., to establish rapport with us) know us and have an earthly understanding of our lives. He needed and wanted to know us.

And it started with the humble birth of a tiny baby: God's gift to us.

Then, with *understanding,* by both God and man, Jesus could take our sins upon his back, die for us and thus, provide us with God's pardon from sin.

And just to think: it all began with a tiny, helpless baby. Only God could have thought of this!

BALM OF GILEAD
(YES, THE ANSWER IS YES)

Misery, Misery, Misery. The people were miserable. In the 8th Chapter of Jeremiah, we read of sorrow and worry and questions and hurts and fears. There was searching for peace and none to be seen. The thinking was that God had deserted them. Not only that, He had put the people to silence. I have often read that one of the worst forms of punishment against someone is to give him or her "the silent treatment." It is frequently used in prisons and is cruelly effective. I have personally seen it used in the military and I have observed it in manufacturing plants and business offices. A lot of people think they can accept and whip the silence. I personally never saw but one person that did. All the rest crumbled sooner or later.

In this particular chapter, it seems the people also had to sit still. "Why do we sit still?" But to sit still and to be silent is double punishment for most humans. The woes of the people continued (no wonder Jeremiah is termed the weeping prophet) with gall to drink instead of water, the horses were snorting and neighing and the land itself seemed to be trembling but it was just the thundering noise of the enemies' horses approaching. No grapes on the vines, withered leaves and summer is past and gone and the harvest never came "and we still aren't saved."

The sad saga continues with threats of venomous snakes and vipers and no hope of charming them. The thundering of the enemies' horses is near and "they are coming to devour the land and everything in it . the city and all who live in it." Everywhere and everything is doom and gloom. And there is no use to cry; even though I want to I 'm too faint to even cry.

Woe is us. Woe is us, even today, in this still brand new centennial. Trouble and woes and uncertainties galore. Why did all of this come upon us? What we need is the very same thing the people of Gilead in the 8th Chapter cried for: "We need a balm." Is there no balm? Does God not have a "balm" for us?

And did none of us hear the Lord when he asked:

"Why have these people turned away?"

"Why does Jerusalem (America) always turn away?"
"Since they have rejected me, what kind of wisdom do they have?"

Note: For those that are faint-hearted **do not read** the following statement the Lord made in the two previous chapters.

"But they did not listen or pay attention, instead they followed the stubborn inclinations of their evil hearts." "They went backward and not forward." (Jeremiah 7:24)

"My anger and my wrath will be poured out on this place..." (Jeremiah 7:20b)

"I am bringing disaster on these people, the fruit of their schemes, because they have not listened to my words and have rejected my law." (Jeremiah 6:19)

"Look, an army is coming from the north." (Jeremiah 6:22a)

For those of you who think all of this scriptural based writing is:
    (1)   entirely symbolic in meaning and/or
    (2)   obsolete by the more enlightened thinking of our age.

Remember we (supposedly) have nothing to fear but fear itself, so sleep well tonight. But, if

Jeremiah 8:22
UMC Pub. House 1986
Afro-Amer Spiritual   music/words
ARR Wm Farley Smith 1941

BALM OF GOD
(GOD ALWAYS PROVIDES)

Because of a hymn written in 1888 by an unknown author, this otherwise obscure verse has become a familiar Christian thought/prayer. Even those of us who can't sing very well have hung onto this 'balm' in scary times. I know I have.

To me the verse is saying that in even this modern day we live, even when all the sophisticated, technological advances, we enjoy (especially in the medical field) fail us; when all of our wonderful earthly resources, including doctors, families, friends, etc., have failed

and make no mistake, at one or more times in everyone's life "they fail us," no matter how hard they tried, or didn't try. Our lives are filled with painful examples: a loved one that should not have died, or the tragic death of a young child or when your doctor tells you

At these non-explainable/unbearable times when *hope is gone,* Christians can muster the mustard seed of faith to find the inner resource (and even it doesn't come easy) to go to 'Gilead" for a spiritual balm. This is a mystical experience which we aren't suppose to be able to explain why and how it works; it usually comes in a quiet way, a quiet peace that: comforts, exceeds understanding, gives added strength, when there was none. Or, maybe the "balm" comes in a quiet way of *acceptance* that someday God will explain and make every thing right. But he is in control. Now, you have "doubt strength" and a resolve to just take it one day at a time until

Regardless, the soothing ointment works and life goes on. We "will understand it better by and by."

Is *there* no balm in Gilead; is *there* no physician there? Why then is not the health of the daughter of my people recovered?

BEST FRIEND
(AND A GOOD LISTENER)

This page could easily be entitled "A Brotherly Friend." Only that would not be totally accurate. For Jesus is the friend that sticks even closer than a brother. It could probably be better entitled, "A Friend in Time of Need " But neither would that be totally accurate because Jesus is not restricted to only being around when there is a need. You can enjoy His company any time and almost any place. If you were to, per chance, go into a "naughty place," Jesus would stand outside and wait. He is also a friend with a lot of patience. So, there is another title: 'The Friend with Boundless Patience."

Do not despair because He seemed to desert you at the door of some "naughty place." He would have sent the Holy Spirit to go in with you (and convict you). I do recall my dear mother telling me something that I could never forget (even though I sometimes tried to forget her message), like for instance, when I wanted to go in the "pool hall" with my high school buddies. Her admonition was to never go anywhere that I would be ashamed to take Jesus.

Over the years my relationship with Jesus evolved without much conscious thought and little effort. He really did become my best friend and I knew immediately that He was there when I had a panic or even a minor need. But just as precious to me was to be able to wake up in the middle of the night and be able to easily and instantly talk to Him, even when I didn't have a crisis or a problem to worry about. We just "talked" like good friends are supposed to. Which, by the way, reminds me of yet another title for this page. Jesus is a "good" listener–Friend.

Assignments:
I.   Silently list some of your dearest friends. Then, still silently, think of at least one time, when even they let you down or disappointed you.
II.   Then, try to think of a time that Jesus let you down.
III.   Enjoy thinking of some additional friendship titles for Jesus, e.g., Constant Shepherd, etc.

THE BIRD WATCHER
(KNOWS WHEN IT FALLS)

One night in a small rural church in the South, an old gentleman stood up during testimony time at a revival service I attended and said, "My Lord is a bird watcher!" I was somewhat taken aback but most of the audience seemed to know immediately what he meant as indicated by their "AMEN's" and applause. And then he went on to explain. "He could have said He watches the mighty eagle or the tiny blue bird or any number of the beautiful birds. And I would reckon that he does occasionally watch these. But the Holy Book said He watches sparrows. And He don't just watch 'em but He knows when one of them gets hurt or falls."

Again the crowd erupted with praise and I too felt the spirit and mood of what he was excited about. "And that's just amazing, he continued. There are plenty of sparrows and I don't reckon they are worth very much. And brother and sister, they sure don't have much color and beauty to behold. Fact is they are sort of drab. But nevertheless, my Lord and my God, in all His power and all His greatness, and in all His love and mercy cares enough to watch out for them. That's wonderful. Cause, like the old song says, I know He's watching out for me too."

BLESSED ASSURANCE
(AND NO ONE IS IN SECOND PLACE)

Room 326. One of many, hospital rooms. But this particular room held a painful and particular significance to me. This was the room where my Mother had died ten years earlier. Just the two of us, alone, that final night. There was very little conversation. She was very weak and her heart was completely worn out. Almost. I felt impressed to do something "special" for this very special mother. I was her only son and we had always enjoyed a close and warm relationship. But more than this, we had always enjoyed a "fun" relationship. I admitted, unashamedly, even in my 53rd year, that I was "a mama's boy."

My special gift that night (which turned out to be my parting gift) was to read the Bible aloud to her. Dozens of chapters. I read a lot from Luke, assorted selections from the epistles and 50 of the Psalms. At best, she slept in troubled naps. Much of the time she was comatose; perhaps bits of semi-consciousness. Regardless, I forced myself to read on and on, but always aloud. Quite loud, so she might possibly hear these blessed words she had loved and trusted and lived by for almost sixty years. I never once grew tired of reading but had to focus on the words so that my crying never became obvious. The tears seemed, at times, like liquid refreshment, maybe living waters.

Reading the Bible aloud seemed so appropriate. For after all, my Mother and Father were the only two people I ever knew that, upon their retirement, had spent a number of months reading the entire Bible aloud to each other. Their beloved Bible was not just a sacred book; it was their heart and life.

Her heart was now very tired. Almost gone. In the scant vanishing hours the very next dayspring would quietly dissolve the final "almost" until the last halting heartbeat, after 74 years, gracefully and silently exited, leaving a lifeless heart, that beat no more – now lying at rest in a still body. But I was blessed. I had the assurance my Mother had passed on to a new life. Room 326 was empty and I never wanted to enter it again and even think about it.

Think about. Most of us as Christians seldom think about the empty tomb and that is as it should be. Rather, we think of where He has gone, i.e. to Heaven. Christ is indeed in Heaven, at the right hand of his Father. And so, as my thoughts occasionally slipped back into the sadness of that early morning "departure," it is only momentarily for my Mother is no longer there.

Now, years later Room 326 holds little or no significance. Instead, I have such fond memories of those beautiful last hours we shared together. And the Blessed Assurance is forever real.

BREAD OF LIFE
(ABSOLUTELY ESSENTIAL)

Isn't it absolutely amazing how effective Jesus could be with one six word sentence? Jesus often preached in just <u>one</u> sentence, tremendous sermons with elaborate content. His ultra-brief "sermons" made an impact with staying (and changing) power. As an example with only six words: "I am the bread of life." Let's begin to list just a few of the points and expand a bit on this otherwise simple sentence and all that it implies.

I am— One of the most profound *descriptive names* of God.

The— It is He who both creates the bread and becomes the "bread."

Bread—We must have it to live. A fantastic one-word-fits-all item.

Of This vital "bread" is of and from and by Jesus. You can't get it anywhere else.

Life— The most important issue we will ever have to deal with; both in this life and in the eternal life to come.

Additional thoughts to dine on and digest:

We **need** bread daily.

The top three things we need are: bread, water, and air.

It is bread that sustains us.

It is essential. Not coincidentally or as a supplement. Nor is it an option. It is not a luxury. It is *essential*!

Bread is actually rather simple and easy to understand. Sometimes we make the mistake of overlooking the basics and/or letting them become commonplace.

Jesus is saying I am the "food" of life.

We can't live without "Him"   . not for very long.

Substitutes may be tried. But none of them will suffice. Not for very long, if at all.

For physical survival, only few things are more important than bread, i.e. air and water.

Interestingly, Jesus could have said I am the air of life, or I am the water of life. I think the message in His declaring He was the bread of

64

life is to speak to the basics that are an absolute "must" in our daily walk as a believer. As to spiritual survival, the sentence said it well and there should be no doubts, to **who** the bread of life is.

To summarize, any of my Baptist friends could quickly add three points, in order to make it proper and appropriate for a Sunday morning sermon.

1. Bread (food) is absolutely essential for life.
2. Bread is a daily need.
3. Bread provides the strength and the essence.

Obvious Point: Let's not rush out to slay giants, or walk-on-water, or start a major TV ministry, until we have the *essence* of Christ mastered in our daily lives and fully know the source of our strength and being.

"PASS THE BREAD, PLEASE."

BREAD OF OUR SOULS
(OR WE PERISH)

Bread of our souls.

This "phrase" may be one of the absolute best to describe the vital importance of what God means to us. It is certainly a classic example of perfect conciseness. These four words sum up our spiritual outcome.

Bread is the perfect example of a staple and an essential food. Without "bread" we starve, perish, die! Our soul must also have the right substance to survive.

Jesus, the Son of God, is the only "food" that will allow us to *live*. We may try a lot of substitutes and we may even "linger" for a while. But only the "bread of life" will provide long-term survival, i.e. **"eternal life."**

BREAD
(TRY TO GET ALONG WITHOUT IT)

Jesus could just as easily have said I am the water of life. Or, I am the air you breathe. However, "bread" was a better, tangible example and an easy one for everyone to understand. Just think of all the words that can be substituted for bread.

Jesus says, I am the *hope* you need.

Jesus says, I am the *most basic thing* you need to be fulfilled.

Jesus says, I am the *foundation* you must have.

Jesus says, I am the only *totally satisfying* thing you can ever have.

Jesus says, I am the *staple* in your life.

Jesus says, I am the essential *eternity* you need.

Jesus says, I am the *love* you need.

Jesus says, I am the *comfort* you need.

Jesus says, I am the *best assurance* you can ever have.

Jesus says, I am the *everlasting*.

Note: We should, never, never again, take "bread" for granted. And we should always give thanks for bread.

And before we eat it.

THE BEST FRIEND
(LOVES AT ALL TIMES)

One of the many wonderful things about a "true love" relationship is that it never becomes un-new. There is unending freshness. You never become ordinary to each other. You never become tired of each other. You never become immune to your feelings of love and joy in a beautiful relationship and neither of you becomes immune to the love and joy that is returned to you by the recipient of such love. Certainly you do not take such love for granted but continue to cherish it day after day and weeks turn into years and years into forever.

Among the many, many components and characteristics of a true love relationship is the "friendship factor." This especially holds true in a committed relationship between the believer and the Lord Jesus. For Jesus wants to (and can indeed) become like our "best friend."

A "best friend" doesn't really need a description or a list of duties and responsibilities. This and other such criteria are understood by both parties.

QUESTION: Have I become *best friends* with Jesus or do we merely bump into each other occasionally? Do we meet perhaps once a week, like on Sunday mornings? Have we really gotten to know each other? Or, do we have to wonder what the other is doing? Do we yearn, with burning desire, to be with each other?

THE BLEEDING SACRIFICE
(THE ULTIMATE GIFT)

A sacrifice, by its very definition, must die or lose. And this morbid gift is usually bestowed so that others can benefit. And how better to assure the certainty of the sacrifice than by giving your most valuable physical possession that best represents "living life." Your blood. Unlike pagan sacrifice, this divine sacrifice of God's only Son was willingly given. And it was done in love, the supreme sacrifice for me.

Then comes the BIG question. It always comes when someone you love does something very special for you. And it doesn't get any more "special" than for God's only Son to die for you. The question: How do I repay such a gift, a magnanimous gift! The first answer is both immediate and obvious: "I can't repay it." "No way!"

We aren't asked to repay! We couldn't any way.

Then, immediately, comes from the Holy Spirit, the only acceptable answer: "Obedience is better than sacrifice".

I Samuel 15:22

THE BOY WONDER
(OFF TO AN EARLY START)

This descriptive term may seem a little odd, but it certainly is a quaint reminder of an incident in the early life of Jesus. I would imagine there were other similar experiences where some action or activity of Jesus grabbed some attention and caught people by complete surprise and bewildered them. Turning ordinary water into wine without benefit of other ingredients?

At the age of twelve, Jesus was lost for several days from his parents. Joseph and Mary must have been frantic. Finally, after what must have seemed like many, many days, they found Him in the temple courts astonishing the Teachers by His questions and understanding for one so young. Imagine the relief they felt. Jesus wondered why his parents were searching for Him, stating, "Didn't you know I had to be about my Father's business?"

When was the last time you and I have shown some eagerness to be about our Father's business?

CANOPY OF PEACE
(DOES GOD GET INVOLVED IN PETTY DETAILS?)

This is a true story.
This is a true "sweet" story.
This is a hard-to-believe story.
This is a simple story.

This is also a story that might possibly raise a deep, theological, philosophical point, which learned and profound minds can sit around large round (or oval) shaped mahogany tables and ponder, after they have resolved how many angels can be seated in alphabetical order on the sharp point of a needle that a rich man could not proceed through the eye of said needle.

First you, dear readers, might wish to know how I know this story is true. I know it is true because the woman who had this experience is sanctified (even though she doesn't wear a bun, nor sniff snuff). She is of high integrity and impeccable character. She is also, in spite of many, many strong points, not a woman who possesses a lot of imagination or matters of a literary bent.

She is the woman you often have read about: She is called "Blessed." She is also called Martha (not her real name) because she is so rigidly practical in every facet of her life. Although extraordinarily practical, as previously stated, she is broad-minded to the point that she reads a number of magazines and periodicals. She does <u>not</u> read fiction, since she considers it a horrible waste of time. She does not, I might add, believe in flying saucers and other such weird foolishness. She just does not have it in her to waste time on stuff like that and other such nonessentials. Do you begin to get the picture of this somewhat straight-laced impeccable woman who is beautiful, talented, energetic and loved and admired by many, but who has no imagination per se?

Since the fascinating story you are about to read (finally) hinges on the credibility of this single individual's reputation for truth and honesty, you might ask how can I vouch for her integrity and the validity and truth of this story? Well it is really quite easy and simple:

She is my wife of 49 years.

We built a new home in a resort area even though neither of us are beach people. Martha doesn't like sand, especially in her house and she really doesn't enjoy water. Her dear mother (now deceased and currently residing in and around the hills of Glory) was also very practical and did not allow "little Martha" to go in or near any containers of water, underline until she first learned how to swim. In addition, our doctors have told both of us to stay out of the sun, due to a propensity for skin cancer. Nonetheless, she allowed her wonderful kind husband to build their dream house. We dedicated this house to the Lord and we are still in a state of wonder of God's grace that gloriously blessed us to own such a beautiful and special place.

Even before we moved in Martha wanted to "name it" like people who live in resort areas are prone to do. Even though our house wasn't on the beach front, she liked the idea of giving it a name and she especially wanted the name to have a spiritual connotation, so as to be a quiet, yet effective witness for our Lord.

You've all seen the cute names on signs attached to the front of vacation homes, e.g., Sea Breeze, Relax-A-While, Stay-A-Spell, or Sum-R-Place, etc.

Initially the house was a second home for us. It was not a rental house but we allowed people to stay (for free). With the Lord's blessings it became a type of "retreat" and a number of families (some who normally could not have afforded such a vacation) were able to stay at no cost. Thus, a sizable number of guests were able to enjoy the house. Now, it has become our primary residence, but still available to a lot of visitors.

"Martha" felt a strong need to give it a name, but she (typical for Martha) wanted the house to have a spiritual name so it would "serve a purpose," she explained. Totally shocked at this unusual behavior, since it bordered on being imaginative, I agreed, but suggested *she* be the one to decide on "what name shall the place be called?"

Several weeks went by and none of the great and clever names I suggested were satisfactory. Then one Sunday, she came home from church (I had not been able to attend that particular Sunday, as was my customary religious practice, since I was suffering with a dire case of the sniffles and not wanting to spread my plague on saintly people) and quietly announced, (Martha's do not get excited, unless there is a guest in the house) that she had "found" the name for our new home. To which I responded in sanctimonious tones, "What name do we giveth this house?" Martha replied, like a proud mother dedicating her baby, "Canopy of Peace."

When I inquired, after silently pondering in my heart, how in heaven's name could my dear Martha have come upon such a beautiful and fitting name, what with her handicap of being born without either imagination, or literary bent, she proclaimed, matter-of-factly, she had just found it in the pew Bible, during the morning service. Knowing Martha, as I was beginning to know her, after two score and ten years, I quickly surmised that she had most likely scanned the pew Bible, (Revised Standard Version) when the good pastor had strayed from his prepared message to tell a modern parable. Like any good Martha, my Martha would have considered it a waste of time, hence, she used this time to good advantage to scan the Bible and look for an appropriate title for the new house. When behold her eyes fell upon these three words, "Canopy of Peace."

We both immediately liked the name and there was never any further discussion until later, when ready to place the order for the sign to be made, I asked for the Biblical reference where she had read those special words. She could not recall, but was sure it was in the Old Testament. Alas, I could not find it. I did some rather extensive research, including an electronic Bible, Computer-Internet Bibles and even Strong's Concordance. The word "Canopy" appears six times in several editions and in Strong's Complete Concordance. But "Canopy of Peace" is not in any one of the approximately 12 translations I've checked, not even the Revised Standard Version. To this day, Martha still insists she *saw it* in the pew Bible.

It is not in the pew Bible (RSV), the only Bible she had access to that Sunday morning. I must leave it up to you, dear readers, to resolve the mystery of the how's and if's of Martha's seeing this phrase in the Bible??

TEN YEARS HAVE PASSED: The only place I have ever seen "Canopy of Peace" is on the engraved wooden plank that hangs on the side of the house, partially obscured by a crepe myrtle. But still visible with its peaceful message.

It still warms our hearts at how many people, some who never even noticed the sign outside the house, remarked about how peaceful the house "felt" and the peace they enjoyed during their stay. Quite often their comments are something similar to "the most peaceful place I've ever stayed."

What thinkest thou, dear reader??

THE CARPENTER'S SON
(DID HE KNOW THEN?)

Advantages to working as a carpenter:
You learn a trade like ordinary people do.
You learn to work with your hands.
You learn to appreciate the smell of fresh lumber.
You see and appreciate the beautiful grains in something as commonplace as wood.
You learn what it feels like to bang your thumb with a hammer.
You learn how it feels to have a speck of sawdust in your eye.
You learn how difficult and cranky some customers can be.
You learn the difference in shoddy work and craftsmanship.
You learn how nice it is to see the smile of a satisfied customer.
You eventually learn to appreciate the restrictions and demands of a tough supervisor. (Even if it is your father.)
You learn that it is best to try and do things right the first time.
You learn the value of a hard-earned denarius.
You learn the discipline and dedication of paying tithes.
You meet all sorts of people: good and not so good.
You learn to accept responsibility
You learn to get up early in the morning and be at work on time. (Even if it is the first work day of the week and your back hurts.)
You learn that women aren't the only ones that gossip.
You discover that some affluent customers can be slow-payers.
Although busy with building things, your work allows you a lot of time to think about other things. You do a lot of thinking.
You notice, with some envy, as others your age get married and start their families.
You are amazed at how quickly the years go by.
You watch in dismay, at the way some people waste their lives.
You learn to relate to the common people.
You wonder how it would be to be a fisherman.
You always remember the first time a hammer smashed into your hand. And how it hurt.
And how it hurt.

THE CHOSEN ONE
(FOR A TOUGH JOB)

Jesus is the *one* that God chose. Odd as it might sound, God chose Jesus to do what He (God) could not do. At least, He could not have done it as well as His Son could do it. I suppose what I am feebly attempting to do is explain some of the intra-workings and the inter-workings of the Trinity.

For how in heaven's name (no pun intended) could All-Mighty, All-Wise, All-Knowing, Creator-of-All, All-Holy God, All-Divine come to earth and accomplish His eternal purpose and objective. He undoubtedly could! We undoubtedly could not have handled it. Oswald Chambers described God's methodology **best** when he wrote the short four word sentence that no mortal can improve upon: "God became a baby."

As infallible proof that God's way is always (ALL WAYS) perfect, if God had done it any other way, then the supreme example of showing His love to us could not have occurred. For God *gave* His Only Son. And nothing else could have illustrated and proven it as vividly and with such intense pain inflicted on *both*, Father and Son.

THE CHOSEN
(THE PERFECT CHOICE)

There are at least sixty-six times in the Bible, where the term *Chosen One* is used. One is used as a descriptive noun. Jesus was the *Chosen One* of God. David was "chosen" at least twice. Saul was a chosen one of a different sort. Moses was chosen and objected, thus spending forty years in exile or "preparation" or whatever you care to call his life after he left Egypt. The Levites were chosen for a special ministry. Abraham was chosen and the twelve disciples were chosen. The thirteenth disciple was chosen. The City of Jerusalem was chosen by God. In a very real sense, all of the Hall of Faith names listed in the eleventh chapter of Hebrews were "chosen."

The question becomes: What do the individuals in this select group have in common? Obviously, one answer is that most of them were *divinely chosen*. One was chosen for the wrong reason. All taught that we should not judge a book by its cover. Neither should you judge a judge by his cover, even if he is tall and handsome. But another answer that might apply is that many were chosen because of their past accomplishments and/or future accomplishments that would come. A few may have been chosen for the wrong reasons. Several were chosen even though they were unlikely candidates, e.g., questionable background, humility, had complexes, speech impediments, or too outspoken.

Obviously, in some cases selections were made because God saw potential that others did not see. And some "blew it" even when the selection was seemingly rightfully made.

There is only one that can be entitled *The Chosen*. That is Jesus! And God made the perfect choice.

Then, somewhere down through the ages and in every individual case, an ironic and seemingly strange thing happens. The selection process seems to get turned around, whereby each one of us have opportunities to do the choosing. And the strange part is that we must decide to choose the *Chosen One*.

Or, we can decide to reject the *Chosen One*.

Kind of makes you think, doesn't it??

COPY LORD OF THEE
(WHAT A ROLE MODEL)

Years ago, I had a fresh idea. At least to me it was fresh and brand new—even though I know many others must have thought of it also.

It had to do with my morning devotions. It seemed that things were getting a little stale. Not boring, but almost. At least I was smart enough to recognize that the problem was mine, not God's. And, it was definitely not **the Book**, I was using.

For me, it was most likely my trying to follow the semi-old-routine, which was:

1. Set alarm clock to get up 30 minutes early.
2. Dash water onto face.
3. Have cup of wake-me-up coffee.
4. Meditate briefly.
5. Read Bible for 12-15 minutes.
6. Pray for 10-15 minutes.

Nothing wrong with the routine, but I needed a change. Then "it" hit. Rather than merely reading the Bible as per usual, I began to copy, by hand, with a number two lead pencil, the scriptures. So, you will get the picture, I began to copy down, usually printing, verses of scripture. I copied a large number of scriptures on "faith" (38 hand-written pages). I copied scriptures on "commitment" (17 pages). I copied Chapter 15 of John's gospel ("I am the vine") and other classic sections of scriptures.

This old fashion procedure took a lot of time. And of course you guessed it.

It slowed me down.

It caused learning to occur.

It caused deeper thinking.

It caused memorization as a by-product.

It caused better retention

It caused the scriptures to stay in my mind longer so I pondered better.

To summarize: I not only learned more but I truly enjoyed this special format for several years, and, still practice this old fashion, laborious tedious painstaking non-computerized method of *"being with the Lord."*

In an odd way, I was reminded of an old hymn I chanced upon years ago, "Make Me A Copy Lord Of Thee." What better way to model ourselves after our Lord, in that He becomes our example or role model and we thus *try* to be a "copy" of our Lord?

The Key Point: What better way can there be to accomplish the modeling process than to spend time in intense study, "digging" into his word (meditating) and *dwelling* on all the inspiration and guidance contained in the scriptures?

THE COUNTER
(THE HEAVENLY AUDITOR)

No scripture in the Bible is insignificant. Just look at the shortest verse in the entire Bible: "Jesus Wept." Without those two words we would have no "proof" that our Jesus cried; that our Lord had this sensation and tender trait. How touching and tender.

Another example: think how wonderful it is to learn that our God of the universe, who spoke worlds into existence would have care and interest in knowing the number of hairs on our heads. I think this is the scriptural way of showing that no detail is so small that God does not know and *care*. Other similar examples of God's auditing detail are the lost coin, or the concern for the single sheep, one out of one hundred.

No detail can escape our Lord and all of these added together, along with unnumbered millions of these we are not even aware of, all go to show in yet another way, illustrating the depth and width and height of His love for us. It is absolutely amazing, isn't it? And the half is not yet known.

CREATOR GOD
(OF ALL THINGS AND ALL TIMES)

Attempting to write a book on the many names of the Lord has been many things to me. First, it has been a BLESSING! Second it has been ENJOYABLE. Then on down the list comes challenging, enlightening, difficult, lonely (i.e. isolation to *write*, to which I am not accustomed). Note, that at times I get verbose (i.e. carried away) and at times I am inclined to mix in a bit of humor. Quite often when I use humor (albeit microscopic and/or camouflaged) I am kind to my dear readers and will add a brief parenthetical statement "bit of humor." Otherwise, my humor might go completely unnoticed.

I could be a mite bold and point out that quite a few people have told me that "I have a creative mind." Really, I don't feel like I am bragging to put it immodestly that I have a *quick wit* because I personally get NO credit whatsoever for this trait or "talent." Regardless, I get no credit for this trait because the Almighty Holy God in all of His mercy and this Great and Good God who is also *the* creator saw fit, for whatever the reason, to make me this way. I was born with it. I might have inherited some traits akin to humor from my Mother (my dear Dad   I called him "Pop" was born without even a funny bone in either one of his elbows). I did not study, nor learn, humor/creativity in school either. This was "something" I was born with and for which I am grateful.

All of this personal non-inspiring stuff about me does indeed serve a purpose. The purpose is simple in a profound sort of way: to cause you, dear reader, to think about yourself in your own privacy and "analyze" yourself. Note, it will help greatly if you are age 40 or above. People under 40 are not capable of being *objective* about themselves. Note the clever way I have used psychology so cleverly to make all those 40 and above feel smug about themselves and knowing they now have to be objective. And those under 40 are now challenged (and offended) that I have cleverly implied that its impossible for the younger group to be objective and therefore, they are doggedly determined to prove me wrong, and show that they can be objective. Pretty clever, huh?

ASSIGNMENT: Find your talent. Even, if it's only *one*. You may have to dig it up. (Note, bit of humor, albeit scriptural based.) Every person has talents that the Creator gave to him or her. If you have accumulated great wealth due to your rich relatives generosity, then this type of "talent" doesn't count. Ask God to help you find your talents. Then I leave it up to you to decide what the next step is. If you can't find at least *one*, then I'm not interpreting the Bible correctly in the talentology sections. Or else, you are blessed (??) with an excessive amount of humility (which means you are going (1) to pay money and consult a real psychologist or (2) wake up and get with it and start thanking God for giving you a talent and ask him to now help you find where you buried it.)

Our Creator has indeed created each one of us differently. We are wondrously and marvelously made. Don't we often fail and take our Creator for granted?

THE CREATOR GOD
(AN EXERCISE IN SPIRITUAL WONDERMENT)

Here is a simple spiritual exercise I "invented" which needs to be "tried-out" on a few brave-hearted souls. This may well be your rare opportunity to be among the first to ever participate in a first time ever event.

Make a detailed listing of as many things you can think of, or until your hands/fingers/brains are too exhausted to continue, that God, our Creator, must have had to consider when the creation act/process was first initiated and each individual "noun" (i.e. person, place or thing) that had to react/interact/mesh/coordinate with one or more other created "nouns." In other words, what things had to fit together reference content, timing, results, dependency, etc. for them not be chaos and havoc and mixed-up confusion.

This simple (bit of humor) "exercise" may involve your having to consider such things as air, ozone, ultra violet rays (benefit and harm), electromagnetic forces, moon, tides, water, water containment, chemistry of blood, of God speaking zillion of stars into existence and instantly affixing, or scheduling their precise orbits and making sure the schedule is not only accurate, but can be maintained for extended periods of eons (eternally), or food chains (you may want to start listing at the bottom of the chain, unless you find it easier to begin at the top of the chain), but don't forget to include the affects of weather, storms, draughts, insects etc. that may adversely affect the various components of the chain. Then, don't forget the intricacies of conception, chromosomes, toxic substances, wars, greed and violence of human kind, radioactive ores that must be contained, until discovered, magnetic pulls on ocean tides, heart beats and available on demand, etc. WAIT! WAIT! PAUSE! RECESS TIME OUT! STOP! HALT! TIME OUT! PLEASE!

Just giving a few examples of what you needed to do became mind-boggling even to the brilliant (bit of weird humor) designer of this exercise. And we had just begun to list some of the basics that needed to be properly meshed into the marvels of nature, universe, galaxies, hurricanes, etc.

Let me skip ahead (with your kind permission) to the point I was hoping to make. After pointing out that our wonderful Creator God most certainly had to be (among other things) a God of numbers, math, high math and above all **preciseness** and exactness in all things He created and taking into consideration all things great and small. (Note, how we just put God in a Box???)

There may well be an exception to all this preciseness, which certainly prevents us from putting God in this box. For when it came to the only thing God created in His own image and the most important crucial decision, those human beings, would ever have to make, and indeed one that had eternal ramifications: that decision of choice, i.e. to choose, or reject, "union" with the Creator God. This was left entirely to the *individual*! Imagine such freedom that God saw fit to delegate but it sure ignored preciseness, didn't it?

THE HOLY CHILD
(AND THEY TRIED TO KILL HIM)

The Christmas story never grows old and even as seasoned adults we hear it with renewed freshness each season. And maybe we also enjoy the story because it still speaks in warm and cozy emotions to the child in each of us.

Did you ever think about the "Divine psychology" God used so masterfully in his *plan* to "save the world?" Suppose, just suppose, that Jesus had first appeared on earth as a grown-man-Christ. With miracles, love, power, wisdom and other attributes, he could have undoubtedly established himself as **The Messiah**. But how much better, i.e. God-like perfect, (and here is where the "psychology" comes in) by Jesus beginning His earthly ministry as a tiny baby, we humans would not be as intimidated and could more easily adjust to the slower process of babe-to-child-to-adult. Perhaps this gradual and natural growth, which occurs unnoticed in our minds and is one of but many factors that enables us to so easily allow Jesus, deity and God to become our friend that is closer than a brother.

CHRIST THE CHOSEN OF GOD
(AND HIS *ONLY* CHOICE)

God makes no mistake!

God chose Jesus, His only Son to be the *way* for us. There are many other "terms" you can substitute for "way." He chose Him to be our Savior, to be our Advocate; to be the "propitiation" for us; to be our "reconciler," thus bringing us to himself, i.e. God.

We had a debt (our sins) we could not pay and he chose Jesus, not just to be our own Messiah, but to be our "Ransom." Once this debt ("barrier") was removed, Jesus could be our "Redeemer" and our " Reconciler." Then, and only then, could he unite us with God. But God knew without the shedding of blood there could be no contact and communication and love between us (pitiful, sinful, humans), until a sacrifice was made. Jesus was that sacrifice but God didn't just require a sacrifice; he also needed some way to bridge the tremendous chasm between his Holy nature and our human-like dirty rags. God knew if He personally came to us, we couldn't handle it. Not even Moses could; he only got a partial view. He had the option of sending angels, but something about that wasn't just right. They were a commodity. The divine dilemma was how to show us, His "creation," in an unmistakable way how much He loved us. So He did what had always been known since the foundation of time. He would **give** us His only Son even though it meant sacrificing him on a cruel cross. Even with all of God's might and power, it would mean that at the worst moment, He, God himself, would have to turn around so He did not have to see the final agony and gasping, writhing cruelty. When He heard those words "Why have you forsaken me?" then He would have to turn his back. Not until and after what seemed like an eternity even to the Eternal God, and he finally heard "It is finished" would He turn his eyes to his Son, hoping the eyelids had been mercifully closed.

Thus, God has completed and implemented the most wonderful magnificent PLAN OF THE AGES. There would never be a need to revise it. It would never need replacing.

The design was perfect, as only God could have done. This unique plan, and only this plan, contained the way and the only way humankind could be redeemed and reconciled back to God. And the plan had at its core Love– running throughout the intricate design. The plan could only be implemented by Love, and this Love, both divine love and human love, had to be freely joined, in order to merge our hearts and our spirits into God's heart and spirit. There were no edicts. Love was to be freely given, by all parties involved.

Finally, (and the *finally* goes on and on) the separate and combined aspects of the Triune God, the Father, the Son and the Holy Spirit were not just at the Plan's core, but as active participants in every thought and action. Loving and touching each and every soul – past, present and forever more.

THE COMFORTER
(THE COMFORTER HAS NO EGO)

This is one of the many *perfect* names for our Lord. And I love the sound. It implies nearness, reassurance and on and on.

Not that other names aren't "perfect," but this title seems to be so apt in many situations and circumstances. Katherine Marshall in her beautiful book "The Helper" brought renewed interest to the Holy Spirit and the many practical and inspiring applications of the Holy Spirit operating in our lives. May I suggest you read chapters 14, 15, and 16, of John's gospel? Read aloud, slowly and carefully.

Certainly most of us remember the meaningful words of Jesus, delivered at such a needed moment in His Farewell Address to His disciples mentioning several times the Holy Spirit, e.g., Helper, Advocate, Comforter and Spirit of Truth. These pensive moments were of extreme value to His followers who were probably in a state of overload. They were hearing so much: deep unfathomable thoughts, "surprises" (they could not believe their ears) but all being tempered with reason, ("it is to your advantage that I go away") and ("He will guide and teach you") but including one very important thing they desperately needed: reassurance, i.e. "the Father will give you another Helper and He will abide with you forever."

These are indeed "rich" and profound truths Jesus gave them. However, the brief condensed moments were like viable compacted "seeds." These divine announcements were planted in that upper room but intended to sprout, grow and develop and from that moment on, as these substantial tenets and foundations of the Kingdom of God were established throughout the rest of an unending eternal salvation of humankind and to all inhabitants throughout the world and for all ages to ensue. Profound and mind boggling indeed.

POINT: Did not Jesus Christ, who came from the Father God and had talked often of Him; now He the Son of God had just quietly, cleverly and divinely announced the third member of the Trinity. The Trinity or the Godhead (and without ever using the word). And it still hasn't been used in the Bible itself, which in no way detracts from the importance or significance of the glory and majesty of the Spirit of

Truth. The mission: bring about the will of God, show the love of the Son, and, all the while operating in the nebulous and intangible reign of the Spirit and the Truth.

> God is a Spirit and we must worship Him in Spirit and, did Jesus not
> say "I am the Truth."

> No one comes to the Father except via the Truth of the one, who also said "I am the way."

The Comforter has come.... He stayed.... and He is still with us.

CUP OF BLESSING
(HYMN DESCRIPTION OF OUR CARING LORD)

As *believers* in a world that may or may not love us or even appreciate us, perhaps, just perhaps, we often make the mistake of thinking that we have to play God and save the world. Especially when, we are overwhelmed by some drastic event, or a major problem, of a friend or stranger, which we are quickly aware, is far beyond our own capabilities. A simple example might be finding you're on board a small boat that has sprung a leak and it is obvious that the boat will sink and the other occupant, who cannot swim, will drown. You have one of two options: swim away to safety, or take the empty coffee mug lying in the bottom of the boat and begin to bail the water. The single cup is certainly not large enough, but it is all you have–and you have it. Perhaps if you do use it, you buy some time   until help can get there   certainly the person that would drown *knows* what you are trying to do. Admittedly, this example is overly dramatic. But how many times do we encounter a tough situation, and not even try to do "something" with whatever "cup of blessing" we do have. No, we don't have to play God. And He is the one to save the world, not us. But maybe there is something we <u>can</u> do.

Sitting in a waiting room of an auto dealership waiting for my car to be serviced was another routine wait. Unlike most people, I really did not mind it. If I have a paper and pen I can write. Good utilization of time and time goes by smoothly. Only one other person waiting. Usually the room would be filled with people and noise and a blaring TV. When no one was around to object, I turned the TV down. Way down.

Now, I was all set to write. Most good writers have laptops and PC's and word processors. I am not yet, if ever, a good writer, and I have no reputation to maintain. So all I need is a pen and a few sheets of paper. So I began to write, and felt as smug as a bug in shag carpet. The other person waiting, a woman seemed forlorn and fidgety. An odd combo. But I ignored her. Pretty soon the waiting room added a few more fellow "waiters." They all stared hard at the TV. I could tell it bothered them. Not enough volume. But like robots or zombies they all sat and stared, as they lip-read Katie, Matt and Ann. They could hear a little bit of Al. Strangely no one thought of using the remote control, which could have solved the dilemma. It was on a chair between two of my fellow waiters, but neither seemed to notice it, right where I had left it under a couple of magazines that dated back to the previous century. So I minded my own business and wrote, still enjoying the peace and quiet. You would think a room full of people would talk and chat, what with the TV so low you could only barely hear Al, but he only interrupted us every half hour on the half hour with the weather.

Eventually, cars were serviced and names were called – except for mine and the forlorn lady's. I probably should have mentioned that early on, I "got" the feeling that I should speak to her, but I ignored the "feeling" which is why I didn't mention it earlier, since it didn't reflect very well upon my Christian behavior, nor my Southern hospitality. Finally, with just the two of us in the room and with the TV volume quiet low, which made it conducive to a conversation, I belatedly obeyed the "nudge" and began a conversation with Ms. Forlorn.

Now, pay attention, dear reader, and see all the things the Lord unfolded within the next ninety minutes on the heels of a two hour period of nothing worthwhile, thanks mostly to my wanting to be alone in my shag rug.

Ms. Fidgety and Forlorn turned out to be pleasant and kind, probably in her late forties or early fifties. She had her "plate" full of troubles, as they say around here. The previous day, Sunday, she had been stranded three times when her car broke down (quit running) three times in one afternoon on I-95 while she was traveling alone (except for her elderly cat) on a thrice thwarted attempt at moving from south Florida to northern Maine.

She (and her elderly cat) had spent the night in an unknown strange town in a lonely motel room. Now here she sat in a strange waiting room on a Monday morning with a soundless TV and a room full of sour faced southern gentleman who obviously do not exude charm on Monday mornings. Fortunately, the morning had evolved to mid-morning and the only person (me) in the room finally spoke, asking what brings you to this place?

Immediately, she told me her story of woe of her thrice broken down automobile and of her lonely elderly cat, now waiting alone at the motel, probably feeling deserted, in spite of the red roof on the motel. The Sabbath day had definitely not been a good day or a day of rest.

After she quickly summarized the previous day's woeful events and being stranded mid-way between two daughters, one in Maine and one in Florida, who wanted to help and couldn't, but she was able to cry on their shoulders via long distance. She concluded by adding a postscript "and I even had someone praying for me now look at all that's gone wrong with this trip."

Feeling a strong need to say something "reassuring" I replied, the trip isn't over yet and you still don't know all that God is going to do. She just stared at me with a puzzled look and it was obvious my response surprised her. Fact is, it surprised me, too.

Then, I did what most of you would do. I decided God needed my help to help her. I know that is ridiculous and I also know God doesn't need my help. But, in my defense, there was no other person around at the time, but me. And I didn't notice any *unaware angels* anywhere in the place.

The next minutes were action packed. I offered to let her (and her elderly cat) stay in our home that night or for the next several nights until her car could be repaired. She was speechless and eyed me somewhat suspiciously.

I told her that while her car was being repaired, I would drive her to the motel so she could check on her lonely cat. We went together and talked with the service manager. Her car needed a new alternator, which was more than Anne's budget could stand and it would take several days for it to arrive.

Meanwhile, we discussed a serious health problem with the service manager about his seven-week old grandson. We discovered that his grand-baby was suffering from a very rare disease, so Anne added the grand-baby to her prayer list and was able to share love and concern.

A man on crutches with a newly amputated foot entered our "circle" and Anne and I shared with him. Anne added him to her prayer list. I silently noted that God was crossing her path with individuals who had **real** problems. Meanwhile, a mechanic came in and answered that a rebuilt alternator had been found for one-third the cost and her car would be ready in a couple of hours.

While at the motel, I arranged for an extended checkout time for Anne and told her to stay with her cat for an hour, while I sat in my car and did some non-interrupted writing.

As we were about to leave Anne's motel, she mentioned that she had no idea where she was and how on earth would she ever find her way back to the dealer or the interstate. I reminded her that God does all things well and directed her eyes to the right and in the distance of about ¼ a mile was the sign of the auto dealer. Then directed her view to the left about 1/8 of a mile, we could see the Interstate 95 North sign —both views connected by one convenient wide boulevard. The Lord had certainly located her nicely.

Arriving back at the auto dealer, we found her car parked out front and ready to roll. I asked Anne if she needed any money to finish the trip and she said "no" but embarrassed me by calling me something that sounded like she said "angel." (A first for me.)

After loading Anne's luggage and cat into her car, Anne and I did two things any two believers should do: standing together at the trunk of her car, we exchanged e-mail addresses and then enjoyed a prayer of thanksgiving and of traveling mercies.

Addendum for all cat lovers: The rest of the trip was uneventful and "Lucy" is living happily ever after   in Maine.

Another Addendum: To share this story is in no way meant to reflect on any good deeds that I might have done, or to mention being referred to in angelic tones. The real reason for sharing this story and the real point that needs to be made is, just think (and it's scary) how close I came to *almost* not doing anything.

THE CHRIST OF GOD
(THE FINAL ANSWER)

Jesus asked a question two thousand years ago: "Who do men say I am?" Peter immediately answered for himself and his fellow disciples, "The Christ of God." And today we must answer the same question of Jesus. Who do men say I am? A beautiful answer might be: "Jesus you are the Christ of God; you are Christ of men; you are Christ for me! You are Christ the King. Another good answer: You are my Lord and Savior. Yet another answer: Lord, you are certainly the Christ, but to me you are a "personal God" that I love so dearly; you are the only One, on whom I can absolutely depend. I can worship at the mention of your name.

To really answer, the question isn't so easy. Jesus was really asking who do the people you associate with day in and day out who do the people around you say that I am? Here is a list of possible answers: truthful answers to a direct question from the Christ of God.

Well Lord, to tell you the truth the people I'm around don't really talk about you a lot   in fact, I hardly ever hear your name mentioned   well, now that I think about it, there are some exceptions, but they are not necessarily "good." But I do hear you mentioned quite often on Sunday, well, when I go to church on Sunday, and I try to be there fairly regular   not as often as I should y   ou know what I mean. And now that I think of it, your name is mentioned quite often on television on Sunday, but I don't watch too much of that religious stuff   know what I mean. A lot of them seem to always be asking for money.

And the other time your name is mentioned quite often, and I really hate to tell you this   is when people are talking   most of the time it is grown men, but not always   sometimes it can be women or, even yet, children many   use your name in swearing. However, most of the time they are upset or mad, but I don't reckon that excuses them. Many times I almost speak up and would like to tell them that they should not do that,   take your name in vain. But I would probably offend them but I reckon you g   et offended, too.

I feel awful Lord. You are the Christ. You are the Holy Christ, the

94

very Son of God. You are the righteous one. Blessed One and Redeemer; my Lord is my God and my Savior. You suffered, bled and died for me. And yet I don't have enough courage to defend the Holy name of the Christ of God. Lordy Mercy!

THE CHRIST
(THERE IS NONE OTHER)

Matthew 16:16

In this verse Jesus seems to be conducting his own public opinion survey. He asked his disciples (in our language of today) "what are they saying who do they say I am?" He then received a sampling of some current responses of that time. But perhaps Jesus wasn't all that interested in what the general public thought or said. Maybe he only wanted to know what his own close associates would say. So he asked a direct question: "But who do you say that I am?" Not surprisingly, Peter volunteered the first response. His answer was succinct, factual and accurate.

Now, let's imagine that Jesus asked us this two-part question:

PART ONE: And what are the people that you come in contact with saying about me who do they say I am?

"They can't use your name in public."

"What? Why?"

"Well our Supreme Court told us so."

"Well, for another example, we aren't allowed to pray before our football games begin."

In fact, your name can't really be used in most of our schools. *"To be honest Lord, your name really gets battered around a lot, know what I mean?"* **("I'm afraid I do. But please explain.")**

"Well, like cuss words; swearing, but they don't mean any harm." **("Sounds like they are using my name in vain. That rule was explained to Moses several years ago. In fact it was given to him, to coin a phrase, "carved in stone.")**

Well, some people feel more comfortable calling you by some nebulous term like the Great Spirit, A Higher Power or maybe just the Magnificent.

However, your names are used a lot in movies or even on television, but nearly always in a profane way.

And your names are common in everyday language by many people, but used in a flippant way, totally non-relevant way.

PART TWO: What do you say or do when you hear all this evil

unthinkable odious, totally non-concerned blasphemous use of the Son of God's name?

Suggestion to Reader: Answer this question in your next prayer to our Holy God, whose name is above all names.

DIVINE
(BUT <u>HE</u> CAME DOWN)

We humans, "mere mortals," have a hard time relating to this term. We understand what it means and that normally makes us uncomfortable. Divine implies holy, high, heavenly, all power, all knowing, all wisdom, unreachable, and far away. It especially implies Holy, Holy, and Holy. All of these words, or concepts, are "foreign" to us and only serve to make us feel more uncomfortable and further distanced from God, the Divine. We feel insignificant, powerless, remote and not worthy. And on top of all that, God is immortal, while we are mortal. Earthly mortal. If we let our minds dwell on it, we feel helpless and humiliated. Therefore, we move our minds away from this and try to think about something else.

God is also LOVE and MERCY. So he came up with a "NEW" plan to replace (or supersede) the "OLD" plan. Oswald Chambers described the new plan best: God became a baby.

Note from the author: I admit (without apology) to using Oswald Chamber's phrase "God Became a Baby" at least four times in this book. I was impacted (permanently impacted) from the first time I read this highly descriptive and accurate and touching phrase. I have also overused the term "Awesome" throughout these chapters, for which I somewhat apologize.

Isn't the phrase "God became a baby" awesome??

OUR DAYSPRING
(A UNIQUE NAME)

This is a very interesting name of our Lord. It could certainly be called unusual, if for no other reason than that the term only appears twice in the entire Bible (KJV).

Job 38:12 **Hast thou "commanded the morning since thy days; and caused the dayspring to know his place;**
Luke 1:78 **through the tender mercy of our God; whereby the dayspring from on high hath visited us,**

Personally, I like the *sound* of the name. It certainly implies a number of positive, upbeat traits, i.e. sunrise, almost sunrise, another day-is-a-coming newness, vigor, spring-in-the-step, eagerness, opportunity, etc. Almost all of us go through tough, trying tribulations. Often we call them "valleys." Job had certainly gone through a devastated deep dark valley. Perhaps, the valley of all valleys. Job had been in the deepest and darkest "valley" for what must have seemed like an unending forever.

Job most likely never dreamt that the eventual exit out of this valley would have such a marvelous recovery experience. "Beauty out of ashes" might be apt terms to describe the metamorphosis.

In the valley of experience most of us go through (and thankfully, never as severe as Job's) we spend most of our valley time wallowing in misery, wading through dismal pessimistic mind sets as opposed to planning and anticipating the joy and good times that eventually lie ahead. In these "despair pits," even when we think of Heaven, our moods aren't necessarily glorious and "won't it be beautiful there" anticipating scenarios.

All the reason we need a "Dayspring God" for He alone can create from the worst of our horrible experiences, hurts, bitterness, wrongs, the **new start resurrection** we so desperately need to even enjoy our survival. Dayspring is the perfect name (and the only explanation) for such a miracle.

"Morning has dawned."
"Dayspring has sprung."

THE DEAD MESSIAH??
(BUT NOT FOR LONG)

It is easy for us to tell about how "they" crucified Jesus. In today's language "they executed Jesus or to put it very bluntly, "they" <u>killed</u> Jesus." "They" are obvious and well-known culprits, i.e. Pharisees, Sadducees, Pilate, Jewish religious leaders, and Roman soldiers. Even the disciples that were closest to Jesus temporarily deserted Jesus. The Bible gives a brief listing on what I call the faithful "final four" which should certainly qualify them for a Hall of Faithfulness Hall of Fame. Jesus said, " It is finished." Wesley penned it poignantly in a Seventeenth Century hymn "tis finished."

Only God himself knew that this "ending" was only a preface to the greatest **"victory"** to ever, ever be won—only a matter of three days away.

In one place in all of the scriptures, these four people are identified by name as standing near the cross. Where were the others? Most likely watching from "afar," if even that close. Shortly afterwards, Jesus would pronounce the most extraordinary and unique benediction ever uttered: **"It is finished."** His own benediction: A benediction of seemingly sadness and despair.

What has to be the saddest moment in all of history ages and eons, past and future: The Messiah died. The Son of God deserted by almost everyone.

Just suppose we had been there on crucifixion day. Would we have done any better? Or, to bring the scenario up to date, have I deserted my Lord when a burst of profanity erupts like a slap on his face. And yet, I ignored or pretended not to hear, as though my Messiah was dead.

THE DESPISED JESUS
(...AND YET ALTOGETHER LOVELY)

The people around Jesus during his short-term tenure on this earth came up with a lot of reasons to <u>despise</u> him.

That's an ugly, harsh, cutting word: you don't hear it used much today. They probably despised him because of his lowly birth (lower than being born in the slums or ghetto).

They certainly talked about his questionable birth. And most gossip is a form of "despisement". (Right?)

They probably despised a small dinky village like Bethlehem (but it sounds "sweet" in a Christmas carol).

The innkeeper was on the border of despising when he had no room for a young obviously pregnant teenager (not even a rollaway).

The King himself despised Jesus (and all those in his age group).

The religious leaders, full of piety and prestige, despised him to death (and they were the cream of the crop–religiously speaking).

Hog farmers despised him. (No one likes to lose $$$ even if it smells.)

He upset the money changers. (Reckon they despised the *change* he made in their business?)

The tax collectors really got "upset" and despised his radical thought on the method of distributing revenue. (imagine giv   ing to the poor!)

Pilate, perhaps didn't despise Jesus personally (but he despised the responsibility that meeting Jesus placed on him). (He tried to wash off the despisement.)

Most of his disciples, when things got hot, scattered or hid or fled or lied. (Perhaps this could be modified and be termed "employer dissatisfaction.")

The above listing does not pretend to list all examples of despisement (or borderline despisement) cited in the Holy Scriptures of our Lord and Savior, the Holy Son of God.

Just two after-thoughts on this subject:

1. Aren't we relieved there wasn't enough space to perhaps list examples of when our own actions exhibited despisement? (Or borderline despisement?)
2. Isn't it fortunate that Jesus had no desire to run for a political office? (Obviously!)

THE DIVIDER
(OUCH!)

Our Father is "tough". But he has a right to be. He sacrificed His own Son. His words are hard and demanding. He does not have to evade or soft-pedal. No one can say the author did not warn us. The intent is to divide! Even divide asunder.

His word is always sharp enough (just like a sword) to slice a critical line between the membrane of soul and spirit, so that the swipe exposes bare truth. And this type of surgery is not elective. It hurts! But if any of us, even as a human and not divine, had given our only son, or even a son, we would feel that we had a right to be demanding.

We can't escape this "asundering" procedure. God's sword is sharp on both sides so it will get us coming or going. If not on the downward swipe as we dodge or run away, then on the upward thrust as it returns. Make no mistake, it will return, but it will not return void.

"...Even to the dividing asunder of soul and spirit..."
Hebrews 4:12

"...it shall not return unto me void..." Isaiah 55:11

THE DONKEY RIDER
(A KING ON SUCH??)

What lessons can we learn from Jesus riding a donkey? Surely he should have ridden into town sitting in a fancy chariot pulled by several white horses. There was a prophecy to be fulfilled so the religious scholars of his day should not have been surprised at his mode of transportation.

Jesus was very specific, once upon a time, while speaking to the church leaders of his day, pointing out how they loved to sit in the most important seats in the synagogue. These seats probably had a "Reserved" sign prominently affixed.

I think about this scripture every time I drive up in front of a church and am immediately confronted with signs reading "Reserved for Pastor," "Reserved for Associate Pastor," "Reserved for Music Director," etc. etc.

Can you imagine a sign in front of the Temple saying Reserved for the Messiah or Reserved for Jesus?

No way!

Luke 11:43

THE DOOR KEEPER
(DO I HEAR A KNOCK?)

There are several references in the Bible to the **Door** and specifically warning people to enter in by using the *correct* door. There would appear to be a door, i.e. "one" door that we, the "sheep" of Jesus: should use. And it could be stated by the process of elimination this is the onlyiest (sic) door to be used. The language gets pretty tough about those that would attempt to get in by some unauthorized door. They are compared to being the same as a thief and robber. Evidently, thieves and robbers were despicable (no good) characters in those days. Today, such characters might try to be excused by coming from broken homes or hard times. Most people have just moved into more modernistic homes trying to ignore the inevitable.

Jesus also is referred to as *the* Way, which is very similar to the terminology about the door. Fortunately, or unfortunately, both of these terms are extremely easy to understand. In fact, they really don't lend themselves to requiring a lot of interpretation or explanation even though as a child, I heard some pretty long sermons explaining and re-explaining what "the Door" and "the Way" actually meant and the procedures associated with these entrances.

I figure I might as well go ahead and explain it to all you younger folks that were not around in the yesterdays like I was. What it meant back then was that there was only one way to "get saved." There are some plain talking scriptures that let it be known that Jesus is the door and we must go through **that** door to get to God. No "ifs" "ands" and "buts" about it.

It appears that modernization of spiritual principles and our more enlightened age of thought would (perhaps??) take into consideration such things as:

If you live a good, moral life.

If your Ma and Pa were good, God-fearing, folks.

It's no big matter what you believe, as long as you are *sincere*.

If you were baptized at some point in your life and/or dedicated as a small baby.

One or more of the above are sure to get you a good seat on the front row of Heaven. Just as long as you can find a loophole around one verse of scripture that states "salvation is found in no one else, for there is no other name under Heaven given to men by which we must be saved."

Therefore, it is clear that Jesus himself is the "Door Keeper." Only, I should perhaps mention that as the official door keeper Jesus has one unusual feature: He lets **us** do the opening, as long as the requirements are met.

In our world today, a lot of "beliefs" have been watered down and explained away. A lot of alternate doors and routes are being proposed, offered or "sold." We could be kidding ourselves and skating on thin (dangerous) ice. All the time trying to ignore what we really *feel;* that the way still leads to the *Only Door*. Jesus keeps the welcome mat out. But He will not force us to enter.

P.S.   Back to an earlier point: Have you ever thought how many seconds it would take to melt the thin ice on which we so merrily skate?

THE DOOR KNOCKER
(LISTEN...SOMEONE IS KNOCKING)

Isn't it wonderful that we have a personal God that stands at the door knocking. Usually we think of him and restrict him to knocking "at the door of salvation." Without a doubt, the "door of invitation" is the most important. But make no mistake about it: this personal God stands at *many* doors in our life. Doors of loneliness, doors of frustration, doors of opportunity, doors of problems, desperate for a solution. Doors of guilt, rejection, depression and the lists of doors goes on and on. Indeed, there is a door for every need, every problem. But the door "latch" is always on the inside. He will never force himself on you.

So, before you decide there is no solution for your problem, or before you decide to remain in your mire or hopelessness; before you decide to quit and give up: LISTEN. It may well be a gentle tapping at the door instead of a loud knock. Listen today, and see if there isn't a door *you* need to open.

"Be still and know that I am God"

THE DUST MOLDER
(DID YOU SAY DUST?)

There were many lessons that God or Jesus taught us <u>indirectly</u> and perhaps we miss them. Our eyes and our minds are upon the bigger picture or the main event. Obviously, we need to be focused on the central issue. However, the little details can be, not just interesting, but important. There are dozens of examples and each one carries the possibility of being sermon material. Well, maybe sermonette substance.

To list a few:

Suppose Noah focused too much on the wood (and the wood grain) and forgot to put pitch on the bottom side of the ark. (After all, it wouldn't show under the water.)

When God chose dirt (or dust) to make man, why did he select such a worthless material (Was there a hidden message here?) The laws of supply and demand didn't do much for our basic, original value. (Was he trying to tell us something about our intrinsic value before he breathed a "spirit" into us?) Even after you add in the various components silica, carbon etc., the value of the substances still only amounts to less than a dollar.

Afterthought to the above: what happens to this "dirt" and all its chemicals after the "spirit" (life) departs? It returns to its original configuration, doesn't it? "Configuration" sounds better (more important sounding) than saying it returns to <u>dust.</u> (Was God trying to introduce re-cycling?)

To summarize this subject and try to ponder just what God would have us learn:

that our God is so great that He could indeed take the most plentiful and worthless (cheap?) material of all and create *potential*.

that he needed only take this unimpressive material and breathe on it, or in it, in order for *it* to come alive.

that it wasn't until the *eternal* factor (soul) was introduced that His creation really gained significance.

God is the Creator and we are the created, the creature, the createe. Whatever accomplishments or successes we might eventually enjoy, we can never, never glory in them because it is God that had made us–and not we ourselves.

Our greatest worth comes because God made us. And our greatest glory comes because He showed His love to us through His Only Son.

THE EAR REPAIRER
("OUCH"..."WHAT"..."WOW")

Sometimes you run across an incident in the Bible that doesn't seem all that important and you might wonder, why it was included? What or why the significance? Such is the story of the "ear amputation" recorded or mentioned in three of the gospels. Mark and Luke do not even identify the "swordsman." Luke only referenced the incident but does mention Peter as the disciple who did the cutting. Matthew gives the most space to the incident, including the incident itself and considerable detail as to Jesus' commentary. He, too, identifies Peter as the one using the sword.

We can probably assume that the act of violence itself and the quick repair of the injury only took *seconds*. A half-second and another half-second for Jesus to quickly and easily repair the damage. Now, back to the opening sentence, as to what we can learn from this two-second, two-act play. Or, at a minimum, what questions can we ask in the never-ending quest for spiritual insight.

Was this yet another impulsive act on the part of Peter?

Was Peter trying desperately to make up for his lax behavior as a disciple?

After all, he had just been caught asleep on the job. A Roman soldier caught sleeping on duty would have been immediately executed for derelict duty.

Also, Peter had just been told by his Lord and Master that he would deny Jesus before the next daylight. Was the bravado on Peter's part to convince the Master? Peter had indicated that others might fail the Lord, but "not me, Lord."   I'll go with you, both to prison and/or death.

As they left the Passover supper, Jesus had told the disciples to "take a sword" or sell a garment and buy a sword. He had even agreed that two swords were enough. What was the purpose?

Did Jesus sense his disciples' fear and know they needed the earthly comfort of a couple of swords? Did he not know that in just a very brief period all of his disciples (except one) were going to run away and hide in the dark?

Moments before the sword was drawn, Jesus had asked his Father, if He could be spared this ordeal, i.e. let this cup pass? When Peter pulled his sword and drew blood, did Jesus, for a brief second, consider calling twelve legions of angels with drawn swords?

Probably not, for he immediately halted Peter and said "enough is enough"   "those that take the sword will die by the sword." (Phillips) And immediately, with no obvious effort, he put the ear back in place.

EVER PRESENT
(... IN NEED IS A FRIEND INDEED)

Let us play *the game* again. You remember, the one where we consider or scan all the names, titles, attributes, etc., and then decide on *the* "Top Ten." None of us like this so-called "game" but we all agree (don't we) that it is a great way of illustrating how wonderful God is, because it is nigh-onto-impossible to stop with *ten*.

I vote for including Ever Present as a major, important, crucial and vital term. Certainly, He is Holy and Mighty and Wise and Strong and Eternal and Mighty and Loving and Redeemer and Savior and Divine and Truth and Life and on and on. However, one thing that is especially wonderful is that 'He" is **ever present**!

When we need Him, He is there. In fact, "there" would be another good name for God, because **He is always there** (which makes God have a three named title, Always There God). Or, said another way: Ever Present.

We don't have to go to Rome, or wherever, Buddas live. Or, we don't have to wait on a particular religious holiday, or until a priest is available, for our confession. Fact is, we know *the* Great Priest. And he don't (sic) live in Rome, Italy, or Rome, Georgia. One might say with a bit of respectful humor, He "roams" all the time, so He is ever present.

We don't have to climb a high mountain to see a wise man or Guru behind a white beard and long gray hair. We certainly don't have to climb a high mountain on a rugged trail of broken glass to do penance in order to reach our High and Lofty God, who is indeed High and Mighty but He is also Ever Present, which has been previously stated thereto.

Our God is not a Supreme Power. He is *the* Supreme Power. Some supposedly Supreme Power gods are everywhere, up there floating around and allowing free spirits to be free spirits–doing their thing. One of the things they supposedly do is become gods themselves. As my grandfather often said, "those little so-called gods aren't worth a half-a-dime," for three dozen of them."

What people need is an Ever Present God, available when and

wherever needed, but one that is touched by the feelings of our hurts and needs and fears. If, also, you know this Ever Present God's only begotten Son, what you really want to do is to be able to call him by his first name.

One final note, even though one can never stop talking, telling, testifying and describing **our Ever Present God**, it is worth noting that He is Ever Present in time of trouble and He never sleeps or goes off on long journeys, which is another reason, He is Ever Present.

Do you begin to get the picture??

OUR EXAMPLE
(NONE BETTER)

Don't we try to make Christianity too complex and too complicated? Don't we try to make it too difficult to learn? Don't we overfill it with rules and regulations and policies and doctrines and traditions and dozens of other do's and don't do's, when our basic manual, i.e. the Bible, already contains a gracious plenty of all the aforementioned. And probably the worst result of all this "overcomplicating" is that we then instill in our own thinking and the thought processes of others, that the implementation or application of Christian living is entirely too difficult a task/lifestyle for us to ever be successful. In fact, in our minds (even though, who said it was "fact") living a *true* Christian life becomes nigh onto impossible and/or improbable.

Perhaps after years (even centuries) of going to the extreme, we need to deliberately go to the other extreme and see if something can't be gained by beginning to re-simplify this complicated, regulated "faith" of ours.

Jesus Christ, our example, on a number of occasions put the essence of the gospel in a few precious words:

> **If you've done it to the least, you've done it to me.**
> **Love your neighbor as yourself.**
> **He who would be first must be last.**

AMEN!

P.S.   And He might well have added, "And stop trying to put me in a box."

114

THE EXAMPLE
(NONE OTHER CAN COMPETE)

I am basically an "old man." As they say, I've been around the horn a few times. I can readily admit to being an "old man" but would prefer that we preface the title with "wise old." Hence, this wise old man usually thinks he is quite savvy at most things and even pretty good at some things. Like for instance, sizing people up quickly and astutely and correctly, in my years working in the human resource field, extensive years of employment and training; even quite adept as a pseudo-counselor. Note lower case "c" on " counselor," since my background is empirical. Now, having modestly (sic) described my impressive credentials, oh, but how it pains me to admit that I still "blow it" in one of my major strength arenas, i.e. sizing people up, which involves compressed psychoanalysis and instant evaluation. I am just about always right.

Having said that, I remember the phrase my grandfather coined " " *almost*" it don't amount to a hill of beans on a dried up mound of red Georgia clay, EXCEPT in horseshoes."

Would you; could you believe that within the last thirty days I completely misread two individuals? They appeared, as easy to read as a book cover. In fact, that is exactly what I did, I read, not one, but two "books" by their covers. I assumed neither one had a personality, neither one had anything on the ball and neither one would I care to get to know at all.

Well as it "improperly" turned out, both individuals not only had a personality, but they had nice personalities and several other good points that I had missed (by a mile), as I prejudged them. In fact, only with a smidgen of effort, I now consider them both as NICE new friends and I do want to know them even better. (I think my grandfather also said something about not judging a book by its cover.) Incidentally, I've given up reading book covers. The Bible, which never misses out on anything important, mentions a number of instances about the dangers of misreading book covers.

Don't get fooled by a book cover that prays loud and impressively on busy street corners.

Don't judge a person by his or her book cover, unless you can really know what is going on in their heart.

Don't judge the book cover of some poorly dressed insignificant looking little old widow woman when she just contributed a much greater percentage than you did.

Don't be fooled by some big mouth fisherman's book cover when he tells you all the wonderful things he is going to do.

Don't judge a house builder's book cover, until after a hard rain.

Don't judge the book cover of a successful farmer (or buy stock in) who is planning to tear down his barns and

Do you need more examples? Read **the Book**.

MY FRIEND
(MAJOR THINGS JESUS DOES FOR ME)

O.K. Here is my list   and it probably took me less than a minute to complete or think of the ten items.

1.   Salvation → A Foundation

2.   Eternal Life

3.   Gave Me Peace/Assurance

4.   Removed Fear Of Many Concerns

5.   Death Is Not The End

6.   Meet Loved Ones Again

7.   Not Alone– Now Or Forever–With Me Always

8.   Peace   So Important To Me

9.   I Have A Source! Comfort/Strength/Guidance/Peace/Friend

10.   Anticipation –An Eagerness Versus A Fear Of The Unknown

The thing "wrong" with my own list is that it contains so many "duplications." In other words, so many *overlaps*. But I cannot help it. **This is my list**. Therefore, I should be able to do it "my way." And so should you have the same prerogative with your list. Perhaps this is another way of saying that "salvation" is a personal thing, i.e. *between God and me*.

FAIREST LORD JESUS
("BEAUTIFUL SAVIOR")

I had this interesting thought, when I suddenly awoke at about 4:00 am: that the Lord is an "artist" and sometimes communicates with us on a rare individual basis by giving us a *visual scene* in our minds. Strangely, this seemed to explain a mystical experience I had 40 years earlier when, while busily getting ready for work. I was listening to "Fairest Lord Jesus" on a 33 1/3 phonograph. I paused in the middle of the room, encapsulated by the ancient melody and closeness in spirit, when I "saw" in the brief part of a second of time (and I saw it in clarity and vivid detail) three individuals that I had known quite well but all had died, within the last couple of years and were members of the same small church I had attended. Other than that and that we knew each other, they did not have a lot in common. The youngest had died tragically at age 19 in an automobile accident, another at age 34, within hours of successfully undergoing open-heart surgery and the oldest (late seventies) died peacefully in his sleep at home. They were peacefully walking side by side at a leisurely pace but no doubt to a destination, doing some talking and sharing, but obviously enjoying themselves. Their surroundings were in a natural park like setting mostly shaded by interspersed shadows and sunlight. Their path was wide enough for three and led down a comfortable slope, beautiful enclosed with trees, shrubs, and ferns. I don't recall any flowers but I think they were conversing as they walked.

There was nothing shocking or surprising in my own emotions as I witnessed this "mini-vision." The scene was so natural and peaceful that I almost felt as if I (about 10 yards away) was a sightseer of which they were unaware. It was indeed a divine experience for me, one many years later I still vividly recall in freeze-frame preciseness.

The only unnatural thing about the entire episode: these three departed friends looked exactly as I had last seen them–except there was no difference between them in their "ages."

FATHER OF THE FAITHFUL
(THE REAL COMMANDING OFFICER)

The story you are about to read is one hundred percent true, but told with bits of jest and humor so as to dilute the morbidity of what you are about to read.

This is one of the most remarkable stories I have ever heard. Perhaps you need to have served in the military to comprehend how absolutely remarkable (improbable) that it really happened. It involves an individual (a close relative) who is also one of my lifelong friends. We have been very close all of our lives. Get the picture? Therefore, I know assuredly that this unbelievable story is _true_.

Fact is, our association since boyhood has involved our being frequently together (except for a four-year period when he and I went our separate ways during the Korean War); he to the U.S. Navy and me to the U.S. Army. Fact is, parenthetically, we tried to join the Navy at the same time but, alas, I was rejected, due to my right leg being slightly shorter. True! Other than this period we have been around each other and known everything about each other and remained closest of friends. We even married sisters.

One important point, involving his character and integrity needs to be established before this unusual story can unfold. This dear friend has **always** had (then and now) a very serious relationship with Jesus Christ. He is _dedicated_. In his Navy days he would most certainly have been known as a religious fanatic! He did not drink any type of alcoholic beverage; he never used (and has never) a single cuss word. The list of holy traits goes on and on, i.e. read Bible every day, consistent in his prayer life, studied the Bible diligently, and He lived and lives a holy and pure life. He had dedicated himself totally to his Lord. I can easily describe him, as the most trusted, trustworthy person I ever knew. The son of a minister, he was raised in a super strict (Biblical) environment and many years after the death of his godly parents he is still "living and walking the talk." Probably the best I've ever known. But still well rounded, hard-working, great husband, father and grandfather. Always dedicated to his church and actively involved. Always paid his tithes, etc. etc. etc. A very sincere, likable person.

Do you get the picture? Now this remarkable, unbelievable story can finally be told. Incidentally, I cannot reveal his name or the name of the ship on which he served, since he is concerned that he might be arrested and charged for what he did 50 years ago somewhere in the middle of the Pacific Ocean.

He served on a small ship that carried a well-known name, which I cannot reveal. There were approximately 267 sailors on board; small enough so that everyone on board knew all their shipmates and there were very few secrets. A lot of men living together in very close quarters, for many months at a time. This particular ship did indeed experience "war." It **is** war and not mere "conflict" when the enemies shoots big holes in you and/or your ship, whilst you are trying to also put big holes in them, even if you can't see the whites of their eyes.

Not to drag this remarkable story out much longer, I do need to go on record saying that all of the facts in this story can be substantiated by official government records with the single exception of the "crime" itself and even that can be substantiated by a sworn affidavit and polygraph (now that the captain and other officers are deceased). During the time this story occurred (1952) there was a U.S. Navy tradition (covered by official regulations, of course) that **no** alcoholic beverages of any kind, including beer, were allowed on board the good ship, with one and only one exception. Just before the ship sailed from port and if the ship was going to be at sea for a long period of time, one load of beer would be taken on board, while closely guarded and supervised; then immediately, placed under lock and key far below deck in a secured area. The precise number of sealed cases was noted and recorded and then double locked. Only the captain of the ship and one other person had the keys. Although everyone on board was well aware of this precious, cherished cargo and true to Navy tradition going back to the days of rum, knew that this beer would and could be liberated and consumed by the thirsty sailors when, and only when, they had been at sea for a very long period of time and furthermore, that they had served obediently above and beyond the call of duty and on the strict condition that the consumption of the beer be allowed when, and only when, there was a justifiable reason for "rewarding" the crew for their hard efforts taking into consideration the extended period at sea, no land in sight for many weeks, reinforced for jobs well done and/or being under enemy fire. All of these conditions had been met and the crew was raring and ready for "B-Day"! The dry-thirsty mob had been on "go" for days when the "crime" occurred. Incidentally, did I mention that the **only** other person who had the key to this precious cargo was the sailor responsible for the inventory and control of "special foodstuff" etc. and this individual had to be approved and sanctioned by the Captain himself? No problem, because the Captain, who was in fact, "The Commanding Officer" personally knew the most trustworthy and probably the only teetotaler on board. You guessed right: it was my friend. Incidentally, did I mention that my friend had been duly "elected" by the crew and duly designated by the Commanding Officer as the ship's Chaplain? The Lord works in mysterious ways, His wonders to amaze even the U.S. Navy.

Incidentally, my friend and "Chaplain" was highly revered by the ship officers and crew because they knew him well and while not many would share all his values and religious beliefs, could easily respect him and even love him for the earnestness and sincerity of his walk with God and the love they sensed from him toward all of them.

As the "unnamed" ship continued its long and winding course over many knotted mile, and weeks of boredom, anxiety and loneliness day after day, their solitary and combined thoughts would frequently dwell on memories left behind, a beloved wife or sweetheart, their children, mom's home cooking, etc. But most often their thoughts were of all that beer. And when, pray-tell, do we get to drink it?

They all admired him and appreciated him in his role as the ship's Chaplain, especially since he had, by his own efforts and initiative just recently pulled off a "miracle." Just before they sailed, he had visited the Top Chaplain in Washington, D. C. (at the Pentagon Cathedral, I suppose) and as a follow-up to several written requests, submitted and ignored earlier by the very long chain of command, much prayers had been offered all the way up the chain to the Ultimate Commander. Thus, via much prayer and persuasion, he miraculously obtained a small portable organ for their humble ship that per Navy regulations did not deserve such splendor. Incidentally, did I mention that the Chaplain could play a pretty mean piano? The crew had good reason to "be proud" on each Sabbath as they convened on the fantail of the little boat; as their music and words echoed (??) far out over vast ocean of billowing waves and roaring winds and their combo Chaplain-Preacher (now organ player) did his thing. After all, they were the only ship of its class (Naval term) that had its own sacred, sanctified organ.

Now to a key point: My friend (who incidentally is my brother-in-law) did not partake of strong drink, even regulation beer. And, alas, neither did he think it wise, nor that God would approve of the crew drinking and "revering," especially after God had just protected them in battle. Thus, after much, much wrestling with his conscience and wondering if he was really "hearing from God," he decided to act with Holy boldness. Not being able to even sleep for several nights, he did, one night arise from his cozy bunk and headed for the storage area, deep (real life drama about to unfold) within the bowels of the ship, knowing full well that this unthinkable crime would never have but **one** single suspect, since the key he held was as though the "only key" since the Captain did not normally hear directly from God. Therefore, it would be immediately known that the real culprit was their own fellow shipmate and beloved Chaplain, and it was he, that "had done it."

As he headed downward, this gentle person, who had never committed a crime, much less ever even had a speeding ticket, nor had he ever even snatched a Baby Ruth candy bar or committed any type of wrong doing. Now here he was saturated with fear and fully knowing that court martial, and nothing less than a less-than-honorable discharge having been found guilty of causing the crew to mutiny on the high seas, or even some other worse fate certainly awaited. But for some time now he had wrestled with this unthinkable quandary. Wrestling with God can't be any fun. So wrestle he did, like Jacob of old. Now, after losing the wrestling match, he crept downward to the beer and whatever punishment would eventually be his fate, as he sincerely felt the beer needed to be destroyed. (An apt term for the type ship on which he served.) Downward and quietly he went expecting any minute to be caught, and for the first time that he could ever recall, he could actually hear his own heart pounding. Then, in the dark of the night he proceeded, without turning on any light, to insert the entrusted key into the lock and then began the frightening and arduous task. Gently, he picked up the first case and marched like a doomed man beginning the trek down death row to the chamber. One heavy case at a time, up several steep flights of steel steps, opened the bulkhead door which caused a light to go on each time he stepped out and quickly to the side of the ship, then feeling the cold railing on the side of the ship, stared momentarily at the dark ugly water many feet below, paused, then breathed a prayer and raised the case over nothing but space and water, then released his fingers from their curled position, as the case of beer, never to touch dry lips, began to fall into the briny deep. As the case hit the ocean, he said "Amen" which he had not thought of doing. It just seemed the appropriate thing to say. Time after time, he repeated the task following the same route for several hours, sweating with fear in the cold night, still expecting any moment to be spotted as the scum of low life he felt to be. On his second try walking through the ship's galley (the cooking and baking area), he stepped onto some freshly baked (and iced) sheet cakes, the bakers had purposely left on the deck (floor), so they would not slip off the countertop during the night if the weather got rough and stormy, but realized in horror he was leaving icing tracks (which Sherlock would have truly loved), as he repeated his criminal act over and over, time after time, but this criminal of God continued his mission trek, with each trip seeming longer and gathering fear each time. The Navy regulation beer carefully crated, weighed approximately 50 pounds, so it required numerous trips from bottom to the topside railing to dump the sinful brew. Thus somewhere around thirty trips and thirty "Amens." must have been pronounced over the one-way "baptisms." Finally, the ordeal was over. Perhaps it would be more appropriate to say, the "mission" was over, or whatever you choose to call it.

If no one had seen him during the many trips, it would be a miracle enough, not to mention the somewhat soiled cakes and the footprints in the icing, along with the telltale snowy white icing footprints on the freshly painted floors of regulation gray. No matter if that miracle did or did not occur. After all, there was somewhere close to 300 thirsty, deserving sailors awaiting the long-overdue celebration of beer. Yea, even free beer!

Even the strong faith of my very devout friend wavered greatly. He returned to his bunk just before dawn, and lay down exhausted, wide-awake. He lay on his back. He waited and waited (and still open-eyed), too tired to pray and awaited his impending soon doom. The best worse case scenario would be to be hung for having committed, i.e. something akin to the Navy's unpardonable sin the theft of and the destruction of government property. Having to walk the plank was not beyond the scope of Naval justice if his fate was left to his fellow crew members.

He waited and waited. For many nights he could not sleep, as he waited for the guillotine to fall on his guilty neck. The only "satisfaction" he had, (and it was resting on quivering, feeble faith) was that he had done what he felt the Lord had impressed on him to do. It would be several long weeks before the ship returned to home-port. The ulcer-building, raw nerved suspense continued. He waited through anxious days and even more anxious nights. How could even one or two sailors, much less a shipload of beer loving sailors **forget** about all that beer? They all knew and yearned for the beer, as sure as God made Granny Smith apples.

And yet, no complaints or requests were ever registered; no gripes were even submitted, and the subject of the beer never surfaced. He waited and waited.

Exactly fifty years later, one half of a century, he is still waiting and wondering.

"PRAISE BE TO GOD WHO DOES ALL THINGS WELL."

OUR FATHER
(AND HE NEVER TIRES OF OUR CALLS)

One of the most "helpful" things Jesus did for His followers was to leave "instructions" as to how-we-should-pray. One of the disciples, unnamed, had just made a request for Jesus to teach them to pray. Think about it. Without the response to "teach to pray," we may not have had the "salutation" to God. We would not have the perfect and most appropriate opening line: "Our Father   " We certainly needed some name, title or designation rather than Dear Sir or Dear Lord.

We indeed do have **many** that can be used, e.g.,
>Most Holy God
>Creator of All
>God of Abraham, Isaac and Jacob
>Great Jehovah
>Omnipotent God
>Almighty God of All Creation
>Lord God Almighty
>Eternal and Everlasting God

There is nothing wrong with any and all of the above. I would suppose all of us have used them from time to time. I once had a well-trained and highly schooled pastor, who seemed to use **all** of them in his Sunday address to Our Supreme God. Nothing wrong with that, I quickly add. If we use every one in this book, we still can't adequately and fully do Him justice. He is worthy of all honor and all of our praise.

But really, don't you think what Jesus wanted to do is to "teach us to pray" and he knew we needed to be respectful in our attitude and in our language. But at the same time not to be overly intimidated, (it's O.K. to be awed) but not fearful of coming into His Holy Presence with a loving and respectful "Our Father." Remember Paul told us we could "approach the throne boldly!" Not because of our own righteousness, but because we had met and knew the Father's Son.

FORGIVENESS
(AND NUDGES LATELY)

I woke up that morning feeling rested! It was going to be a great day. I could feel it in my bones. Then, suddenly, without warning, my dear wife, almost like a snake (only she didn't rattle first) struck without warning and before I knew it, we were in a disagreement that soon merged into a full-blown argument. This was an "unusual" spat my wife and I were having. What made it unusual was the fact that I had not done anything to provoke or cause the exchange we were having. And after 41 years of marriage, I was in a pretty good position to evaluate such matters. Without any doubt I was completely innocent (an unusual experience in its own right) and never mind the fact that she was trying to recover from some extensive dental surgery that certainly explained her irritability, she was going overboard in talking to me like I didn't deserve to be addressed. I am proud to say that I kept my cool for quite a while, turned both other cheeks, and was feeling pretty smug and godly-like, knowing full well that she would apologize later, and being so full of humbled behavior, I would slowly but gracefully accept the apology. It was all so scripted and planned. As my temperature, pulse rate and ruffled feathers subsided, the spirit of Christ began to nudge me. These sorts of nudges, while ever so slight, have the strangest ways of being so realistic and persistent. Assuming I actually had been completely innocent and possessed a no-fault position, it still didn't give me any right to respond (even momentarily) in a harsh manner. Please note that I wasn't even wearing a "W.W.J.D." bracelet. But I knew that in spite of my innocence and regardless of whether or not I ever received an apology, I had to forgive and apologize.

So I did.

Then I had my good day back again.

THE FIRST MARTYR
(AND THEN THERE WERE MANY)

The Bible is really a down-to-earth plain talking book. Certainly there are beautiful words, comforting messages, great literature and poetic-like selections, challenging parables, faith, activities, miracle words of comfort and reassurance, and especially the stirring and all-together precious red-lettered words of our Savior; beautiful messages of love and hope and peace. Even eternal life!

However, and make no doubt about it: Conversely there are no sugar coatings and glossing over cover-ups, where spiritual insight and stark reality have to be delivered, so that believers and non-believers are forewarned of life and death, Heaven or Hell, ultimate issues.

To take a "parable" from a classic country and western song, God never promised us a rose garden (certainly not on this earth.) Not withstanding, I have known people who desperately searched for the scripture that supposedly said He did. Some of these are the same ones still trying to find that beloved verse our grandpappy's often quoted about "God helps those who help themselves?"

Think about it: Some of the "best" most committed, most dedicated Christians that ever lived, died, cruelly died, for their belief and trust and faith in a little known man named Jesus, who never even got the chance to pastor a church with a steeple or appear on Sabbath morning TV. Many of these "fanatics" actually choose their cruel, painful, agonizing end. In most cases, all they had to do to save their life was to "recant." Recant is a word that has largely gone out of style even though there is still a lot of "recanting" going on. Oh, by the way, these early "fanatics" were called martyrs. That word is nigh on to archaic even though we still occasionally see it used, when some lowly-paid unknown missionary-person is killed for their faith, usually in a hot, humid, miserable jungle in some backward country we've probably never heard of. Tour groups, just about never, never go there. When some missionary, probably a "loner," who was foolish enough to struggle and work his or her way through college, then spend another few years studying to learn a strange and difficult language that no one important ever speaks, only to finally arrive in strange country "X" knowing in advance, they have to depend upon limited funds to be hopefully sent in by those few faithful ones that remembered to mail their pledge in and knowing that when they (and perhaps their family) arrived in country "X," they would have to stay in this seemingly God-forsaken place for three-to-seven years before being able to return to the land of the free and the home of the affluent.

Then (I'll skip over the morbid details) some young reporter is given the assignment of writing the news story (that will eventually appear on one of the back pages, probably Page 7) and he, a young Jimmy Olsin type, will have to look up the word he's never heard, or had to spell before. "Hey Mac, how do you spell one of those freaks who die for Jesus? "

Lordy Mercy, this kind of writing gets me down-in-the dumps, besides its mostly made-up-fiction, isn't it? So let's move onto something with a little fun in it. Let's play a game, or at least something sort of like a game. Many people play "games" with religion or even with their faith. But I've got news for us. God doesn't play games!

What do you have that is worth dying for?

THE FIREHOUSE GOD
(ALWAYS ON DUTY)

Here is a strange statement. In an odd sort of way that we normally might not think of, God has allowed us to become **"creators."** The word absolutely must be placed in obvious, bold quotation marks, because, to be very up front about it, we really aren't *creators*, since we don't have any official authority and neither do our *creations* have any staying power or lasting significance. So, be forewarned before you go running off on some creating binge.

The reason we think we might think that we can **"create"** is in a sense God's fault, (smile, you know I'm kidding) because He gave us such freedom when he endowed us with one such inalienable right called free moral agent. Do you begin to get this picture? Right off from the starting gate we know we can accept or reject God.

And suppose we try to halfheartedly accept him (I think it's called lukewarm.) then we become **"creators"** of a sort when we try to make a god of our own choosing. We want a god we can put on a shelf and pull him down if we make a mess and need our God to clean up the mess.

We really do like a god that's like a fire truck safely tucked away in a fire station   just per chance we do have an emergency and need to call him out. We prefer a god kind of like an insurance policy. We don't want our god to be too public.

Don't call me, God. I'll call you, if I need you.

THE FINGER TIPS OF GOD
(NOT THE HEART   BUT VERY NEAR

As far as I know, this title was one that was "invented" by me, even though it is logical to imagine that many other people may have used the term. It came to me as I enjoyed a beautiful spring morning. The fresh breeze, the smells all around me blended into an invigorating aroma of new life and vitality. Many scenes and scents from flowers and trees floated around, up and down and in and out. Like wisps of hints on tangible and intangible beauties there alone with all this surrounding me was like a silent and peaceful bombardment of sights and sounds and smells and sensations. Sensations that could not be adequately defined, or described. Something close to divine, if not Divine. Had I held the "thermostat," I would not have lowered or raised it, even a smidgen. Everything was perfect and could not get any better. Yet, with every moment, the glory of Divine grew larger and nearer.

Many birds and a nearby stream provided the sounds. They were the sounds of new life and new energy. And yet the sounds were unobtrusive. Everything was blended into the "perfectness" of the day to be experienced. Green was everywhere. Green grass, green leaves, and green hills. And all of the greenery was politely interrupted, by the sprinkling of blossoms on the trees and the wildflowers interjecting into the green of the blanketed grass that ran in every direction.

I would hear a bird, then birds in plural and songs of chirps of wrens and sparrows. They all claimed this springtime space in assertive claims of many sounds that blended into a musical masterpiece. A composition, not of Mozart, or Chopin, but of God's nature. My own senses were heightened and intensified, both visually and orally, as I saw a sprinkling of wild flowers and heard the accompaniment of birds, with the constant strong, yet peaceful, flow of the stream of water, unhurriedly passing over and around the rocks worn smooth by gallons of drops and eons of time. The rays from the sun sparkled, as the water lifted to allow the penetration of the sun and then was as quickly gone and as quickly replaced, to continue the endless light show over and over again. Through it all, the birds never ceased and every time I noticed the flowers, it was as though new colors and shades and tints and hues had been added and blended into colorful scenery and unalterable serenity.

Standing all alone, and yet at perfect peace within the spirit of this sanctuary of nature, I quietly knew that this moment would be as close to God as I would ever share on the face of this earth. For all of this was made by God and without him nothing was made. In a panoramic view of the entire scene, I fully realized that I was only seeing and hearing and smelling a miniscule part of the whole. Then, my senses narrowed to focus on the beauty of some flowers and trees just in front of me. Almost like a microscope, I could begin to see the fine details. There was enough beauty and enough detail in one flower, or on a leaf, to view "forever." I could have easily reached out and touched the nearness—but I didn't dare. Somehow I knew Heaven would be even more beautiful. True Divine and glorious moments like this would be eternalized. Then my thoughts, somewhere deep within me, were summarized. Not summarized by me, but capsuled for me as a lasting memory of the moment.

Yes, this is as close to God as you will ever get while on this earth, for you are standing very near to the very fingertips of God.

THE FEAR REPLACER
(THE DEVINE ERASER)

One of the worst problems we can face is "fear." It can be worse than a dragon. At least, we can usually see the "dragons" which are our enemies. But sometimes a particular fear can haunt us day and night and reach the point where it is with us without escape. Always in our thoughts, every waking moment and we can only momentarily escape it by sleep and that sleep is slow to come. And then, it pounces back into our minds the instant we awaken, usually in the middle of the dark of the night. Fear becomes nausea, amplified by imagination, constant depression and a problem without solution. Dreaded and unknown and no end in sight. Our human efforts and intentions have long since proven futile. We beg God for the answers to problems we can't even describe. We wrestle like Jacob, only our daylight never comes. And we don't have a ladder.

Then at times the "answer" surprises us by suddenly being there. It didn't arrive; it was just there. And we wonder why we didn't grasp it earlier. Many times it is not the answer we sought, nor the one we expected. It arrives **not** as a "solution" but rather as a much-needed *respite* of peace. Peace, so desperately needed. The "fear" that plagued us for so long was not resolved into lived-happily-ever-after dreamland. However, with quiet confidence and assurance that settled softly upon us, we knew that God had not given us the spirit of fear but replaced the spirit of fear with power and love and a sound mind. Very similar to a peace that was beyond comprehending.

Another example of: "I can do all things through Christ when He strengthens me."

The "Dragons" of this world are often so large that we "fear" we have not the strength, knowledge, or courage to slay them. They belong to and are controlled by, the power of that negative sinful force, the Bible describes as the "The Prince and Power of the air." It is He that would hold me hostage from the peace that God gives. Peace I can have, as I avoid His Dragons out across the world. Then, I am reminded that I have a 'sword' available to me to slay the Dragons. I reach for the word of God, my sword, with it drawn in a position of poise with power, I read these words: "Greater is He that is in me than He that is in the world."

And again, He replaces the fear with the Power of His word. Not even a dragon of Satan can withstand the sword of the Lord.

THE FIRST NOEL
(AND THE "MUSIC" GOES ON)

There were only a small number of individuals who saw and experienced the "First Noel." They can almost be counted on our ten fingers. I'm talking about those precious few that were around when Jesus first arrived on earth.

Mary and Joseph
There was an innkeeper and perhaps his wife.
A small group of shepherds who were fortunate to be working the night shift.
A trio (perhaps 3) of foreign visitors who were rewarded for (1) begin alert and studying, and (2) their willingness to undergo the hardships of a long journey.
An old man, who was devout and trusting and who must have had almost as much patience as Job. One thing we do know: the Holy Ghost was upon him!
A very old (but very devout) widow woman who had spent most of her life fasting and praying. (Fasting and praying must have been important and worthwhile back then.)

These, I believe are the only persons we know that are recorded as having seen and experienced firsthand the First Noel, when Jesus was a tiny baby.

So, if we suppose that six shepherds came in from the field that night and if we suppose that there were three wise men and add Mary and Joseph and the two senior citizens in the temple, we have a grand total of 13 individuals. These individuals knew there was something indeed special about this child of such lowly birth. These "thirteen" were certainly a very lucky number. (However, I really don't think we, as Christians, should even have the word "luck" in our vocabulary.)

This calculation obviously does not include the innkeeper (and his wife??) because he probably had one room "saved" should per chance an unexpected VIP arrive and need a room. Most motels and hotels still have this hidden practice today. Therefore my assumption is that had he known just who Jesus was, then Jesus would not have been born in a stable. But let us not be too hard on this innkeeper, because according to prophecy Jesus **had** to be born in a stable.

Interestingly, there are a few others who *almost* knew first hand the tiny first Noel Messiah. King Herald had the rare opportunity. Only, he was too lazy or too proud to get involved, so he delegated his royal privilege. And he certainly delegated to the "wrong" group, when he asked the wise men to locate the First Noel.

Finally, did you know that it is possible to be **"very religious"** and still miss out on "heaven" or something heavenly in the form of a small baby from heaven???

Addendum: A few years later another group of "religious people" working in the temple also missed out by not recognizing "the First Noel," but by then He was about twelve years old. John the Baptist did recognize and acknowledge the deity of "the First Noel" when Jesus was a grown man.

After Thought: Isn't it sad to think of all the people, down through the ages and even to this day that have "missed-out" on seeing or meeting Jesus. And think of all those that were *almost persuaded.*

THE FORERUNNER
(WHAT A RELIEF)

Isn't it both interesting and wonderful how sometimes one of God's names will only appear *once* in all of scripture? Forerunner is an example of this oddity and you have to be old fashioned and use the King James Bible to find it. And when you do find it, what refreshing thoughts are uncovered and discovered; that Jesus himself is our forerunner, taking it upon himself as our forerunner, to go to God first, for us and serve as our *advance man.* A somewhat military sounding assignment, but indeed an important one.

And while I may not always be so swift on my feet or my brain, I figured it out real fast that I am mighty (delightfully) pleased to have Jesus as my forerunner.

I have no desire to face a Mighty God alone, much less a Holy God, much less a Mighty and Holy God, who has all knowledge. This means he knows about the time in Cassel's 5 & 10¢ Store, when I was about 8 years old, I "lifted" a rubber eraser from the counter. I needed a new one to put on top of a worn out pencil eraser. (They were only one cent each then.) Furthermore, absolutely no desire whatsoever to face a Righteous God who would take one glare at me and only see filthy rags, for sins much worse than the stolen eraser.

Do you see my reasoning for such fear and trembling and trepidation, besides being scared speechless out of my wits? No, I want Jesus, my personal "forerunner" (High Priest), to go first and announce to His Father, that:

"I am here today, Father, to tell you that Jack has been redeemed by my blood and all his sins have been paid in full. Therefore, he is fully qualified and ready to enter into your heavenly temple and your Holy Presence."

AMEN!

"…Christ has gone ahead to plead for us from his position as our forerunner…" (Living Bible and KJV)

Hebrew 6:20

THE FORGETTER
(GOD CAN'T REMEMBER??)

There are a number of divine traits that God, alone, possesses and this is one of them. As mortals, we do ourselves proud when we are able to forgive someone who has done us a grave injustice, odious harm, unthinkable betrayal, etc. But it seems to be virtually impossible for us to forgive and forget.

This is not to say that forgiveness is not in itself a noble deed. Indeed it is. And it takes tremendous effort, will power and extreme self-discipline, not just to make the forgiveness act deciding to forgive, but the more difficult part is usually to *maintain* the decision to forgive. Good intentions and hard-earned determination have a way of eroding away. Thus, the pain of the offending deed returns with a renewed vengeance and the conflict begins all over again. How sweet it would be, if we were able to forget and thus, end the bitterness and the pit-of-the-stomach sickening sensations that begins yet another round of eating away at your inner being. Even sanity seems to stand on the brink and depression moves in again, seemingly like this time to stay until W hat a relief, if forgetting could be inserted on top of the act of forgiveness and both buried forever—once and for all. Instead, the memories of the hurtful incident are seemingly encased in cement like icing that petrifies the total mess. At times, it is as though a large silent parasite is constantly at work in your very innards. What can you do?

Most individuals find that they have two options. One, continue to "exist" with the "parasite" and eventually be buried together after years of remorse and bitterness. Or, number two, tell God that the problem has you whipped and you are ready for His help. Since God has forgiven and cast the "memory" of whatever it was He forgave you for, it stands to reason, that this is the only workable recourse you have for such deep seated hurts.

At times like this (I think most of us have been in this predicament), I turn in desperation to my *faith* for help. I need my faith here and now. Not necessarily just when I am about to cross over Jordan to the Sweet Forever. And God has never failed me.

To put it briefly and to the point, you use some select scriptures, quote them to God, and then expect him to honor his word.

1. My help comes from the hills, i.e. God.
2. Pray two ways for your "enemy"
   (a)   daily
   (b)   sincerely/earnestly/diligently
3. Ask God specifically to bless your "enemy" and even suggest specific blessings, i.e. good things to happen to someone, who has spitefully used (or misused) you.
4. Remember to cast your burden/cares on God. He told you to do this.
5. Move, live and have your being on Him, not in your misery.
6. Force your mind and your thought process to the positive. See/read/memorize and cite daily, continually and constantly Philippians 4:8. Live by this verse.
7. Give the negative to the Devil (and tell Him where to take it).

THE FORSAKEN CHRIST
(WE WOULD NEVER DO THIS)

One of the saddest verses in the Bible:

When Jesus reaches the absolute lowest (worst) critical point in his life; the most crucial moment, for after all, this was the overriding reason he had been sent to earth, i.e. to be sacrificed by horrible and cruel death. Crucifixion!! To be Crucified! This is the pivotal moment. And what happens?? All disciples fled and forsook him. This is drama, *real drama,* in the life of the *man* Jesus. And he is virtually alone. Well, almost alone. One disciple stayed nearby. But what if John???

But what if John, the gospel writer, had   ???

Then all the disciples forsook him, and fled.
Then all the disciples deserted him and fled. NIV

Matthew 26:56
John 19:26

THE FORSAKEN CHRIST II
(ALL ALONE IN A CROWDED WORLD)

I imagine that Jesus had a lot of lonely times in his life, especially his early life. Before he became known he probably spent time alone in meditation and thought. I wonder what his prayer life was like. Was he ever "homesick" and wishing he could be back with his father? Or, as a young boy and later as a young man on earth, had he completely separated his divine nature and now existed mentally and emotionally as he did physically?

We know something of his forty days alone in the wilderness so that certainly involved loneliness. Did he realize then or think about the busy life that lay ahead, with crowds pressing around him and people everywhere pressing around him and wanting to see him, or touch him, or just how curious they would be? Their "wanting" to see him would come for various reasons: desperate needs that encompassed the worst in pits of despair and all sorts of human health needs. Did he have empathy even then to wake each and every morning of your life, open your eyes again and have only darkness or nothingness before eyes that could not see and had never seen? Or, every new, new day began like the one before and the totally useless arm still hanging there, flopping uselessly and of no more value than if the arm had never been there. Or, waking a short distance from the pool. The nearby pool that might as well had been seven miles away. But the pool was the only hope you had ever had, and if the angel did perchance come today, and if someone was there to help you more toward the pool and if you could, against unmentionable odds, be first. Another day, of impossible hope. The list of human misery and desperation was unending. Another would awaken to his new day with the ever-present stench of hogs nearby. But this odious cloud of filth was not the problem. His problem could not be defined for his mind only half-worked and constantly battered back and forth between scant fleeting bits of scattered sanity accompanied by many voices inside the head that seldom shut up and when they did, the silence was ever more frightening. In the rare moments of borderline sanity, there was only time to wonder if he was ever going to make heads or tails out of an ever-tumbling mind. The list of pathetic individuals with pathetic hopeless needs would go on and on. And perhaps human Jesus didn't know but could only await the unknown like mortals.

In these times of being alone, could he possibly imagine that very soon he would be speaking to large multitudes. That he might be yearning for solitude and rest from the crowds that seemed unceasing. A crippled man being lowered through the roof into an already packed room with suffering needs. Or another time, when an older woman with a desperate need couldn't get near him, but at the last moment managed to barely touch the hem of his garment.

How complex. It was *both* good and bad, but not all of masses had such dire needs. Many were there just out of curiosity. In almost every crowd he could sense the odd mixture of crying desperation for hope intermingled with jeers, hate, jealously religious hypocrisy, bewilderment and the ever always there curiosity. At these times he might be so tired and overwhelmed that he yearned to be "home." And at these times, he could even envy the small animals, like a fox, cuddled up in a den of his own.

Perhaps one of the worst moments of being alone that lay ahead would be unbelievable and not imaginable. Needing to be alone in prayer (well, almost alone), so he could make sure that he was in his father's will for his impending death seemed so near. He prayed and prayed in the darkest of hours of a night that held no hope of sleep, only fear and dread, and his prayers were the most intense he had ever prayed. So much so, that his sweat mixed with blood. And then, the unreal shock of finding the precious few he had taken with him so that he wouldn't have to be totally alone (he could not bear the thought??) on this the worst and final night of his life on earth where he could have had some decent sleep   or, when he finished praying he found these, his dear/close friends sleeping. Surely they could have kept awake, but   . And later Peter really made the history books: three denials!

One final example indeed may be the most pathetic of all. Certainly, it is one of the saddest statements in the entire Bible. It's recorded twice, so we should read it twice.

141

"Then all the disciples forsook him and fled."
"And they all forsook him and fled."

Question: Have you ever deserted or denied the Christ; your Christ? I've heard a lot of sermons on Peter's shameful actions. Are there any "sermons" in your/my life?

THE FOUNDATION
(BEWARE!)

One thing the writer of this book will always do is *keep things simple.* If per chance I do exceed this promise, then it most likely means that I have also exceeded my ability and my learning. Please allow me to illustrate an important subject and keep the explanation simple and easy to understand.

Question: Jesus can be described as our "foundation. So what is a foundation?

Answer: It is something solid on which the rest is built. Or, on which everything stands.

Question: Does everything have a foundation?

Answer: Yes. Everything has a foundation of some sort or the other.

Question: Does an airplane which flies in and through the air have a foundation?

Answer: Yes, we just explained that everything has a foundation including an airplane. In an airplane there is a foundation made up of a metal structure, which holds the engine, or engines and this structure is in turn held together and supported by the basic metal framework on the basic aircraft. Thus, when the airplane flies in and through the air, the foundation absolutely must be doing the job it is designed to do.

Question: But in simple terms, why is the foundation so important? For example in the case of a building, be it a tiny house or a large skyscraper, we seldom, if ever, actually *see* the foundation.

Answer: If the foundation isn't structured properly and built of the right materials then nothing, absolutely nothing, can stand; at least for very long. And whether you see it, or not, is not important. What is important is that it is there.

Question: Did Jesus ever illustrate or explain this subject in easy-to-understand terms?

Answer: He certainly did! And his explanation was even simpler than the one just used. He gave an everyday type example: "Build two houses: one on the rocks and the other on sand. Then, wait until it rains.

Question: I see. I see. What do you suggest for the best; the *ideal* building material, for a foundation?

Answer: The Solid Rock.

GOD IN A BOX
(BUT PEOPLE KEEP TRYING)

The "worlds" we live in are filled with logic, regulations, customs, rules of conduct, established modes of operation, "establishments" galore, societal traditions, parental expectations, constitutional laws to establish foundations on which we build structures for state laws, county laws, and city laws to delineate the days on which you can and cannot water your lawns. We are even instructed on what and how to discard our garbage.

Centuries ago, the Greeks and Romans and others began growing and cultivating governmental and religious rules and regulations that follow us and condemn us to this very day. We have multi-cornered churches throughout America, often two or three at one intersection and others located between intersections in empty stores or no-longer-used drive-in theaters. Most, if not all, creeds, faiths and doctrines have their own Scribes and Pharisees who have prolifically written on parchment, tablets of stones, hard drives and floppy discs, the jot and titled do's and don'ts, as supposedly handed down by God and/or those who (supposedly) have dogmatically heard from God the clearly deciphered thus-saith-the-Lord edicts. Many of these "divine" doctrines are amazingly similar while others are so dissimilar and vastly different that they must have evolved downward from the University of Postbabelmentarism. All of which causes a small degree of discomfort to all the good people of like-minds who are heading merrily down their single track of tradition when suddenly said single track branches into various and sundry directions. Point: We are a *people* programmed to think that **everybody** must conform rigidly to our "standards." Generally, that is true, but . just look at all the myriad of church denominations that dot our landscape. I am not implying that this is good or bad or **who** is good or bad; right or wrong. All I'm doing is *wondering* why so many and are they all necessary?

All of which brings us back to the orderly, logical and regulated, fences and boundary lines, cocoons that customarily enveloped our lives and thus goes a long way in explaining why we are so prone to build "boxes" all over the place in which to place our God. Such boxes are unintentionally intended to restrict, limit and/or control our God so that He conforms to **our** thinking. And when this doesn't work we organize committees, task teams etc. in order to reinforce and lengthen our constitutional hierarchy, in order that new or stronger boxes can be built—all for the express purposes of putting and keeping God in a box.

Now, for the big, huge, brilliant climatic ending to this thought-provoking essay, so hold onto your hats:

Thou cans't not put God in a box! Or translated, *you cannot put God in a box!*

P.S. I would suppose that while you were reading this, 1.5 new churches were started in towns and cities all over America. How many were started because their own church was overcrowded with standing room only, and thus, built for reason of growth in the Kingdom of God? Or, were some, perhaps, built on foundations of ego and pride? Or, perhaps, it was simply that somebody got mad at somebody.

I bet the Devil grins (sometimes).

GOD IS A PARADOX
(A WHAT??)

Is this "title" for God in any way disrespectful? Not at all. It merely illustrates, once again, that God's ways are not our ways and our ways are not God's ways. This name also points out in so many ways the mysteries of God. We may not understand them, but we can certainly marvel in them and at them. I absolutely love Psalm 139.

The best definition I could come up with for this occasion is a paradox, two things that don't seem to go together, yet, they do. And it would not be incorrect to say "two or more things." The list below was easy and enjoyable to develop, and one purpose for showing it is to cause your own thinking to pursue this divine thought which obviously centers around God's son, Jesus, and then have you add to the list.

Where do we begin? How about in the beginning? Or we could begin at the end, only there is no end to God. That very idea is a type of "paradox." Our Great Creator God, who created it all, had no beginning. Wow! Let's quickly move on before you think I am going to explain or expound on *that*!

To accept God, we must accept something we cannot fully understand or explain, but we *accept in faith.*

The prophets of old, for hundreds of years foretold of his birth and gave some very specific details, and yet when He finally came, even though the prophesies had been recorded in the most sacred of writing, they refused to believe. The pitiful handful that did believe was not the key religious leader. In fact, after waiting hundreds of years, they not only wouldn't believe but "they" killed him.

The very select "chosen" people, of which Jesus was one, did not accept Him, their very Savior.

Jesus was from the lineage of King David and when he arrived as the spiritual King, the earthly King of the Jews, Herod, would go to great lengths to have him killed.

They had long awaited the Messiah, expecting Him to arrive as a great king and save them and build a great kingdom. He came, not on a great white horse, as a king, but paradoxically speaking, as a helpless little baby, born in a stable and located in an obscure village.

Perhaps one of the greatest paradoxes of all, God came as a baby. Who could believe that??

On the day He finally did ride into the Holy City, he was on a donkey. King's don't ride donkeys! No way!

Another *odd* thing: a paradox by its very definition can be somewhat odd or peculiar; He was birthed by a virgin.

His central message was one of Love and Hope. He proved "Love" by dying and "Hope" should have died also.

Death did not destroy Him. Isn't that a paradox? Remember the definition: two things that go together but don't, or is it two things that go together, i.e. death and destruction, but *don't*.

That God the Father, who created all and owned all, would "risk the most important thing He ever planned for humankind, and yet the entire "plan" became the responsibility of a small baby, who so happened to be, His Only Son.

Thus, weird listing of paradoxes could go on and on. But they don't make a lot of earthly sense, do they?

But on the other hand, we are talking about **divine** matters and **divine** love.

Personal Note: And now I am suddenly struck with a "new idea" that I should have thought of years ago: Am I not one-half of this paradox?? Why should God love me? Why should Jesus die for me? Why did He go to heaven to prepare a place for me? He is Holy and Pure; at my "best" I look like a bunch of filthy rags. God gave His all. I can only surrender my "all."

GOD IS LOVE
("Needs to be read aloud")

Love Excelling. Amazing Love. Understanding Love. Divine Love. Love Eternal. Forgiving Love. Everlasting Love. Undeserved Love. Unfailing Love. Unsurpassable Love. Tender Love. Tough Love. Gentle Love. Love that gives. Love that keeps on giving. Unconditional Love. Unbounded Love. Devoted Love. Love without measure. Soothing Love. Peaceful Love. Calming Love. Love that cannot be explained, except: Merciful Love. Healing Love. Marvelous Love. Love in the midst of darkness and storms. Love that brings light and Hope. Love that is Light. Love that is Hope made real and intangibly touchable.

Heavenly Father Love. Love that is tender, like a mother's love. Touching Love. Sometimes a light touch on the hem. Desperately need love. Love sometimes to one who deserves it least. But needs it most.

Sympathizing Love. Empathy Love. Love that can be felt and sensed and experienced, yet not fully explained. Love that weeps. Love that sweats blood. Love that hurts. Love that Cares. Surprising Love. Love that surprises. Feet washing Love. Feet washing by the Son of God. Amazing Love. Marvelous Love.

Love from a Creator God. God of the universe. God who spoke stars into existence. Yet, Love from One who held children on His lap. Love from a Shepherd. Love from a friend. Love from mighty God. Love from Almighty God. Yet, Love from One closer than a brother. Love from the Master. Love from the Master who lowered Himself to serve. Serving Love. Always Love. Love always, even unto the end. Love beyond the end. Everlasting Love. Eternal Love. Securing Love.

Love from a Savior. Love from a Savior that would die for you. Love from a Savior that *chose* to die for you. Even a horrible, painful disgraceful death. And His Father's love *gave* this, His sole Son. The Supreme Gift. The Supreme Sacrifice.

Love that bled. Love that thirsted. Love that twisted and squirmed and died in agony. Sacrificial Love. Forgiving Love. Love that surrendered. Love that gave all. Dying Love. Yet Love that would not die. Undying Love. Arising Love. Love that would not be silenced nor sealed. Arising Love. Victorious Love. Victorious over death, hell and graves. My grave. Your grave. Amazing Love. Marvelous Love.

Eternal Love. Love for eternity. Love from the God of all creation. Love for all of mankind. But Love personalized and individualized for me. Unexpected Love. Unearned Love. Unmerited Love. Pardoning Love. Deep Love. Deep deep Love. Deepest Love. Matchless Love. Marvelous Love. Awesome Love. Love painfully illustrated and exemplified. Hard-to-describe-Love. Unfathomable Love.

Resurrected Love. Love that resurrects. Great Great Love that is Humble Love. Love that was humbled. Love by Example. But the Example cannot be matched. Matchless Love. Marvelous Love. Amazing Love. All Love Excelling.

Love that *became* God. Only Son Love. God is Love.

GOD IS LOVE II
(JESUS LOVES ME, THIS I KNOW)

Probably the best definition a human can give of our Creator: *God is Love.*

But how much Love?

Answer:

      Why does God love us?
      When does he love us?
      How does he love us?
      Where does he love us?
      How much does he love us?
      How long will he love us?

GOD IS LOVE III
(BUBBLING LOVE)

Love has many adjectives, synonyms and meanings. We love Jesus and we love football, hot dogs, onion rings, music, also, puppies and kittens, as well as the Blue Ridge Parkway, and the list of things we love goes on and on. But the love of a believer in Jesus comes from and <u>because</u> of Jesus, who touches and changes the believer and then this God like love begins to bounce off onto others, i.e. spouse, family, friend, strangers even enemies. And the love is "returned" to Jesus. At times it is expressed and at other times it needs no words. But the love, which is of God and from God, becomes a non-ending vivacious circle.

We, Americans (especially here in the home of the brave and land of the free), use the word LOVE for so many, many things that our expressions and intent are carried to excess.

Then, we use the same four-letter word to express our love for God and God's love for us. This ought not to be, dear readers. The love we have for Jesus most often comes because we know and sense that Jesus loves us. As this begins to happen, a type of chain reaction is produced, whereby we feel and sense love from Jesus. We feel like He has "touched" us, then our own love is activated. We then want to do two or more things at once, i.e. we immediately want to show love <u>back</u> to Jesus (and usually we do) but we also have difficulty on being able to feel like we can adequately express all the unbundled love back to Jesus. We immediately and naturally begin to want to give or share this radiant love for Jesus with others. We soon learn that love is contagious and hard to contain. It is also hard to define or express. But oh, the joy unspeakable and overflowing with glory, like rivers of life and bubbling springs that never dry up and joyous rejoicing and exceeding gladness...Oh, the joy of trying to express such Divine Love that is ours.

Joy, Joy, Joy!

Isaiah 12:2-6

GOD OF GRACE
(OTHERWISE IT WOULD BE IMPOSSIBLE TO PLEASE HIM)

If you were asked to list the most commonly used word in our "English Christian vocabulary" certainly "grace" would have to be high on the list. Especially if you recall how frequently this subject is preached in many churches. Or how very often the topic of "grace" is mentioned or referenced in most Protestant churches. And just think of the many sermons that are based on the book of Romans, a classic book on "grace" by a writer who knew first-hand about "grace."

One might describe the prolific pro-grace doctrines as being widely proclaimed since grace doth abound so much and in our lives and since there is so much sin around us we can with assurance know that grace doth abound even more.

A compilation of scriptures on "grace" tells us that we are admonished to approach the throne of grace, be strong in grace, let mercy and peace and grace be ours from God, know that it is by grace that we are saved, beware and do not fall from grace, but know that God's grace is sufficient and great grace is upon us.

Here are some "counts" I took from Strong's Concordance. The word "grace" appears 38 times in the Old Testament and 127 times in the New Testament. Now that you know this profound statistic, you should be prepared for the quick quiz.

1. Which Old Testament book mentions "grace" the most?
2. Does the word appear in all four of the gospels?
3. Which New Testament book mentions the word most? (Besides Romans)?
4. Which unusual term appears once each in the Old Testament and the New Testament?

GOD OF OUR THOUGHTS
(AND BEFORE WE THINK)

Did you ever listen to yourself pray? I mean *really* listen? Especially, if you are called upon to pray publicly? Or, even to pray in front of a small group? Perhaps even if you are praying aloud in front of just one person? Even if that person is your dear, dear spouse?

It seems to be a natural human trait for most humans to pray to our divine God and not be able to sound as though we are sincerely and genuinely talking to our Lord and **not** to our earthly audience.

Have you ever noticed that there seems to be a direct correlation as to how earnest our prayers "sound" according to the desperation or emergency in which we are praying?

I can remember being trapped in a back seat of an automobile involved in a terrible head-on collision and the stench of raw gasoline all around me and the horn which had stuck, blowing ceaselessly, adding unnecessarily to the deadly drama. Did I pray in solemn and sanctimonious carefully spaced hyphenated syllables, "Most High and Holy Lord God, I beseech thee that thou, O God, would bestow upon this your humble and unworthy servant, extended tender mercies and to protect and shield me from this impending disaster within which I sitteth."

No! You guessed it. My prayer was brief, concise, sincere to the point and readily understood. In fact, it was very similar to the prayer of an eight year old friend of mine, in Sunday School years ago, when the teacher had each person in our small class to say a one sentence prayer and when the prayers had rotated to my shy friend, he managed after first swallowing a gulp, "Lord, help us!"

There are also some great examples of short-to-the-point prayers in the Bible. The thief on the cross only needed one sentence. The Pharisees in Luke's gospel was long-winded, but in contrast the publican smote his chest and begged for mercy in one sentence.

Lord, teach us to pray.

GOD OF THE WHY'S
(AND THE "WHAT'S" AND "WHEN'S" AND "HOW'S")

We all experience or read about sad experiences. Sadness is a part of life. I don't suppose anyone escapes it. Probably few tragedies are sadder than when a small child (or small children) are suddenly taken. How one *ranks* the degree of hurt, loss or anguish, I don't know. I have often read that a mother losing a baby or young child is the worst. Even worst than if she lost her spouse or mother.

My own family went through a horrible loss many years ago. The father loaded five children, ranging in ages 5 to 15, for their Sunday morning routine to church, less than a mile away. The mother (my grandfather's sister) was not feeling well, so she stayed behind, something she had hardly ever done. This left space, for one person, so an aunt of mine, an eighth grader at that time and a straight "A" student, rode with her cousins and their father. The 1934 Ford and the seven people started to church. Near the church, the street passed over one "railroad crossing." This route had been taken by Uncle Jim for many, many years, including many, many Sunday mornings. Only this time, the car was hit by the train. Everyone in the car was immediately killed, except Bernice, the passenger cousin. Bernice survived, but with multiple injuries, including a brain injury and was never able to return to school.

Days later, six coffins were carried into the small church, which had a capacity of less than one hundred people and the joint funeral for the father and his five children began.

That was at least 70 years ago. Our small town had never had such a massive tragedy and it would be 48 years before a greater number of people would die in a common disaster.

The small church only had a seating capacity of less than a hundred and probably measured 30 feet wide and perhaps 40 feet long. It's hard to imagine the six caskets, but all my life my family members have told and retold the story. If you can imagine the scene, then it's hard to imagine anything sadder.

As in almost any tragedy, or sudden death, the questions begin. They never end. But they begin in a non-ending stream always

155

punctuated with multiple oral question marks. Most times I had heard them as whispers—but sometimes in screams. Why, Why, Why, Why????

We all philosophize. "We" encompasses ministers and pastors and preachers and teachers and news commentators and relatives and neighbors and all the rest of us. The "We's" have a lot of opinions and guesses and speculation and do-you-suppose?? A lot of our questions are asked in whispered tones. At times, we seemed ashamed to question. Maybe that is why we often whisper. But the whispered ones don't seem to get any better answers than those screamed in desperate WHY'S?

If you patiently read this, thinking there might be some satisfying explanation or inspiring point waiting at the end, you will certainly be disappointed. I can't get answers to my own WHY'S. And I have had a lot of WHY'S. Frankly, I don't know what I would have done without Romans 8:28. And even when, in the worst of times, Romans 8:28 didn't help *enough*, I'd back up to Romans 8:26 and groan. I am being totally serious: groan and moan. When you've used all the great answers, including classic scriptures and you've been consoled and counseled—and none of it has been enough   and the hurting is still hurting and the loneliness is breaking the heart apart, into chunks of worthless nothing, I can groan and let the Spirit have the impossible problem.

One final comment   only don't read it, if you can't take the blunt: Some things simply can't be answered and aren't meant to be answered—at least not here and now. If we could answer, then we would be as smart and wise as God.

And we aren't.

P.S.   A bit of personal stuff I learned from my Father, as we sat outside a critical care unit waiting on his wife of 54 years to die, and good-hearted, well-intended Christian friends, would stop by to give comfort. A local pastor also stopped by and not being acquainted with my Mother, asked my Father:

"How old is she?"

"Seventy-two."

"Oh, she's had a long wonderful life."

The pastor then walked away and my father responded quietly, "Not long enough. I wish people wouldn't say that."

OUR GOD
("PAPA")

There are some cultures and religions that do not feel they have the "right" to ever pronounce or write the name of God, Jehovah, etc. The usual reasons involve the fact that "He" is so mighty and so holy and so tremendously superior to we puny mortal humans. A case could be made that there is some validity to this line of reasoning. One ridiculous example, (just to make the contrasting point) is to imagine one lowly ant praying to a mammoth elephant.

There is at least one group that has another line of reasoning which is somewhat different but also has earthly validity as measured with a divine yardstick: that we should never use a name, since no one name or term (or even a group of descriptive) can even begin to accurately describe the Mighty Being. They base this point of belief on the fact that we can never know or understand all there is to know or understand about "Him." Therefore, any word(s) we used could not encompass the marvelous unknown factors that would need to be included in addressing such a Supreme Being. Let's admit, they have a logical point. Any and all points and questions raised above aren't really of any concern to the true believer.

We already know and admit that God is so very, very, Holy, Holy and so very powerful and mighty beyond description and understanding. Furthermore, we readily admit that to refer to ourselves as puny is an understatement of all times. We furthermore know and have known for a long time that our goodness (if any) is like filthy rags. A rag is worth very little value and even that value diminishes with filth and dirt.

We do understand that any God (and there is only one true God) that can create a world from nothing and fling stars from his fingertips is beyond description by mortal tongues.

As to what name or term we should use?? This was resolved so beautiful and so simple by the gift of the approachable Jesus who taught us to pray to "Our Father or if we prefer "A bba Father, knowing that we have an Advocate with Our Father and that Jesus said

that He and the Father are one.
   Hooray for Jesus!!

Matthew 6:32 and Father are one
Romans. 8:15 Abba Father
I John 2:1   Advocate
John 10:30   Our Father

THE GIFT
(THE GIFT OF GOD)

Jesus is <u>the</u> gift of God to all of mankind. A "gift" never cost the recipient anything. A gift must be "free" to make the definition, i.e. to qualify as a gift. But the individual who bestows the gift is responsible for the cost. A gift has a cost, a value that is then transferred freely to the recipient. So there is a "giver" and a "givee." In simple terms: God gave us His Son (which happened to be His *only S*on), so imagine the value. He, God and His Son *paid* the price for this invaluable gift.

I've been a Christian for many years, over half a century. To put it modestly, I know the basics. Certainly I could pass Christianity 101. So why do I (almost everyday of my life) keep pondering in my mind, over and over, as to what I can do to "pay him back" for all he's done for me; that I need to earn my salvation? Could it be that all I need to is love him and show this love by devotion and commitment? Could it be that all I need to is "love him back" and show and share this love with others? Could anything so wondersome and incredible be this simple?

Could it be??

THE GIFT OF LOVE
(A SACRIFICE OF LIFE AND LOVE)

Jesus was in full agreement for his Father's will to be done. This
˅as not a mere pledge of love with a nice-sounding "commitment of
˅" that He might or might not have to live up to. Or, die to. All too
ʰe time came for Jesus to "agree" to be killed. That reads rather
ʼoesn't it? All too soon the time came for Jesus to " agree " to
ˇced.

ˍid not go to the cross, and to his death kicking and
He did not yell and try to make a scene about how unjust
was. He did not proclaim and preach about how He was,
doubt, a fulfillment to numerous scriptures from their
ther did He utter in loud dismay, about all the great
˅vidence" of the love He had exhibited and preached, or
ˍple He had caused to be healed or the hungry crowds
ˍ there any name-dropping about who His father was.
ˍbout His long and impressive lineage of well-known
King David who reigned during the "golden age"
ˍondly remembered by multitudes.

ˍld appear missed a lot of opportunities to defend
ˍarely answered Pilate when given the chance. His
ˍment was "thou sayest it." And shortly thereafter in the
ˍse suffering and agony, it must have entered His mind
thaⴀ ˍd still call 10,000 angels or more and back out. They were
still at hˍ beck and call. Earlier, He might have been able to recant.
He, the Very God of Mercy did not even ask for mercy even in the
worst of pain, thirst and struggling misery.

Just a sip of water. Instead, in four astounding words, that for all
ages transcends our thoughts: **He became our sacrifice.**

To most of us the word "*sacrifice*" is one we rarely use. It is nigh
onto archaic. Besides, we actually have difficulty relating to it. Not
much sacrificing going on, is there? About all we have left are
historical examples or theoretical points to ponder. A few picayune
instances might include petty items we give up for Lent or when
appeasing someone. Most of the sacrificing we experience is in

baseball, which is a poor example to compare.

But now we have a vivid and poignant instance of a hurting example of sacrifice. "Sacrifices" are supposed to be painful. On a bright sunny morning over a Pennsylvania countryside, on September 11, 2001, the passengers on Flight 93 experienced and died, when we refer to their deaths, a type of multiple sacrificing.

Even thinking about this incident of sacrifice *hurts*!

GOD IS GOOD
(ALL THE TIME)

Way back when, and perhaps even farther back, when I was being brought-up as they called it "back then," one of the first things I learned, was to be thankful for my food, which meant we always prayed before we ate. It is now described as "saying Grace," but way back then my folks called it, "saying the Blessing," which as I do recall, this made a lot more sense to a one year old, than trying to explain the beautiful theological concept of Grace, i.e. God's unmerited favor, and besides, sometimes my Aunt Grace ate with us. So you can see the potential for confusion, back then, when I already had enough trouble learning the basics of life, which at that time, I had not yet been introduced to higher education with all the ABC's, which I was not yet comprehending in my young, albeit brilliant brain, because I certainly do recall the confusion of understanding A, B, and C and why other ABC's were called things like LMNOPQ or UVX. All of this is unnecessary *aside* to my original, early-on point of being thankful for my oatmeal or red eye gravy which turned to a semi-solid white grease, especially in a cold kitchen "warmed," (and that is using the word loosely) by a wood-fired kitchen stove without a clock. Perhaps later on I thought, upon the joyous occasion of my mother getting a kerosene stove, things would get better, but the room seemed to be even colder. (And the kerosene stove still didn't have a clock.)

What I realize now, but I didn't grasp then, is that perhaps I came nigh on to starving because I learned that back then, we were poor and it was the Hoover days and back then I never heard a kind word about whoever Hoover was but my Mother explained that he was a publican. I later learned in Sunday School about them and the Far-a-sees and many, many years later on, I bought a Hoover to pick up dirt. Now do you begin to see why I had a hard time learning the "Anglish" language in George-gee. Now I have almost gotten on yet another "aside" because my point was that since food was scarce as hens teeth (try figuring that one out) and that when the furniture factory wasn't running (Where would a factory run?), my daddy would take a long walk out in the country, and if the Lord blessed him, which he often did, my daddy would get a job-for-the-day of hoeing cotton and the "blessing" amounted to one dollar (Hallelujah) but he told us that another blessing came, and he seemed to like this blessing better than the dollar-a-day because the farmer's wife would feed dinner around noontime so he got a good meal which didn't cost anything and besides my Mother didn't have to cook. But I understood that the farmer's wife said the blessing over this blessing, which later on I understood. And years later, my Mother used to scare me in retrospect to death, when in describing the Hoover days, she would wax poetic and say: "Many be the day, I cooked the last food in the house but we never went without food, Bless the Lord."

Now, many times on television I see little starving skinny children that don't have food to eat, and always say or think, there, but for the grace of God, went I, or put another way, then but for the blessings of God could have been me.

So, now I can understand why I never began a meal, even in a busy crowded restaurant, even if I'm dressed like an executive and sitting with other dressed-up-like-executives, some of which I've just met, but I never eat without asking politely "do you mind if we say a blessing?" And before they can usually answer, some are in mild shock, I say a brief prayer out loud, thanking the Lord for the day, our health and the food, but what the Lord really knows I am saying is:

God is Great, God is Good, Let us thank Him for this food.   *Amen.*

GOD OF COINCIDENCE
(WHO KNOWS?? THE LORD GOD KNOWS)

In an earlier life I lived, back in my thirties and forties, I had a rather strong interest in what would normally be called " coincidences." Like most people I've experienced my share of highly unusually happenings or events. Most of mine have been rather mundane; seemingly of little or no value and not really interesting per se. The only thing that was interesting at the moment was the "odds" of them occurring and usually made more interesting by the timing of the event.

Let me list an example that typifies the point of an ordinary run-of-the-mill coincidence. While visiting in Florida, I was making a business phone call to an attorney in Washington, D.C. I had never met or talked with this attorney before, but had a need to employ an attorney licensed to practice in the District of Columbia. I had earlier agreed to help the friend of a friend find her birth mother. Stephanie, whom I had just met, (age 39) had been left in a small hospital in Washington, D.C. when she was only three days old. After seven months in foster homes, she had been adopted by a nice young Navy couple. Afterwards she had enjoyed a good life for the last forty years. Both of her adopted parents had recently died and so now Stephanie felt she would like to find her birth mother. This type of search happens quite often so there is not a lot of interest at this point in this example. I talked with several attorneys I knew but none of them had any personal attorney contacts with D.C. attorneys. I just preferred to have some sort of contact or recommendation rather than choosing one out of the phone book or even from a legal directory (which I had available). Therefore, I told a friend who worked in the office about needing to find a D.C. lawyer. She then called a secretary of a friend in Chicago who's job involved working with attorneys and asked if she knew of any attorneys in D.C. Her friend gave a name and it was days later before I found the time and the mood to place the call. Now, this non-event "plot" slowly progresses. At this point, two ordinary businessmen "met" by telephone, brought together by a sequence of ordinary events that had to evolve from Washington, D.C., 40 years earlier, to a Florida phone call that had to be preceded by a somewhat unnecessary phone call to a secretary in Chicago, and then the call from me in Florida, finally reaching the D.C. attorney. To add a few other superfluous details, my friend who called her friend in Chicago was from West Virginia and she had first established her connection with the Chicago secretary, while both were attending a seminar in Seattle, Washington. Now, all the characters in this "play" have played their role and whatever happens next, exciting or otherwise, is about to happen.

The opening of the telephone conversation to the D.C. attorney was the usually "first-time" phone call and involved some idle chit chat before we got down to the purpose of my call. He casually mentioned that he had just returned from a trip to visit his father. For absolutely no sound reason, I asked where his "home" was and he replied Tennessee. I then responded that I had just been in Tennessee a few days earlier. Again, for no real reason, I volunteered that I had spent a few days in a remote area and a town so small (pop. 350??) that I was sure he had never heard of the place, i.e. Roan Mountain. His response was immediate, "Sure I've heard of it" that's where my father w   as born and we had driven several hundred miles back to that area to search for some of the family's burial spots in small private cemeteries. I then told him that three days ago, I had climbed a steep hill behind the farmhouse where we stayed and had unexpectedly come upon a rather large family cemetery completely hidden from the view of the country road one-half mile below and not easily accessible by the road. Thus, the two of us were both in **Roan** Mountain for a few moments out of our total lifetime, both walking in two obscure family graveyards about the same time.

That is basically the coincidence. If you were expecting a dramatic surprise, e.g., the attorney turned out to be a long lost relative of Stephanie or for me to have found the lost grave of his father's great-grandfather, I have to disappoint you. Nothing like that happened, or anything to make CNN News. Just a series of ordinary happenings that for unexplainable reasons (and perhaps there were no reasons) occurred. Maybe that is the best explanation. They just "occurred." Or, did they?

When some seemingly insignificant coincidence occurs, we are momentarily surprised; may talk about it for a day or so and then it fades away into some storage area of the brain, perhaps to fade away from conscious memory. Some coincidences do eventually prove to have affected some life or lives, e.g., two people meet for some unpleasant reason, (as they bump fenders, fall in love, marry, and then live happy ever after). Or, another scenario: after this romantic introduction via bumped fenders, they live happily for two years and then go different ways down two separate paths of bitterness.

There are endless questions that the subject of *coincidence* raises.

Does God cause or allow them to happen?

If so, does He pay any attention to them?

Does He take a laissez-faire policy on them?

Does He let "them" have the freedom of a natural storm? Example: A hurricane, which is the result of forces of nature but allowed to roam according to laws of nature and "rain" on the just and/or the not-so-just?

Does He selectively use them for divine purposes?

Does a coincidence apply for a period but may be superseded later by our free moral agency license?

Does the hand hooked rug principal apply, i.e., the underside appears to be a total disorganized mess of loose ends, multi-colors, not making any sense, with hanging threads and no apparent design, but the Maker knew all along what He was doing and the top side eventually illustrates His perfect plan.

Does the ultimate "cause and effect" appear later?

Another personal coincidence of mine occurred against all the logic and reasoning that can be imagined. The statistical odds of "it" happening (without my describing the happening) were astronomical according to a couple of my mathematical guru friends who play with "statistics" like I play with the TV remote control. One estimated 2 or 3 million to one!

Who knows or cares if he was off a million or so. The probability was somewhere way beyond belief. In this particular case I did feel that there was some spiritual cause served or to be served, even though I could not, at that time, tell what it was or what it might be at some later date. On one occasion, I was describing the experience to a dear friend who had enjoyed years in a very staid dignified traditional church background. I had just told her that my only possible explanation was that I had obeyed a tiny almost indescribable "nudge" I had sensed. My pastor had once preached a sermon on how God sometimes nudges us and you have to be sensitive and listening for such. When I did respond to the nudge I felt very foolish. But a moment later, I was totally shocked at the outcome.

The conclusion I summarized from the experience was that either God had indeed nudged me **or** else the statistical odds were absolutely high-as-the-sky. My dignified (somewhat "frozen") elderly friend's response to my experience was something to the effect that what occurred was certainly interesting but that she had a problem with the so called nudge that I supposedly got from the Lord. My own response, delivered in a kindly manner, was that I understood her reservations but quite frankly, I had less problem believing the Lord was involved than believing that it happened against such tremendous odds.

In writing on "coincidence" I fully recognized that this subject is far beyond my level of understanding. I do **not** have all the answers. In fact, I don't claim correctness to any great extent. What I firmly believe is (1) we do not have all the answers and probably never will, but (2) God does. What I do think is that God uses some coincidence (but not necessarily *all*). If he chooses to override laws of probability, it's no big deal with Him. If He chooses foolish things to confound the wise, then He can certainly use simple, simple events and timing to show that we, in all our greatness, wisdom and knowledge, are still not able to explain such no-brainers as chance meetings and perfectly meshed timing. Certainly, we mortals do not have the wherewithal to judge the actual results that may occur later as individuals may be spiritually influenced for good by some small word or deed we uttered that was planted as a seed that would be harvested later in God's divine time and in His own blending of time and everlasting results.

Remember, we quite often never get to see the hooked rug when it is finished and turned topside up, to reveal another facet of God's never ending Kingdom in action.

GOD OF COMFORT... AND DISCOMFORT
(AGAINST ALL EARTHLY ODDS)

All of us *believers* should probably keep a diary of the remarkable "events" we encounter in our daily lives. They will vary greatly in variation of subjects, topics and experiences. And they will vary greatly in the intensity of the happening. All the way from "isn't that interesting" to "unusual; remarkable; absolutely fascinating to unbelievable" and "that had to be a miracle!! Your collection should be limited to an event you have personally experienced, eye-witnessed or personally knew one or more of the people involved in the happening; not something you have read, seen on TV or overheard. In my case, I enjoy interviewing/ questioning the story so as to learn all the facts.

I can almost promise that over a period of time you will be pleased and "blessed" by reading and re-reading your collection. You might entitle it "Miracles"??? and let the Holy Spirit be a part of the process.

My own collection may not be very long but I've enjoyed it and certainly found it worthwhile. It is also interesting and when you share one of *your* miracles, only to have your skeptical friends and acquaintances try to *explain away* the happening, so as to remove any possible divine involvement. A lot of very "good" people prefer to keep God at an arms length relation, (or better yet, keep Him in faraway heaven) because they become uncomfortable if God gets too real. Could it be because a remote God is much easier to ignore? This is evidently some law of spiritual-physics that says the closer a mere mortal comes in touch with the Holy God the more their comfort level diminishes or disappears. Personally, I don't like to hammer a "divine event" down into someone's hard stubborn skeptical head. It is more effective to share the facts and then let them do their debating with the Holy Spirit. However, since I am quite often guilty of trying to help God (even though long ago I recognized that He really doesn't need my help) I do have a pretty good "comeback" I can quickly offer. "Quite frankly, dear friend, I have less a problem accepting the fact that God had a direct role in this, than accepting the statistically, probability that it just happened to occur." Then, I can turn and politely leave "it" with them. One final note on this preface. It is of vital importance that you have total confidence in the integrity of your facts and/or the individuals who have relayed the "happening" to you.

Start journalizing.

I first learned of this true story from an in-law relative, a devout Christian who was personally involved in the first part of the story only and then was a close observer of the rest of the story as it unfolded. Thus, I have no doubt about the integrity of the story you are about to read. Here are the facts and key points in a simplified format.

1. My relative worked in a financial position with a small, but growing business.
2. Located on the outskirts of a large city in the "north."
3. The owners were devout Christians and the Lord had greatly blessed their efforts.
4. Unable to have any children they had applied for adoption (and even hoped for twins). The adoption was eventually approved and the anxious wait began.
5. Suddenly the business experienced several problems and they were forced to file for bankruptcy.
6. They lost their home, were virtually overrun with creditors and many stressful problems. The stress was unbearable.
7. Obviously, the sudden turn of events seemed certain to have their adoption request canceled.

The adoption procedure called for an adoption fee to be required, in what at the time seemed impossible. Amount "X" which amounted to $10,000 was needed on an immediate basis, needed to be paid to fulfill the requirements of the Adoption Application. My contact in this story decided on his own to write them a check for "Y" amount from his meager savings account.

My contact then called one close acquaintance and shared the story. No amount of money was requested or even suggested to this person and my relative did not reveal that he had mailed a check; therefore no amount was ever stated. This person then on his own called people and relayed the story. The number he called is not known. And from this point, we can only assume what happened. Either way, several people called or various people took it upon themselves to call one or more. Result: the exact amount needed for the adoption fee was received by checks from people totally unknown to the adopting parents. Only one person knew the storeowner since she had once purchased an item from him. The owner really did not know her, or even remember their meeting.

Here are the several divine punch lines.

1. The family was packed and ready to move to another state when they "felt" the Lord say "No, do not move!"
2. The checks arrived promptly and every check was for the same amount, i.e. $500.00.
3. The total of the gifts from all the givers (except my relative) was $10,000 the exact amount needed.
4. There had been <u>no</u> discussion among any of them, except that my relative did not tell the amount he was giving and did not ask for the person to give anything. My relative did tell what he was doing with no elaboration or suggestion.
5. Sometime later, a dedication service was held in their local church and that was the first time they had met each other. They had all been invited because of their address being on the checks.
6. Finally and divinely, <u>everyone</u> who contributed attended the Dedication Service.

A note to skeptics: how many times have you been involved in a reception, party, event, etc. and had 100% attendance?

GOD OF MY SALVATION
(CAN I EARN IT?)

It was easy for David to know who the God of his salvation was. Even early in his life he could name at least two times when he had almost been killed. Therefore, he knew the how and the why for placing his trust in God. I have *almost* been killed. How many times can you name?

David had another reason for knowing whom the God of Salvation was. Being a shepherd is a lonely life. But there are definite advantages to a lonely life. Loneliness can silently erase you, if you allow it to. Or, if you discipline yourself, loneliness can build you and strengthen you. Loneliness gives you time to meditate   to think about God and His glory; of God and His goodness; of God and his grace. David used his lonely time to good advantage. He meditated upon God's word day and night. He wrote Psalms. He sang Psalms. He learned to play an instrument. He called upon God and talked to Him and prayed to Him. And he obviously did a lot of praising God and being thankful! All of this helped David to really *know* this God of his salvation.

Often times I hear children complaining to their parents and whining, "I'm bored." Worse than that, I hear their parents worrying because their children might become bored.

Hogwash! Give them a pencil and an index card and tell them to go write a Psalm.

Lead me in thy truth, and teach me: for thou art the God of my salvation; and on thee do I wait all the day. Psalm 25:5

The Lord is my light and my salvation; whom shall I fear?

The Lord is the strength of my life; of whom shall I be afraid?
Psalm 27:1

The Lord is my strength and song, and is become my salvation.
Psalm 118:14

How can we help but rejoice and be glad?

173

GRACE BEYOND EXPLAINING
(MANY TIMES IT IS INVISIBLE)

One thing I have **not** done a lot of in writing this book is to tell any "war stories." There is a very good reason for that: I have never been in any "wars." I barely missed the **"Big One"** that Tom Brokaw wrote about. You will not find any mention of me directly or by name, but I did pull my little red wagon through the neighborhood and collect scrap metal "for the war effort" but I thought I was doing it to "whip the Japanese." All of that now is so long ago, but at the time I wonder if any of the scrap metal I collected ever made it to Japan in the form of a bomb or bullet. If so, then perhaps, just perhaps, I could have gotten some of the metal back in the form of one of the several Japanese cars I've since owned. Oh yes, I remember: I once owned a German Beetle (a Japanese Beetle would sound more appropriate, wouldn't it?).

This "return" of my scrap metal sounds plausible, at least to me, since the Japanese perhaps (just perhaps) used the fragments of *my* bomb or bullet as scrap metal to make my Toyota.

Those former enemies (and I was actually taught in school to hate them) have sure improved their quality since then, because I do remember when we patriotic red-blooded Americans used to "smash to smithereens" those cheap brick-a-bricks, ashtrays and stuff they turned out. Now, you can hardly destroy a Honda. Incidentally, ain't life strange? In the intervening years (and I've got a lot of intervening years under the bridge, so-to-speak) I have been fortunate to have a number of Japanese friends. And, I really can't recall the last time I hated a former enemy.

So what is the lesson to be gathered from all of the above? Maybe it is that God is working in every facet of our lives all the time, day after day, year after year. Even in a major war. Most of the times, we don't even know God is there. Not just because He is invisible and "intangible" and He seldom speaks and when He does speak He normally does so in a "quiet, still voice." Later, we do see his "footprints." Only most of the time He uses footprints of grace–so we then know He was there. No doubt about it.

Someone said, "there are no winners in a war." Most of us, even as the "victors" never felt like happy "winners" when we received (or, knew someone who received) a telegram "regretting to inform us " The enemies I was taught to hate went on to commit atrocities and do horrible ugly things. I had no intention of ever doing anything but **hating them forever**, much less **"liking them."**

I don't feel I personally deserved any credit for this "transformation" in my intense and long-standing feelings. But how much better that this change occurred and the bitterness faded into far away thoughts, tinged with sorrow, regret and sadness, that the evil and ugliness were released, due to the application of conscious and subconscious acts of forgiveness, soothed by the ointment of grace. Put another way, only God can give us "beauty for ashes."

All of this goes far back in my mind to the first time I heard Jesus "talking" during the Sermon on the Mount. I can almost think ("think" is stronger than "imagine") that I was there, but I was in a Sunday School Class taught by Miss Norma, who spoke about Jesus telling us we need to forgive our enemies and actually pray for those that did bad things to us. It sure must have stuck in my brain, because it is still there—and I still hear it.

The grace of God is absolutely beyond explaining. During the World War II years, the deadly feared it-can't-be-true-but-oh-God-it-is, "I regret to inform you" telegrams were routinely delivered by the only taxicab in our small town. I spent the summer with my grandmother then. Many, many times (daily mid-morning times) I saw my grandmother in her bedroom, kneeling before an old-fashioned storage trunk. She had a lot of reasons to pray—a son, Broughton, in Germany trying to cross the Rhine River in bitter battles and her baby boy, Dwight, on a small destroyer involved in the helpless fear of Kamikaze planes on suicide missions trying to dive directly onto gray decks. These two sons were no better than thousands of others who would die. But Broughton had a small son he had only held briefly, during his final leave and he had a farm to work and people who needed and depended on him. And Dwight wasn't even married yet, but his number one reason for wanting to survive? Simply put, he was too young to die.

Thus, on what could be called an ordinary day in the early spring of 1945 in Toccoa, Georgia, the *"Death Cab"* was making his rounds, delivering regret-to-inform-you telegrams. He stopped in front of the house and looked at the name on the mailbox. Everyone in town knew the color and the sound of the *"Death Cab."* Eyes from behind curtains of many houses watched surreptitiously. Usually no one admitted they actually waited and waited for the cab's morbid arrival. Most people didn't really want to watch. The very thought amplified the fear you were trying to keep beneath the surface–as though it wasn't there. On this day I was just 13 years old. I watched.

Everything seemed frozen in time. My heart stopped, or so I thought. It should have been pounding. It seemed like forever. That cab was the center of the universe. Thousands of miles away were the unending fog banks on the Rhine River. Dismal!

The weather was staging the drama for thousands of men still dying, when the war was "almost" over. Several thousand miles in another direction, only farther, the havoc of a bloody war continued. Could a desperate pilot find a destroyer on a raging Pacific Ocean, bobbling almost like a small kid's toy? But for now the cab was all that mattered. Then the cab moved on to find the right address, probably only digits higher than where Broughton and Dwight's next of kin lived. As far as I know, my grandmother never saw or heard the cab stop. She was on her knees at her trunk.

GOOD MASTER
(THE BEST KIND)

Many time the disciples and would be disciples, would greet Jesus with the term "Master." This was generally understood to be a term of respect. Note that this term carries with it an immediate designation of submission and acquiescence. As its harshest meaning implies slave to owner.

Some of the old timers of our Christian faith would more quickly accept the application of the term, stating that we modern day disciples have watered down our Christian tenets and principles. That we need to more boldly acknowledge Jesus as Lord and Master. There are a number of Bible verses that are tough and hard to dilute or explain away. Excerpts from some tough scriptures include: if any man will come after me, let him deny himself, and take up his cross and follow me   if you would be perfect, go and sell all you have and give to the poor .   All who live godly must suffer persecution . And even though it doesn't say exactly this in the scriptures it may be implied that God didn't promise us a rose garden   . At least, not in this life.

THE GOOD WARDEN
(ENJOYS GIVING PARDONS)

I spent several years collecting material in preparation for writing this book. I began by taking only names directly from the scriptures, which is the most obvious place to look for names and titles for our Lord. Later, I expanded my boundaries in several directions, e.g., general usage in our "Christian vocabulary," even a few secular names, like "the man upstairs" or "somebody up there was looking after you" and " a higher power." Personally, I abhor these pseudo names for the Holy One, who has a name and that name is above <u>all</u> names.

Then, I really hit a "gold mine" when I began to use hymns and Christian songs. What an absolute wonderful and massive resource of, not just, names and titles but also traits and attributes of our Lord. Many of these are as descriptive and recognizable as the names and titles. And they have become acceptable and "common" in our Christian vocabularies.

To list a few: Amazing Love, Balm, Calm Assurance, The Dove, Our Example, The Fountain, The Giver, Helper, Inseparable Love, Joy, Our Keeper, Lowly One, Marvelous Grace, First Noel, Open Access, Personal God, My Quietner, Rest in a Weary Land, Still Small Voice, Thou Who Changes Not, Unseen Hand, Victory, etc.

Many of my friends were concerned about the letter "Q." But they shouldn't have been because I have five (5) that begin with the letter "Q." The letter "X" troubled me most, until I discovered some creative ways (praise the Lord) of including the lonely 24th letter of our alphabet. Please note that Strong's Exhaustive Concordance did not give me an iota of help. However, Dr. Strong sure came through for me with twenty-one times for "Zeal."

Finally, the letter "Z" could have presented difficulties, unless the Lord gives you the Zeal to discover that Jesus was a Zealot for his Father and once used a whip to illustrate his zeal. Which is yet another way of describing how Jesus is our "Perfect Everything" from "A" (Alpha) to "Z" (Omega).

Incidentally, I am still trying to remember when and where I ever collected "The Good Warden" as a possible title for our Lord. After all, no one I ever met wanted to be in prison. But I suppose that if one had to be in prison, then, one would certainly want to have a Good Warden. (Right, Paul??)

Ephesians 3:1
Ephesians 4:1
Philemon v. 1
Philemon v. 9

HOLY GHOST
(THE "ORIGINAL" COMFORTER)

The subject of the Trinity or the Godhead may be the most difficult theological subject of all to explain. Especially for most of us as younger children when we first begin hearing about God the Father, Jesus His Son and the Holy Ghost. Unfortunately at a very young age we already had our scary understanding of "ghost" deeply ingrained. And it would be several years, perhaps 10 to 20, before we would have enough maturity to even begin to grasp the understanding (and difference) of the Godhead, and the complexity of joining and/or separating the figures of the Trinity, or Godhead. I can easily remember my own relief when church terminology began to change from Holy Ghost to Holy Spirit. It seemed a kinder gentler concept to accept.

Let's imagine another scene of Jesus gathering some young children around him, as he once did in the gospel stories. If he gathered them once, is it so unreasonable to think that he would have done so a second time? Even another time? And can't we imagine him explaining these subjects to His audience.

Perhaps He said something like: Eventually, I must leave you on this earth and go back to my father in Heaven. But do not worry, because I will not be leaving you alone as orphans. No, please don't be concerned. My father will send a comforter to be with you when I leave. In this way, may this Holy Presence be with you at all times and all places. No matter what you are doing or where you might go.

"...I will be with you always..."   Matthew 28:20b

HE IS ABLE
(AND WILLING)

Evidently, two blind men had heard about some of the miracles of Jesus. In 16 action-packed verses of Matthew's ninth chapter, four (4) miracles occur. A father appealed to Jesus and asked him to revive his dead daughter; a woman with a long-term bleeding problem is healed, by touching the hem of Jesus' garment; a man who had never spoken is delivered of a demon and is able to speak.

The one I find especially intriguing involves the two blind men. Jesus, the one with all the answers, asks them what might seem like an unnecessary question: "Do you believe that I am able to do this?" This direct question transferred a tremendous responsibility to the questioners.

Perhaps the lesson for us is that in our petitions to God we should first "get our house in order" by building our faith and deciding that He is able. Doesn't this seem a logical first step?

Indeed, He is able! Maybe, Jesus just wants to hear us say it.

Matthew 9:28 *And when he was come into the house, the blind men came to him: and Jesus said unto them, Believe ye that I am able to do this? They said unto him, Yea, Lord.*

181

HE IS OUR PEACE
(WHO ELSE...NONE OTHER)

We live in a world of constant tumbling turmoil. Wars and rumors of wars, perhaps the unimaginable nuclear holocaust. What will the scary and uncertainty of the future bring? We live in our own *world* of fear: cancer, M.S., Alzheimer's, heart failure or tragic accidents that may happen tomorrow, or today. Or, an elderly parent facing mere existence in a nursing home. A relative with a long, perhaps forever, prison confinement. A child or grandchild determined to play with fire, or a wrong crowd.

All of the above is but a brief listing of life's possible and realistic horrors. Almost everything on this list could be your dreaded lot. And most everyone can add to this list, e.g., blindness, living alone, comatose for years in a hospital or home for the afflicted. Consider the gloom and doom and be depressed, but the worst of it all is that you and I have almost no control over the eventuality of these depressing possibilities and fears becoming reality. Stark reality!

Our faith, as wonderful and precious as it is, does not offer us a guarantee that one or more of these undenounceable threats will not occur. However, the one thing we do have as *assurance* is that our God is our "Peace" and that He is able to provide us with His peace in spite of and in the midst of any "storm" that we face. Furthermore, this unbelievable peace can indeed be *our peace* even if it is beyond our comprehension as to why we should have a "calmness" and inside-peace. That doesn't make sense when on the outside the raging winds of fears, doubts, uncertainties and even unanswered questions are tearing us apart. But did not the writer of Philippians say it better and with fewer words: a **peace that passes understanding**, which to further explain five words, that don't need explaining: a peace that can be ours when there is absolutely no earthly and no logical reason it should be there.

Because of Jesus.

Philipians 4:7
Ephesians 2:14

HIS WINGS
(ALWAYS HOVERING)

One of my favorite stories about Jesus is where He is overlooking the City of Jerusalem. As though he was speaking and pleading with all those who lived there. Jesus compares the people, like chicks being gathered under the wings of the mother hen. Spending a lot of time on my grandparents' farm when I was young, I saw this picture "scene" many times as the little chicks in the backyard scurried to run and hide beneath the mother hen's wings.

It seems you can almost hear the sadness in his voice, when Jesus speaks to the inhabitants of this great city, seeing them running to and fro in all of their busy activities. Too busy to concern themselves with the impending danger and threats–and all the time oblivious to the ever present hovering wings of a protective and loving heavenly father.

Apparently, a lot of things haven't changed in 2000 years. Isn't it easy to imagine Jesus overlooking the town or city where you live today and hearing Him call out to the people? Only today there are many more people and they scurry about, not just as pedestrians and on horseback, but in automobiles, airplanes and mass transit. There's too much noise and their radios and boom boxes are turned up. Way up. The volumes are not turned loud merely to hear the music, as much as they are playing loudly, so as to make it difficult for our minds to have "room" and time to think, much less hear the call of Him, who would so willingly save us.

The silence, when there is any, makes us uncomfortable. And all the time His wings are gently brushing us.

Psalm 46:10: **"Be still and know that I am God."**

HOLE OF EVERY CONTRITE HEART
(WHO CAN REPAIR?)

This is a horrible story to tell. I've never told it but once before in all of my life. And it is from many, many, years ago. I wish I could forget it. I've tried. I really have. Many times. I'm so ashamed. Specifically, I'm so ashamed of what I did. I have no reason for having done such a horrible thing. I have no excuse for what I did. It was odious. Odious is about the worst, ugliest word in my vocabulary. It is a synonym for despicable.

It happened over fifty years ago. And after all these years, I don't mean to imply that I still think about it daily or frequently. I may even be able to go for a few months (now that a lot of years have gone by) without thinking about "it." And it is not anything as "painful" now as it once was. They say that "time heals." And it does. Only it doesn't always heal. At least it doesn't always go away. Time makes it better, a lot better. But something like a scar remains. Maybe it is a mental scar that will never completely disappear.

Like once when I was in the second grade, so I would have been about seven or eight, I jumped into a fresh pile of dirt, where a well was being dug. My left hand fell hard on a broken piece of glass. A broken piece of a coke bottle, I do not recall. A very bad, deep, nasty cut occurred in the palm of my hand, in the fleshy part near the base of the thumb. The cut was somewhat in a shape of a triangle, with the "base" being nearly an inch wide. The injured hunk of "meat" was about one-quarter of an inch thick. It was barely hanging on to my hand, but still attached at the top of the triangle. *Now* it is obvious that I should have had several sutures (we called them "stitches" then). But back then, nobody we knew hardly ever went to a doctor. Unless. This wasn't bad enough to be "unless." My mother treated it with tender care, which meant she washed out the red Georgia dirt with kerosene and then wrapped my hand with a clean rag. I reckon Band-Aids had not been invented then. I never saw one, until I was in high school and in fact, never went to a doctor until I was in the eighth grade and that was because I had to see a doctor before I could "go out for" football.

Enough of these obvious diversionary tactics. Any way the hand

184

injury eventually healed but left a bad scar. The scar kept fading away and finally, maybe forty years later, you can no longer see the hand scar. But the mental scar of the bad, bad, thing I did, while faded, remains still.

The "crime" also involved a long ago boyhood friend of mine. For whatever reason, we, Jimmy and I, decided we wanted to "kill something." This cannot be blamed on "TV violence," since television had not been invented then. At least, not in our part of the world. I will not go into details about the actually killing of the cat, except it involved a lot of rocks and one baseball bat. When the job was finished, we actually threw the pathetic cat into a large briar patch.

Almost immediately, two small boys, about seven or eight, became very sad about what we had done. Remorse! And guilt, guilt, guilt. I remember we cried. No one saw us kill the cat. No one saw us cry. Finally we prayed, which was a very unusual thing for us to do. We actually prayed for God to make the cat live again. The cat was still dead. No doubt about it! Very dead.

Getting to sleep that night wasn't easy. As far as I knew, the cat experience had already been replaced by the here today–gone tomorrow retention of a young child.

When I woke up the next day and not feeling very good about myself, I slowly walked outside. Then I glanced at the bottom step leading up to our back porch, the spot where the cat normally stayed. The Cat was there ready for another day!

THE HOLY COMFORTER II
(JUST AS PROMISED)

While gathering information on the subject of the Holy Spirit I began to think about the many names the Bible and the Bible scholars use in referring to the third person in the Godhead. You could probably name most of them, but let me list in alphabetical order those that are most familiar.

Advocate
Breath of God
Comforter, The
Godhead
Helper, The
Holy Dove
Holy Ghost
Holy Operative
Holy Spirit
Hovering Spirit
Spirit of Christ
Spirit Divine
Spirit of Grace
The Baptism
Three-In-One
Trinity

When referring to the Holy Spirit, you will be pleased to note that I did **not** use the term *"it"* which is still common in some churches today. I do feel that (fortunately) the use of this term is falling into disuse. The term is objectionable to me personally. However, God is more understanding and forgiving than any of us. Who knows but it could be that God, who looks on the heart, has always been able to *accept* the term knowing that no wrong was intended by His somewhat unsophisticated saints.

As an aside, I would further think that He is not particularly bothered by incorrect grammar. I can well remember Uncle Luke, an elderly saint of God's in the little church where I grew up. He was an "exhorter" called of God but his "anglish" weren't too good (sic). Like he would often say, while exhorting (at some length I might add) that "as shore as a gun is made of "arnn" (iron). Jesus is coming agin." To which Sister Urilla would quickly add, "Praise the Lord, you is right!" In my naughty mind, I would sometimes say to myself (not out loud) that "you is both right."

Looking back, I am ashamed at me and some of my teenage friends for laughing at Uncle Luke and his "backward ways." However, I can tell you this: When one of us became ill, I mean really sick and in those days we seldom went to a medical doctor; our parents couldn't afford them except in life or death situations, we would go to Uncle Luke and ask him to pray for us. His "anglish" and grammar was not a concern. In case of severe health concerns he would anoint us with oil and pray over us—just like it said to do in the Bible. God was good. And he still is.

While compiling my list of names for the Holy Spirit I decided to check my Thesaurus and see what this non-spiritual little paperback book would have on the word "comforter." There were three options listed: (1) one who comforts, (2) the Holy Spirit, and then came the one that brought a smile to my face, and presented me with a brand new thought for a very appropriate name for the Holy Spirit: Number 3 read, "woolen scarf."

Do you get the connection I received? The Holy Spirit is many things to many people, ever-changing to meet our ever-changing needs. But the symbol of the Holy Spirit, or if you prefer, the Holy Comforter being just that: a nice cozy soft warming reassuring *presence* for us. Not just somewhere off in space; not just nearby; not just waiting until we pray and ask for "Him" to come. He is already with us, in us, and all around us, a very present help, in time of trouble, or grief, or hardship, or anxiety, or fear, or "unknown" or whatever besets us. Indeed just like a nice warm and welcoming comforter we can pull around us and feel safe and secure. Then, let the storm winds blow and still know that *all* is well.

THE HOLY GROAN
(A VERY PRESENT HELP)

The eighth chapter of Romans could easily stand alone! Every word in this chapter is rich, awesomely unforgettable, powerful, etc. In fact, I once had a pastor, who could never, never refer to "the eighth chapter of Romans." He literally could not say, "our text this morning is found in the eighth chapter of Romans. He always said, "our text is found in the *mighty* eighth chapter of Romans." He used or referred to this chapter very often. But it was always prefaced as the *mighty* eighth chapter of Romans.

And do you know? He was right! It was always mighty. And it is still mighty. Well, I got this idea once. And it came at a strange time, in an unusual place and under somewhat difficult circumstances. It came at around 3:00 a.m., as I sat alone in my home. Sick and miserable, but not sick enough to die, even though I wasn't too sure of that. One thing was certain, I wasn't going back to sleep anytime soon. So sitting there I began to read the Bible even though I was not in any mood or condition for any type of study or meditation. But I began to read aloud, because it helped me to concentrate and focus beyond my misery. As I did, a beautiful and totally unexpected thing occurred. (Need I mention that I was reading the mighty eighth chapter of Romans?) I do know that it is said that God works in mysterious ways, his wonderment's to perform. But 3:00 a.m. in the early morning, in a place or time I was not expecting to be suddenly overwhelmed by the beauty and the "spirit" of words I had read and even memorized (without trying) years earlier. And in the midst of hearing once again this familiar text, I began to weep. Profusely weep. I was especially moved by verse 26. You don't hear a lot about this verse; overlooked because it is so close to the classic and oft-quoted 28th verse.

I remembered a time when visiting a dear friend of mine who was very ill and in fact had been basically comatose for several days. I wasn't sure she could even hear me. She had not communicated with anyone for a couple of days. But I spoke aloud and told her that a lot of people were praying for her...that I knew she did not feel like praying, but we were, and that all she needed to do was (1) just say the name of Jesus, but (2) if she couldn't do that to just *think* the name of Jesus and (3) if she couldn't do that to just "groan" and the Spirit would do the rest. Isn't that what verse 26 said to do?

Thinking aloud about this verse and chapter, I, of course, remembered what my pastor, that we lovingly called "Rev. Bill," said about this mighty chapter.

The 3:00 a.m. idea was this: I will read and read and reread this chapter, until I have exhausted every new thought in it. You might call this a "spiritual experiment". For always before, every time I read this chapter, I always got something new, i.e. something *special* from these words. I felt that if I read it deliberately and carefully enough times, the words would eventually "give up" all the content and thoughts one human mind could gather.

I will always remember, as I sat there at that early morning time and place, reading the eighth chapter, how I suddenly and unexpectedly began to quietly weep, overcome by the never ending strength and comfort of these familiar verses. I phrase it this way because the verses had such power and inspiration that they were impacting me just as though I was hearing them for the very first time. For full impact, this chapter needs to be read aloud. I beg you to read it aloud to your solitary self.

My objective was to read slowly and carefully this same chapter over and over until I had exhausted all there was to glean from this mighty chapter. I must have read it over one hundred times within the next several weeks of the experiment. Going into this "experiment," I fully recognized that I was indeed reading *inspired-by- the- Holy Spirit language;* not merely great literature or words penned by an intellectual giant.

To summarize the experiment results: I never once finished reading the chapter when I felt like I had come even close to exhausting the depth and meaning of Paul's inspired words. I doubt that any great literary work of Shakespeare, or any other classic masterpiece could stand the same test, as did the beautiful, magnificent eighth chapter of Romans. In my opinion, you can indeed "exhaust" the thought and genius of great literature but you can never uncover the breadth and depth of God's inspired word. They are "spirit" and spirit is non-ending.

May the Lord add his blessing to your reading of this mighty and very special eighth chapter of Romans.

My friend, Doris, recovered and left the hospital several days later. It was a few weeks before I saw her again. She seemed eager to talk and immediately asked me "Did you visit me in the hospital? I can't remember for sure, if it really happened? But I felt like (maybe it was a dream) you told me that if I could not pray...then to just *think* the name of Jesus. I can remember for several days, just lying there and not being able to do anything but "think or mumble" the name of Jesus. I feel that is what got me through."

TO GOD BE THE GLORY (also remember verse 26)

THE HOLY GROAN II
(WHEN ALL ELSE FAILS)

Haven't I told you before? Haven't I told you over and over again? Jesus needs a lot of names and nouns and adverbs and verbs and adjectives and pronouns to describe Him. And there still aren't enough. Sometimes when you run out of names and titles and descriptive terms and maybe you have used them *all,* (not very likely) and you still need another one, because deep down in your innermost being, you *feel* another word coming on; then you can "groan." Some of you dear readers think I made that up. Right? Wrong! Read the eighth chapter of Romans. It talks about this predicament, which is a nice quandary to have.

Some of my Methodist friends haven't seen this verse yet. This piece of scriptural dynamite tells how God sees into the hearts of his people, and knows what thought the Spirit is trying to say. And the Spirit goes on to plead with God, on behalf of his people and in such a way that it is in accord or agreement with God's will.

THE HOLY DOVE
(GOD'S GENTLEST TOUCH)

Here is something I never thought of before. At least no one ever taught me this or explained it to me. And it obviously never bothered me or I would have thought about it. And after all, it is probably not all that important. Nevertheless, I think it is beautiful, sweet and fascinating. Only God could have planned it. On the other hand, perhaps it is nothing to get excited about. A lot of people might consider it one of those little details; maybe, even a petty detail. I think not. I don't think there are any petty things in God's Kingdom. And even if it is a small detail, well I say this; little details can be important. Even little details can be crucial. I'll give you an example. And it is one we learned when we were cute little children. Remember the story of the small hole in the dike and that if someone (one person mind you!) had thought it was too petty to worry about, then all of Holland and all the tulips and windmills and gouda cheese, along with all the people, would have been washed into the sea and been no more. One little kid as best I can recall stuck his finger, a tiny finger, mind you, in the dike and saved the entire country and all that dwelt therein.

The spiritual detail I thought of and I also thought of the answer: Why did God use a little dove to fly down and land on Jesus immediately after He was baptized by John? Well, technically I suppose it wasn't a dove, but the Holy Spirit came as though a dove and it must have looked like a dove. Only this one was white in color, and that is probably why we call it the Holy Dove. The question I had was: Why a dove? Why not an angel or Moses, or Elijah, or even Abraham? Or why not send an angel? After all, this was an important occasion. Then the answer came to me so easily and I would think you have already got it figured out. If one of those famous people from the Old Testament had personally appeared or an angel, or several angels, they would have caused a commotion. Nothing was to take the attention away from God's only Son. So, you can see why a gentle little "dove" was perfect and fitting for this unique event. A small detail appropriately handled by God himself.

God does all things well, including the small stuff. Exceedingly well.

I suppose you are waiting on a "purpose" to this story. Okay! Why not turn your life and all the messed up details over to Him?

THE HOLY OPERATIVE
(ALWAYS ACTIVE)

Often times when dealing with (or trying to explain) a complicated and/or complex subject, it is best to back off and then come back another time and *face* the subject with newness; just like it is the very first time you ever heard the topic. Such a subject is the Holy Spirit or Holy Ghost. Remember as a small child the first time you heard of the Holy Ghost?? And perhaps, even worse, you were introduced to the subject via discussions or sermons on the Trinity or the Godhead.

What I propose to do at this point is to break this divine and lofty subject into its basic parts. This was the way the U.S. Army used to teach us raw recruits the M-1 Rifle, i.e. break this scary, but virtually important weapon down into its component parts and learn them first.

Oh no! Right away we appear to have a problem. A "spirit" is intangible and therefore cannot be divided into parts that we can handle and touch. However, what we can do is give it a simple definition and then list in simple terms what it does.

Only first, we need to make a point: the Holy Spirit is not an "it." The Holy Spirit is a person albeit *divine* and thus the "third person" in the Godhead. First and foremost, the Holy Spirit is obviously spirit and moves in the spirit realm. This spirit largely operates with and within our spirit. I would not think we are even expected by God to understand everything about the Holy Spirit. But we certainly need to be sensitive to and receptive to this precious "Helper" who is available to us.

Now for a very simple definition in one lengthy sentence:

> Jesus, in telling His disciples (and us) that He must leave us (and the earth), said he would *not* leave us alone, but would send the Holy Spirit to be with us, and to be our "Comforter" or "Helper" and that this spiritual entity not being confined to a body, rather as a spirit, could and would be any and everywhere at the same time and since we had already been told that God is a spirit, the wonderful "Being" is really God with us and in a very real sense, the Holy Spirit became the "replacement" for Jesus on this earth.

Finally and most importantly, let us not forget that all of this glorious information was given to us early on when it was foretold, and later announced, when "God" came to earth in the form of Jesus, that His name would be Emanuel: "God with us."

THE HOMELESS JESUS
(NO ROOM IN THE INN)

This title may grab you as somewhat melodramatic. But it is scriptural. The Son of Man had just been approached by a learned person, a Teacher of the Law, who volunteered to become a follower. He was most likely surprised when Jesus answered him ."Foxes have holes and birds have nests . I don't even have a place to lay my head."

Jesus did preface this startling statement by describing himself as the Son of Man. As such, He had chosen to arrive amongst us as lowly and humble. To put it mildly, in a manger, escaping to Egypt for a while, living and working in Nazareth (Can anything good come out of that dump?) and living largely as an itinerant. Paul says that . "He became poor for our sakes "

A case could perhaps be made that Jesus discriminated in that he paid more attention to the poor than He did the wealthy. However, he talked to everyone that would listen. He was criticized for eating with the affluent and His invitation was extended to *whosoever will*. So that debate didn't get very far, did it?

The point I think Jesus would want us to consider is: there was no room for Him in the Inn and there was no "room" to lay his head and it would appear that throughout much of his earthly ministry the general public had no room or time for Him. There were, of course, exceptions with large crowds, but did many come for the free food or went to be entertained, i.e. to see a spectacular miracle?

So, what about today? How much "room" do we make for Him? Surely, He knows we have jobs to do. We've got to bring in paychecks for the crucial things in life, e.g., food, clothing, shelter and other necessities. Would you care to defend the division of your expenditures into categories of "essential" and "non-essential"? And how do you define *essentials*? How many bedrooms and bathrooms can you put in a house before one of them crosses over into the "non-essential" category? How many cylinders do you really need in an automobile to make it go down the road fast enough to get a speeding ticket?

All of this is outrageous and ridiculous, isn't it? We have enough trouble trying to explain why we can't afford to pay our tithes. Besides Jesus didn't say a word about how many cylinders we should have or should not have in our nice air-conditioned automobiles. And we wish He hadn't said all that stuff about, if a man takes your coat, give him your shirt, also.

Matthew 8:20
John 14:2
II Corinthians. 8:9
Luke 6:29

THE HOLY SPIRIT
(A VERY PRESENT "HELPER")

The Holy Spirit "quickens" us with the spirit of God. Does this sound a bit strange; perhaps eerie? In more up-to-date terms the Holy Spirit:

accelerates
acclaims
advises us
amplifies us
anoints us
applauds
baptizes us
blesses us
brightens
calms us
cheers
comforts
consoles
directs
discerns
devoids us
encourages
enlivens
eternalizes us
exhilarates
feeds us
fervor's us
gladdens
goes beyond understanding
graces us
guides us
hastens
helps us
hovers over us

"joys" us
kindles us
leads us
leavens us
lifts us
makes alive
mediates for us
notarizes us (seals)
nudges us
pilots us
probes us
quickens us
quietens us
questions us
restores
revives us
rouses
sanctifies us
settles us
soothes us
speaks in a still voice
speaks spirit to spirit
speaks to us
stirs up
stimulates
stirs our soul
stirs up
strangely warms within
teaches us

immortalizes us
inspirits
instills peace
intensifies
interprets our groans
invigorates
invites us

transforms us
unctionizes us
under girds us
verifies us
examines us
"zaps" us
"zeals" us

To be continued, because I'm sure I omitted a lot for you readers to add.

I AM THAT I AM
(GOD OF THE NOW)

And God said unto Moses, I am that I am Exodus 3:14a

As a small child, I can remember hearing this verse read by a minister and I can clearly recall thinking to myself, "that is the strangest thing I ever heard." Why in the world would God (and I already knew that He had all wisdom) want to be called "I Am that I Am."

As the years have passed and my own knowledge has grown, this name becomes one of my favorites. This is not to imply that I now have a full understanding. I don't. But I do have enough experience to recognize the tip of this profound divine "iceberg." A number of scriptures shed insight on a few of the splendid facets of the I Am God.

> **"...I am Alpha and Omega, the first and the last**
> Revelation 1:11
> **"...fear not; I am the first and the last.**
> Revelation 1:17b
> **"...I am He that liveth, and was dead; and behold, I am alive forevermore..."**
> Revelation 1:18a
> **"...I hold the keys of hell and of death.**

When you put all of the above thoughts together the essence of *I Am that I Am,* seems to be saying, God always was and always will be, which is to say He was in the past and He will be the God of the future. However He is not the "past" and He is not the "future" because God can never be described, defined, restricted or enveloped in time.

Why? Because He is **eternal**, and being "eternal" God can never, never be tied to any clock or calendar, or historical devices of man, including futuristic projections. Put another way, God is now. God has never been a "was" or past tense Deity. And listen to this: God will not be the God of the future, since this too implies some time limit will have to be fulfilled and a new time limit started in order to move the

God-of-the-Now from here to there. This, dear reader, cannot be, because it has already been stated that God cannot be bound in any way to a time restriction or any sort of measurement of time. Put another way, in trying to describe this most profound subject in simple terms (and profound things cannot be described in simple terms) God is the <u>current</u> God, always has been current and forever more will be current.

Thus, the descriptive name "Current" must be capitalized, therefore God is Current, God is Always, forever and forever.

Amen.

I AM
(FILL IN THE _____)

Just when we humans think we are beginning to get our act together just when we are feeling a little smug thinking tha t perhaps we can understand God after all, then, the "holy carpet" gets pulled out from under us and all over again, we realize how inadequate we really are.

That must have been how Moses felt. He had just survived the burning bush experience and removed his shoes to stand on Holy ground and then he gets the great news that God is going to use him to intervene for the children of Israel.

At this point, Moses wants to know what to say to the children of Israel when they ask, what is *his* name? What an odd name Moses received. Perhaps Moses thought that he was about to hear something impressive, profound and regal, like "The Most High and Majestic, Holy Lord of all creation who is Almighty, All Powerful and All Wise."

Instead, he is instructed to say, "I AM has sent me to you." Some Bible scholars have said that this seemingly oversimplified "title" may be the most all-encompassing name of all the glorious names and titles that can ever, ever be uttered. In other words, this particular designation can be used as a Divine Prefix, whereby any believer can proclaim the Divine Prefix and then fill in the blank or multi-blanks to their heart's and spirit's content.

> Ex. 3:14   And God said unto Moses, I AM THAT I AM: and he said, Thus shalt thou say unto the children of Israel, I AM has sent me to you.

I AM _____

    Fill in the blank(s)

I am *your* God.
I am from everlasting to everlasting, (and beyond).

I am the God you need *now*!

I am the God who understands your pain and hurt.

I am the God who saw you last night when you were lonely and afraid.

I am the God of *all* answers.

I am the God who gave you Jesus.

I am the God who would have given you Jesus, even if you had been the only one.

I am He who changes not.

I am He that will never forsake you.

I am the God who knows how many sparrows fell yesterday.

I am the God of all knowledge and I will never laugh at you.

I am the God who knows your thoughts before you think them.

I am the God who walks with you when you think you walk alone.

I am the God who forgives, even when you think you've exhausted your quotas.

I am the God who has forgotten when and where I buried your sins.

I am the God who can be whatever you need (if you ask).

I am the God who once turned my back on my only begotten son.

I am the God who became a baby...to understand you.

I am yours.

　　−can be continued eternally−

IMMANUEL
(GOD CAME DOWN AND DWELT AMONGST US)

The young man was really in a "stew." A quandary might sound better. He was, to put it mildly, caught between a rock and a hard place. Most of us have been "there" and it's not any fun. You fret, you agonize, you analyze, and you can only talk to a scant few trusted friends. And you certainly do a lot of praying but answers do not seem to come. Your days are long and hard and you can't do anything but think about the problem. You long for the nighttime so you can escape in sleep. But sleep doesn't come. Or, only comes in miserable bits and troubled pieces.

The problem was his girlfriend. They were virtually engaged and he loved her. Their courtship had been just as he had always dreamed. She loved him. He loved her. Then, she broke the news. She was pregnant!

It was almost more than he could handle. People were beginning to talk. More "whisper" than talk. It was beyond more than he could handle. His only recourse seemed to be quiet and a quick divorce to save her from embarrassment as much as possible. As the pressure built, Joseph stepped up the intensity of his prayers, just like we do. Just like most of our prayers in time of desperation, his style of praying changed. No longer long flowery phrases that beseeched the Almighty Supreme God of Abraham, Isaac and Jacob for divine intervention and unworthy mercies. Joseph's words, full of fear and trembling cut through all the formalities and synagogue tones. Instead they were abrupt, brief, and sent in desperation from his own heart to the "heart" of God with to-the-point, just talking-to-God, like "Lord, I've got to hear from you." "God, where are you? I need to hear from you now". "Lord, you alone can help me." "Lord, what am I to do?" "Please Lord, Please."

Have you ever prayed like this? When you thought God had gone on a long journey. And forgotten you? When you felt forsaken and sure that, this time, God was too late. God is never late! And he wasn't late this time. In fact, He sent an angel to Joseph. Joseph happened to be (mercifully) asleep. The angel, so as to not overly disturb Joseph, entered the vestibule of dreamland and spoke to Joseph in the dream. The full transcript of the angel's message is found in the opening verses of the New Testament (verse 23) but he was merely repeating what the prophet Isaiah had said precisely, what would happen a year earlier, including the name of the child.

Perhaps a modern translation would have the angel tell Joseph, "Hey Joe, stop worrying. God's got everything under control   Mary, your virgin wife will give birth to a son, and you are to call him Jesus   All of this is happening to fulfill what God told Isaiah long years ago." The virgin will give birth to a son and they will call him "Immanuel" which means "God with us." Do you understand this, Joe? God is coming to earth and going to be with you and Mary and   all the rest. Imagine! God with us.

IMMANUEL II
(IMAGINE THIS!!)

Ever wonder, why God needs so many names? Answer: Because!

Because He is so mighty and so wonderful and so Holy and so splendid and so caring and so amazing and so loving and so marvelous and so eternal and on and on the names go that we pitiful creatures with even our best intellect and life experiences, need all these names, titles, adjectives and phrases to even *begin* our insufficient descriptions of the Almighty God.

When some of my friends first learned that I was planning to write a "daily devotional" on names and attributes of God, they were genuinely concerned about my lofty plans and more than one person kindly reminded me that "there are 365 days in a year." I enjoyed receiving this oft asked question and usually responded by saying, I already have nearly a thousand "names"

For a moment just think of the beautiful and fitting name *Immanuel*. And is there a better three-word definition in all of the earth's language: *God with us*! This cherished term only appears once in the New Testament but it says so much and does not need commentary. Our great and wonderful and mighty and holy, holy, amazing God that we cannot even describe is *ours*. This awesome, almighty, amazing yet tender and loving and caring God *is with us*.

Matthew 1:23
Isaiah 7:14
Isaiah 8:8

INEXHAUSTIBLE GOD
(TRY TO...BUT YOU'LL GET TIRED)

___We never know when God is going to speak to us. Seldom, in an audible voice. Most often a nudge. Sometimes, an *impression* that never fades away like most do with the erosion of time. One of my lasting impressions came at an odd time and totally unexpected. It was about 3:00 a.m. in the dark morning hours. I was in a tremendous amount of pain and discomfort, trying to read the Bible. Not especially for spiritual reasons: mainly to get my thoughts away from my misery. I was trying to plow through what my pastor calls, "the mighty eighth chapter of Romans."

Like most, I had read this particular chapter many, many times. But as often happens in scripture reading, a "new" thought comes. Then the *impression came*: you can never exhaust God   you can't even exhaust this one chapter, no matter how many times you read it.

So that night I began, as a type of "experiment," to read this chapter over and over and decided to keep reading it every day with the objective in mind that I would keep reading it, until no new thoughts came to me   until it just became rote reading with no benefit or encouragement.

I continued to "experiment" every day for over two months (I did not keep an exact record) but I never did exhaust the breadth, depth and scope of these words. I continued to get new and different thoughts, each and every time I read it. I never did "use up" all the power, assurance, peace, blessing, comfort, knowledge, wisdom, encouragement, hope, clarity, insight, personal applications, meanings, understandings, imports, or essence.

If, perhaps, you think my experiment with this particular chapter was ridiculous or not structured properly, or that perhaps **you** can exhaust it, then try it for yourself.

I dare you.

THE INTERNAL GOD
(THE GREAT INSIDER)

In the Old Testament times, most people seem to want a *visible* God. They utilized a lot of statues, idols, graven images, etc. Even the Hebrew children occasionally succumbed to this ridiculous desire. Once when the Number One leader was absent they insisted that the number two guy, Aaron, build them a "god" that they could touch and see. So, with a few pounds of gold he gave them exactly *what they asked for* in the shape of a shinny golden calf.

At least to us, it seems ridiculous. But you can be more understanding when you realize that all of their "neighbors" had big fancy *idols* that they could see and touch. After all, it is certainly easy to know there is a "god" when you can see and touch. It certainly removes the nebulous factor of "faith." And you must admit: a huge statue of polished marble or gleaming gold is impressive to behold.

It was such a common problem of that day and age that the topic of "graven images" made the Big Top Ten list.

Since our thought processes move so quickly, quirkily and superficially, our immediate response to "graven images" is to wipe it away, like a bothersome gnat in December that should have died in October, when it frosted. In other words, we don't have "graven images" any more. Certainly we don't have a golden calf. Right?

Wrong! We have nice "wheels," large screen televisions, boats we use on weekends (but not to go to church in) and we have golf, tennis and football (Wow, do we ever have football!!). We also have careers and professions that consume us and we idolize prestigious things like club memberships. The list goes on and on, but I'll not list other "idols" like wealth, golf handicaps and tennis on Sunday because it is the only time you can play with the boss. So does it count, if we don't bow down to the cherished items on this list? Maybe not; so long as we don't put them before God. (Gotcha!)

Our God is a lot of things, *many beyond description*. Just let's not sell Him short because He is "internal" and yes, even invisible. But if you choose, you can sense His presence and "hear" His voice, albeit usually small and still, and you can catch his nudges (albeit light touches) and you can sense His presence.

Sometimes, He just sends a quiet reassuring signal (which you could easily miss, but it will be your fault), which says in a beautiful soft way,

"Be still and know that I am God."

INWARD LIGHT
("IF YOU HAVE TO THINK ABOUT IT...")

The Bible uses the word *light* on numerous occasions, usually in a symbolic way. Jesus used the term approximately 20 times. We are to be "lights," e.g., like a candle people can see. Many times, reference is made to the *light* in us.

The light in us will combat the darkness, i.e. the evil that constantly tries to flood us. Who in the world wants to be covered or saturated with darkness? The inward light of Christ in us can be accurately depicted as the Holy Spirit operating, much like a flood- light that can be quickly adjusted to change its beam. Thus, causing our thoughts to focus on a need, a person, a personal deficiency, a warning, a danger, a friend needing prayer, a missionary 4000 miles away, to name a few instances. I'm sure there must also be a spiritual rheostat on this "light." Since there is a "small still voice" perhaps there is at times a tiny, subtle light. We need to have our sensitivity dial finely tuned, so as to not miss the light or fail to hear the soft voice.

Once I heard the president of a large fortune 500 company speaking to his top management group on "ethics." The occasion involved the introduction of a new policy manual and a renewed emphasis on the necessity of high ethics in the corporate culture and the responsibility of each and every manager to always make sure that their own ethics were never in doubt. The question then arose about how do you deal with borderline situations, when a decision involves a gray area that is neither black nor white. The president's response was quick and to the point,

"If you have to think about it, it is usually wrong!"

I was impressed. Then I knew he had undoubtedly read the original "manual" on ethics.

Certainly not a bad technique to apply in our daily walk as a Christian.

THE INSEPARABLE CHRIST
(ALWAYS HAS...ALWAYS WILL BE)

"I will be with you always...."

The Apostle Paul is often described as the greatest writer of all times. Any way you choose to measure or evaluate him. Let's be bold and compare him to the Magnificent and Ever Popular and Highly Memorable Shakespeare. It would require many, many pages to describe this esoteric writer and his numerous literary masterpieces.

Still, there is no apples-to-apples comparison to the Apostle Paul. In the so-called secular measurements, achievements and specific results, i.e. total readership pages published, number of years in active publication, general worldwide recognition, etc. One specific measurement (if it were possible to obtain the data) would be the number of individuals who could quote from memory significant passages from each of these two great authors.

Of course the most meaningful comparison (again, assuming that the data were available) would be to measure the changed lives that resulted from reading their masterful works. Certainly none of these remarks are meant to speak disparagingly of the great William Shakespeare.

The intent here is not so much as to compare the two, but to emphasize the eternal importance of what Paul sensed, lived and died for.

EXERCISE NUMBER 1. Develop your own Top Ten list of classic, memorable, meaningful verse or short selection of verses in any of the books in the Bible generally attributed to Paul, the Apostle.

EXERCISE NUMBER 2. Develop several imaginary scenarios such as: You are standing on the deck of the Titanic moments before it sinks .

You are about to be marched into the coliseum arena and face death from a number of hungry lions, as the Roman crowds cheer wildly

You are trapped in a car that has fallen into a deep ravine, hidden by a thick blanket of vines, bleeding slowly to a death that you realize is minutes away

You are in a nursing home; it is after midnight and you are all alone, but still with a mind that is clear enough to know that your tired, worn-out heart is struggling to beat even a few more times, and your breathing is almost

You have two options:
    1. Quote a beloved passage penned by the aged Apostle Paul.
    2. Quote a beautiful line from Shakespeare. ????
    "Who can separate me from the love of Christ... Romans 8:35

THE INSEPARABLE LOVE
(ABSOLUTELY NOTHING CAN)

One of the most beautiful, reassuring, all-encompassing sections in the entire Bible comes near the end of the mighty eighth chapter of Romans. The question is posed in Verse 35 as to who or what can separate us from the love of Christ. Paul then goes on to answer the question. In doing so he, in effect, draws protective circles around the believer, i.e. above (height) and below (depth).

> life and death (beginning to the end)
> distress and stress (emotional bombardments)
> trouble, hardship, trials (the worst "life" has to offer)
> left without the bare essentials (no food or clothing)
> threats of physical harm (danger and sword)
> current threats or future concerns (things present or things to come)
> external powers regardless of their source (angelic or demons)

Then, in closing out this extensive list and just per chance he has omitted anything, Paul includes a classic "extra" by saying "nor any other creature" can separate us from the unbreakable unending, inseparable love of Christ.

In the "super bowl" battles of our lives and no matter what offense Satan throws against us, can we name a better *defense* than reading aloud these powerful verses.

THE INVITATION
(A WIDE-OPEN INVITATION)

Without any doubt, Jesus Christ is the "invitation" of all times and all ages. Not only is He the Invitation of all times, but He is the invitation with absolutely **no** discrimination. His invitation is to all, everyone, rich and poor, unattractive and beautiful, smart and not so smart, Ph.D's and those who cannot write their own names, charming personalities and those who are nigh-on-to-impossible-to-like, mean people and goody-goody people, obnoxious types and dear darlings, those without status and those with overly inflated egos, lonely people and popular chaps, evil people and would-be-saints.

The above listing is definitely not complete. And if it were complete, the all-encompassing listing could be summarized by saying that the invitation from Jesus is to *whosoever will*.

With sincere humility (Is there any other type?) my thoughts on Jesus as a "living invitation" is with certainty scripturally based: Did He not say

> **"Come unto me all ye that...."**
> **"Take my yoke..."**   Matthew 11:29
> **"Follow me and...."**   Matthew 4:19
> John 3:16

And Jesus told the story of one man who issued an invitation and then sent his servants, to go out and "compel" them to come, and when that failed, he told his servants to go out and beat the bushes of the highways and wherever and compel them to come in. Some might accuse this "host" of being a mite heavy handed. However, in his defense, he wanted a room full of people. Leviticus 14:23

An invitation in the Old Testament contains some of the most beautiful language. But of more worth than the flowing poetics, the words themselves speak to the heart of mankind's search for solace in all of life's turmoil and emotional roller coaster experiences. Words of answers for peace, now years old still address with calmness and assurance, up to date solutions to 21st Century quandaries and pursuits.

Ho, everyone that thirsteth, come ye to the waters, and he that hath no money; come ye, buy, and eat; yea, come, buy wine and milk without money and without price.

Wherefore do ye spend money for that which is not bread? and your labor for that which satisfieth not? hearken diligently unto me, and eat ye *that which* is good, and let your soul delight itself in fatness.

Incline your ear, and come unto me: hear, and your soul shall live; and I will make an everlasting covenant with you— Isaiah 55:1,2,3a KJV

All other invitations from Christ are important, but they must remain in the shadow of **the** invitation. The golden invitation in John's gospel (3:16) has to be the "best known" and most crucial of all times. Millions have accepted it. Sadly, millions have rejected it.

Once again this aspect of the "whosoever doctrine" points out the most unique feature of God's love. When all is said and done, considered and evaluated, pro'ed and con'ed, the ultimate (eternal) decision is "ours." To be technically correct, there is no plural pronoun anywhere in the decision process. It will always be *singular,* mine or yours; not ours. The invitation will **always** require an individual R.S.V.P (Mama can't send it in for you.)

Have you sent yours in?

JESU
(ONLY FOUR LETTERS...STILL ABOVE ALL OTHERS)

You never know when God is going to use the ordinary to drop a new revelation into your lap of assorted experiences. One Sunday in a routine church service, my wife and I stood with the congregation to sing "Jesu Jesu." I thought, "What is this strangely titled song doing in our nice hardback hymnal?" Why not call him by his real name, "Jesus?"

It was only then that I saw a footnote at the bottom of the page that indicated Jesu was the Son of God's name in Ghana. In my brief "revelation" I could easily imagine a group of dark skinned natives singing this same song in a shabby little building or perhaps a thatched hut at the edge of a hot jungle. I caught myself feeling smug and superior to them. Do you know it only takes a second to think ugly snobbish thoughts and visualize something you've never seen? At first I attempted to brush this "scene" away, just as one might brush a single South Carolina gnat away. It was interrupting and it was annoying.

There was nothing constructive or worthwhile about my thoughts. They probably weren't even accurate. And I know they were not Christ like. But nonetheless they continued down this superiority pathway of snobbery. I had just driven to church in one of my two nice automobiles, (both late models and "loaded" including air conditioning). We had slept comfortable in our nice home in a very nice neighborhood. Our home had more space (3 bathrooms) than we needed. My wife had decorated it well. And here we stood in our Sunday best in one of our town's better "first class" churches with nice plush red carpet, stained windows, a grand piano and a grander big organ, with very nice air conditioning and perfect acoustics. But at this point, the revelation rudely butted back into my thoughts, and I saw so plainly that small group of shabby natives in a hot humid hut standing on a carpet of dirt and singing to Jesu, Jesu. And then the scene and the revelation abruptly ceased, but not before one final thought came indelibly into my mind. Only, this particular thought didn't cross my mind. It stayed! That is what *indelibly* means. It's still there. And it keeps coming back often.

Oh yes, the thought is God loves these poor pathetic people just as much as He loves me (maybe more) and He doesn't regard me a bit more (not even a tiny bit more) than he does that little humble group.

I don't really remember much about the pastor's sermon that morning. But I sure do remember the "message" that was sent to me. I still have it!

Prayer: "Thank you Lord for interrupting my smugness and hanging my filthy rags out" in front of me—so very visible."

JESUS
(TWO SYLLABLES ALWAYS)

I spent some time just thinking, i.e. mulling over in my mind (so this is totally subjective) the more common names of the Lord that I use in my prayers. Then, I began placing my "top ten" names in order of preference or usage. In fact, I don't know that one can arrange them in a *proper order* since your circumstance and current needs will most likely dictate which name you use. And let's admit it: it probably doesn't matter to "Him" which one you use, does it?

Most likely, we don't really think about it or plan "in advance" which holy name of our Lord is most appropriate. Whether we like to admit it or not, much of what we say in prayer is learned behavior we always heard our mother pray: "Precious Jesus," or a pastor invoked in synagogue tones: "Almighty God" or many other titles used by various individuals.

My "top ten" might read: God, Father, Heavenly Father, Lord, Father God, Lord Jesus, Master, Precious Lord, Savior, and of course, simply "Jesus."

That list reads well, as I carefully and deliberately arranged them in the comfortable solitude, at this particular time, sitting peacefully by the ocean.

But in a crisis about to hit me on a busy interstate, I have yelled, "Jesus save me!" Or, another time in a falling aircraft, I only had time to say the name one time, "Jesus!" But it was enough.

JESUS BRINGS LIFE
(BUT I CAN KILL IT)

Jesus said he came to bring life and not just your basic plain vanilla form of life, but to bring abundant life. Anyone who has ever enjoyed this type of abundant "life style" and then lost it through their own fault (it is always your own fault when you lose it) has lost the vital force and presence. When this "sadness" happens, you can be assured that a number of things are going to change.

You are going to miss your closest friend.

Especially when you wake up in the middle of the night and you were use to talking intimately with him.

You now have a big hole or vacuum in your life. You try to fill it. You can't.

Your worries, concerns and anxieties are magnified. They begin to overwhelm you.

Driving on the interstate will become scarier. Not to mention, flying in an airplane.

You begin to lose your "self-confidence" and then discover it wasn't so self-based after all.

You know you need to read the Bible, but it becomes increasingly difficult.

You feel empty. You miss the joy.

The list goes on an on. You miss the peace that is no longer present.

You begin to wear false faces but you know what is real. It goes by a lot of names: hidden depression, less than lukewarm. You try not to use the word backslider.

Running throughout all of it. You live, not with an abundant life, but with misery and miserableness.

The list goes on and on and on, you feel an emptiness; a void, an ever increasing guilt is now gnawing you; slowly eating you alive like silent parasites.

The list...you wonder when and if it is going to stop.

The list goes on and on. You recall or remember a term from long ago when you first learned to fly a plane: you wonder if you've passed the point of no return?

Jesus is the only one that brings life. And especially, eternal life. Who is deserting whom?

JESUS CHRIST IS LORD
(GET READY TO KNEEL)

This "three-parter" will be brief and to-the-point, and as simple as ABC.

A. <u>A sad thought</u>: many of us live and work in environments and conditions where we routinely hear the Lord's name used in vain (*vain* is a nicer word than "cussing" or swearing) more often than we hear it used as a spiritual or divine term.
B. <u>A sobering thought</u>: some day everyone is going to bow on bended knees and confess that Jesus Christ is Lord.
C. <u>A confident thought</u>: how wonderful to be in a position of lovingly, willingly and enthusiastically confessing ("stating eagerly and emphatically") that Jesus Christ is **my** Lord and Savior. Now!

"…because of this…God raised him (Jesus) up to the heights of heaven and gave him a name, which is above every other name, that at the name of Jesus every knee shall bow in heaven and on earth, and every tongue shall confess that Jesus Christ is Lord to the glory of God the Father!

Philipians 2:11
Living Bible/KJV

JESUS IS
(ALIVE...AND REAL)

Complete the following sentence: JESUS IS_____.

A rather easy assignment, wasn't it. I would suppose that you inserted "Jesus is the son of God." Or that you wrote Jesus is my shepherd; perhaps, Jesus is the Messiah, Jesus is King of Kings. And the list obviously goes on and on and on with biblical names, titles and descriptive terms. Over 1,000 were collected in preparing for this book. And that exercise in itself was a spiritually broadening and rewarding experience.

The first time I actually used this collection of "Names of the Lord" was to teach an adult Sunday School Class. This was a last minute substitute assignment, which I am sure we all have experienced. I had not done any preparation, nor did I really need to. The material itself, which on that particular morning was a handwritten list of about 40 names lifted straight from the scriptures, easily carried the lesson. Brief personal comments were natural additions to each term. And I had never, never had a group give such rapt attention to any class I had ever taught. Not only were they paying close attention, but it was apparent they were eagerly awaiting (and trying to anticipate what the next "name" would be). I failed to mention that I presented the names in alphabetical order, i.e. Alpha to Omega.

At the end of the class there was a spirit of unity, so real you could almost feel it. But out of time, I needed to make some sort of closing summary statement. And it seemed so apparent to everyone as to what needed to be said. Having just spent all this time listing and discussing those beautiful names and phrases of our Lord, we had only barely scratched the surface, and we needed many, many more words, nouns and adjectives and words far beyond our earthly intellect   and still, there would never be enough, to fully and completely describe this wonderful, wonderful amazing Jesus.

In retrospect, the beloved apostle had already discovered this and so said in the very last sentence of his gospel.

John 21:25

JESUS NEVER FAILS
(AND I NEVER THOUGHT HE WOULD)

Growing up in a rather strict fundamental bible believing home, I had it all around me, talked, preached, lived and believed that **Jesus never fails!** We genuinely believed that. Admittedly, there were a few times (only a "few" mind you) that thoroughly tested our belief in this basic principle. In other words, family faith and personal faith were put through the fire. And I can honestly say, our faith may have trembled and been shaken to the core, but we hung on, sometimes by an unspoken thread, and our faith held fast to the solid rock. I'm sure there were silent times when we started to doubt, but we held on and even when our faith almost faltered, we still knew our God was close by and that he could not and would not fail us. And he never did! But

Once, when what I would easily describe as the absolutely best "Christian" in our entire family died. By human standards with which we measure, Ray was without equal. I loved to be with him. When he walked into a room, he was *the room*. He exuded the love and spirit of God. At age 34, he died. Total shock and it-can't-be-true disbelief. Anyway you wanted to measure Ray, he was Tops! The Best! All the super adjectives belonged to him; most dedicated, most committed, turned-on, hardest working, prayingest. He virtually worked 25 hours per day. Oh, did I mention? He was a minister but not just any minister. This servant of the Most High could preach and sing. He built churches. He was a special pastor, loved and beloved by young and old. He was dynamic and charismatic and fun to be around. In his spare time (ha ha), he preached revivals and camp meetings.

We probably all have a "Ray" we have known. Some great Christian, we have known. One we have loved and lost. Some dear one that needed to live many, many more years, Perhaps, *the* first "why do bad things, like dying, have to happen to wonderful people????

Then for days and weeks and months we wonder and question and ponder and speculate and ask: Why? Why? Why? Years later, the discussion of unanswerable, questions continue with slowly diminishing frequency and bewilderment. But deep within the deep recesses of our own private minds, the question without answers are in a hibernation of trust, awaiting an eventual revealing of the underside and yet-to-be-revealed *divine* revelation of Romans 8:28 "vaults" that God will answer and explain–in His own time.

"And God will wipe away every tear from their eyes."

Revelation 7:17
Revelation 21:4

JESUS THE LOWLY
(THE ONLY GOD TO EVER CRY)

So many, many, things about Jesus were "lowly." He was so often the epitome of lowliness. On almost all occasions, He was gentle, He was meek, He was humble. He wept, his heart was "lowly" and easily touched. He felt compassion. " come unto me all you that labor and are heavy laden." You read it in the red print and you sense it in the black ink.

To list a few examples of his humble beginning, in today's vernacular, we could say that Jesus was:

born in "disgrace" unanswered questions, rumors, etc.
his earthly parents were humble; lower class
birthed in a barn in the small Judean village of Bethlehem (not highly regarded)
cradled in a used, wooden feed trough
no mattress only straw; no nice baby blankets or comforter
became a "fugitive" while still an infant had to escape hurriedly in the dark of night
exiled from his own country had to live in a heathen country
eventually raised in a small (not highly regarded) village
brought up in a common working class family environment
probably didn't have a lot to eat and probably only meager clothing
limited education and limited role models.
often a migrant no place to lay his head.
stigma of being raised in "can any good thing come out of Nazareth?"

The list goes modestly on and on, nothing newsworthy or spectacular. And all of this was before he was old enough to ride a mule.

JOY OF ALL THE MEEK
(AND THE SNOBS TOO)

The poor, downtrodden, lower classes, masses in faraway places, visited only by missionaries, the hungry, the starving, those in ghettos, the hurting nameless, the unimportant multitudes etc., certainly don't have a lot to enjoy in this life. Most likely, these groups (and let's not ever forget that "groups" are made up of one-by-one singular *individuals*) are perhaps referred to in the Bible as the "meek." Their plight and suffering obviously touched the heart of Jesus. They were singled out on several biblical occasions for special and deserved mention.

These were my thoughts when I first heard the phrase: "joy of all the meek." And I have tremendous faith that my God, who is wise, compassionate and loving and "who does all things well" will someday (and eventually) in His own way, make it up to these miserable and unfortunate ones. These desperate and pathetic "had nots" and "have nots" will someday have inherited the very Kingdom of God.

Jesus said so!

THE JEALOUS GOD
(AND HE LET IT BE KNOWN)

The term "jealous" usually carries a negative connotation. Most psychologists quickly point out that being jealous is just about always a telling indicator of "insecurity."

But by no means and in no way is our God insecure. A solid rock is stable, i.e. secure. As a foundation, our God is totally secure. And not only is He secure, our God is unchangeable, unbeatable and unstoppable.

If God ever had a problem (since Lucifer rebelled), it sure was not and is _not_ insecurity! (Note exclamation mark!)

Furthermore, he was very straightforward, up front and very clear about his "jealousy." And furthermore, he made his point immediately, i.e. in the first section of the "instruction manual. And finally, furthermore, he in fact carved it in stone." (bit of humor) when he clearly and concisely explained: "Thou shalt have no other Gods before me." Note several things about this particular verse.

It was the first commandment out of the Top Ten.

This particular one, along with the other nine (9) were definitely _not_ suggestions. They were (in military terminology) the Top Ten Top Priority Direct Orders from the Top Commander. Hence, they are called the Ten Commandments.

Based on the above, it must have been the most important.

Had there been a first draft of this commandment (and there wasn't!!) Note that the exclamation points are mine, not God's, but I reckon God spoke these in exclamation point language, because "shalt not" sounds like a pointed finger type of emphasis. But had there been a first draft or had there been an amplified version back then, it would most likely have read:

"Now hear this! And I'm going to say it up front. I don't intend to have any other dinky gods before me. If you try to pull any of that foolishness, talk about smiting, I'll smite your little false gods into smithereens and while I'm at it, I might smite you too. Do you get my drift? And hear me out. I'm only going to say this once. Well, I may say it again in Deuteronomy, since I've got to get this point into your stubborn heads.

Let's face it. I am a jealous God. Make no bones about it. And later on I'm going to prove my love to you, even if it takes sacrificing the most precious thing I've got   . but let's not get into that right now. I've got these other nine to cover."

Does God have any doubt whatsoever about your loyalty or allegiance to Him?

JESUS TOUCHES US
(AND WE KNOW IT WHEN HE DOES)

Time for another true-life story. Let me warn you in advance that there is absolutely nothing exciting about what you are about to read. It is about an ordinary event that occurred between two average people going about their daily lives. Just another day at work! It occurs in a textile mill made up of the routines of day-to-day happenings. This was just another day, like all the days before and like a lot of days to follow. So be prepared to read about almost nothing happening and just a routine conversation between ordinary people in another "average" day. Thus, the *scene* is set.

Speaking of "scenes," let's imagine that we have the characters on a stage and they reenact the events. You will be bewildered at almost nothing occurring or involved. But pay close attention and see if you can spot anything interesting or of any significance. There are two acts in our "play" and they are very brief. They both take place in a chemical lab. And we really only have two individuals in our little play that have speaking parts and they are also very short. Our two acts in this play (same scene) take place two years apart. Now let the "play" begin.

ACT ONE:

The textile chemist, with his back to the audience, is busily mixing chemicals and checking the results. He does not notice as Jan enters from stage left and walks toward him. Just as Jan walks behind him she hears him utter a short statement. She momentarily pauses, with a puzzled look at what she has heard and with a slight shrug of her shoulders continues her walk across the stage and exits stage right.

END OF ACT ONE

ACT TWO:

Two and one-half years later:
Scene Two: Chemist is sitting at an office desk near the laboratory

229

table. There is a knock from the door (stage left).

Knock. Knock.

Chemist: "Yes, come in please." Jan enters.

Jan: There is something I want to talk to you about.

Chemist: "Certainly, Jan. Have a seat and tell me what is on your mind."

Jan: Thank you, but I'll just stand. This is something that has been on my mind for a long time. It's rather strange but, I need to ask about

Chemist: By all means, let's talk. What seems to be bothering you?

Jan: This is somewhat awkward for me. Its been over two and one half years perhaps three years I doubt if you will even remember it. It concerns a statement I heard you make.

Chemist: I must admit, you've sure got my attention. Please go on.

Jan: Somewhere around two to three years ago, I happen to be walking through the lab and you were busy at the lab table mixing some chemicals. You were so busy you never knew I was there. Just as I walked behind where you were seated, you spoke out loud and said something strange. And I have thought about it ever since. I didn't understand what you meant. And I still don't understand your statement. So I need to ask what you meant?

Chemist: You are right, Jan. I don't remember anything about it. But what on earth did I say? What did I say that you would remember and puzzle over for over two years.

Jan: You said, "Thank you Jesus." What on earth did you mean?

END OF ACT TWO.

The reason for sharing this story is that it provides a beautiful opportunity to ponder and wonder (a cute phrase I coined) about how our God, (1) might be working in the daily routines of our lives, and (2) the "lessons" we can learn.

SUGGESTION: Why not immediately close the book and then take a few moments to ponder and wonder about what God would have us learn from the true story you have just read.

OBSERVATION: It is apparent that Jan had little or no experience, or exposure, to individuals who enjoyed their faith on a personal and practical level. It happens all the time. I often meet people who do not believe in bothering God about small things, i.e. praying about a headache, a needed parking space, a child's need to pass a routine school exam, etc. On the other hand, the chemist, who was a close friend and who shared the story about Jan, had long enjoyed a close, personal relationship with his Lord. Therefore, he thought nothing of thanking God when, after working on a troublesome blend of dyes, he suddenly found the perfect "mix" for a shade of mauve a customer had requested. Not a bad example of "giving thanks to God in all things."

POINTS TO PONDER AND WONDER:
God can and does work:
>In the small, ordinary things of life.
>When we least expect it.
>Even when we didn't know He was working.

There is more than one way to:
>Testify of Him
>Witness for Him
>Show His Goodness
>Show His Love

We need to practice/exemplify precise verses:
>"pray without ceasing"
>"in all things give thanks"

"love one another"
"let your light so shine"
"you shall love your neighbor"

We need to realize
    nothing is too small or insignificant for God
    the importance of keeping our minds stayed on Him
    there is power in just saying His name
    we do not know when others are watching us
    no word of scripture will return *void* i.e. empty, without results
    we can *pray* by just saying His name
    we need to *pray* without ceasing
    we can *practice* the presence of Jesus, i.e. live in His presence
    we quite often never know the result of *our* efforts
    we quite often never know the ultimate end of the story

ADDENDUM:

Even though the chemist and Jan worked for the same company and in the same vicinity for a number of years, they never had but this one conversation. In that one meeting the chemist was able to share Jesus with Jan and explain why and how he enjoyed a personal close relationship with his Lord. Shortly thereafter, the chemist was downsized and moved to a new career. He never saw Jan again. In about a year, Jan died of cancer.

I Corinthians 3:6 **"I planted, Apollos watered, but God gave the increase."**

KING OF KINDNESS
(ONLY ONE KNOWN EXCEPTION)

This is a title for Jesus that I sort of made up myself. Therefore, any of you "dear readers" are cordially invited to argue with me.

How dare you? Jesus was and is the supreme epitome of "Kindness." It began when his Father and our God gave Him, i.e. Jesus, his only Begotten Son, to us i.e. undeserving humankind and indeed gave the kindest gift of all times. And then throughout his earthly life, Jesus always lived and exemplified kindness. (Well, perhaps there was the one exception, that time in the temple.) His life was filled with examples of kindness, time and time again, i.e. saving the wedding host from embarrassment, sensitivity to the little old embarrassed lady with the issue of blood or the time they tried to shoo the little children away from bothering him.

These are only a few examples. Why don't you add to the list and make your own list. And while you are at it, make another personal list of *Kindnesses* that the King of Kindness has shown to <u>you</u>.

P.S.   One time he even showed kindness to some demons and allowed them to enter a herd of hogs. Amazing kindness?

KING OF THE JEWS
(AND THEY BLEW IT)

A sign was placed over Jesus as he hung on the cross. A seemingly, minor detail. Even this, one of the final ugly acts that added more insult to an innocent, resulted in yet another dispute. Think for a moment of the various reactions to this hastily printed sign that would have evoked in different ones in the crowd, who saw the sign that day. It was intended as mockery, insult, a cruel joke and most of the crowd recognized it as such. Some wanted it modified to say, "he *said* he was King of the Jews."

Most of his disciples and some followers would have been hurt by the irony of the words. They were mocking him by displaying the title. Yet, there were people that knew in their heart that he indeed was *the* King of the Jews.

Some in the crowd had once believed that he was. Now their faith had been shattered --- never to be put together again.

Yet some of those with shattered faith would later have reason to become converts. There were those in the crowd who had always thought he was a fraud, a troublemaker, a "nothing" from Nazareth, an illegitimate son of Joseph who would never amount to anything.

Quite a few people, some younger, would remember his kindness, holding little children in his arms, have seen him weep outside Lazarus' tomb, or been fed on a hillside, or healed from years of hemorrhaging by touching the edge of his garment.

Still other individuals had had their life forever changed by the wonderful man, the woman at the well, the man, blind for years, saw and read the sign, the dying man lowered through the roof on a cot and now very much alive and well. They all knew and accepted that he was the King but they never expected this disgraceful ending to one so wonderful.

Some were casual observers or curiosity seekers. They had personally touched him or had been very close to him, i.e. placed a ring of thorns on his head and into his scalp or swung a whip that tore his back into fresh bloody bits of raw meat.

Perhaps the one who handed him vinegar when he thirsted for water or the one who drove the spikes or the one who won a seamless robe or the soldier who thrust the spear   maybe later these people had to make a decision: become an early convert to the once disgraced King, who became Savior. Or, reject him and spend the rest of their lives trying to escape the despicable role they played in rejecting the King of the Jews. A life time of guilt that occasionally might subside; only to rise and plague again and again.

All of this was 2000 years ago. Or did it end? Was that the end of this type of encounter? No way. It was only the beginning. Since then every person who ever "met" Jesus has had to decide if he was indeed the King. And this moment of encounter was much like seeing and reading the sign. Then, and only then, came the moment of decision: Accept, or reject?

LAMB OF CALVARY
(SNOW WHITE INNOCENCE: RED BLOOD)

This title of our Lord, perhaps more than others, causes extreme mixtures of emotions to churn our minds. Visual and oral. Thoughts and images. Dread and relief. Defeat and victory. The range of evoked emotions is extensive and piercing. More than memorable, they are unforgettable.

For me, it was Jim Bishop's, "The Day Christ Died," that explained in a vivid and most painful way, the details and intensity of the suffering of Christ. But after extensive reading, I personally don't think any words can come close to describing the intensity of suffering caused by crucifixion.

The comparison of Jesus to a little lamb being slaughtered is vividly descriptive. The little lamb is so pathetic; so was Jesus. The lamb is alone. So was Jesus. The little lamb didn't struggle or protest against his captors. Neither did Jesus. The little lamb is innocent. So was Jesus. Death was cruel but the lamb died the easiest with a quick slice of the throat. But death by crucifixion involved several coordinating horrors: small puncture wounds involving some blood loss. Very painful and jarring puncture wounds using rough-shaped spikes through the arms, involving more blood loss. A large crude spike fastening both feet to the rough wood of a cross, involving more blood loss.

The naked body was harshly and uncaringly lifted off the ground and the body was suspended with all of the weight struggling to defy gravity from three points so the total body's weight was hanging violently and pulling and tearing at the spike wounds, with all the weight. Then with what would seem deceivingly as the *worst* moment, the cross and the Lamb of God, crudely attached, were dropped into a three foot hole in the ground, jarring every bone and muscle, as it suddenly struck the bottom. All three wounds were unmercifully torn into wider gaps, but the handmade crudely formed spikes did their duty. They held with no mercy shown. The body's entire weight was now hanging on the <u>top</u> of the two and/or three wounds.

And now the suffering, which was unbearable but had to be borne, began in ever-increasing earnest. The unimaginable suffering was insultingly complemented by "incidentals" of no small mete. The unbearability of it all repeated and repeated and repeated and seemingly never to end.

Dying on a cross could last for days. Death came with long agonizing cruelty, displayed by the public exposure and "incidentals" of insects, birds, heat, thirst and cold nights, sometimes freezing. And at some point in the evil process, a new (and worse yet) pain joined in the prolonged agony: muscle cramps. Then, truly adding "insult to injury" was the public humiliation of jeers and shame. After all, crucifixion was reserved for the lowest of the worst.

The Romans had crucifixion down to a cruel and fined tune art, so the dying process could last and last. Death was technically caused by asphyxiation. In other words that will always sound surreal: Jesus Christ, the Son of the Holy God, finally died by smothering to death. The "human" within the man wanted to die earlier but the reflex-driven <u>fear</u> of not being able to breathe would override excruciating pain and would let His arms sag, thus allowing the weight to move to the feet shifting the weight to the bottom of the spike in order to raise his body, so that the diaphragm could have enough space to exhale one more time. The cruel cycle was repeated over and over. But finally after what seemed (to the victim and to onlookers) like an eternity, his tired body ran out of "one more times." With the words "It is finished." Thus, Jesus Christ, the Lamb of God, pronounced his own death.

LINK TO GOD
(OUR ONE AND ONLY LINK)

My younger generation friends would call this name for Jesus as "cool." It is brief, to-the-point and describes exactly who Jesus is and his purpose on this earth. Certainly it is a succinct statement of His major purpose for *being*.

To continue with this youthful line of reasoning, God is absolutely too awesome for us to go directly to Him and we are too puny to get near the Divine God of All Power and we know (because his word told us so) that whatever righteousness we might think we have is going to look like filthy rags to the ALL-SEEING eyes. Some times we get desperate enough that we think if I could just touch the hem of His Royal Robe but even the very thought of being that close terrifies us. So what a quandary we are in. Or in teenage talk what a pickle or jam we are in.

So what is the solution, if there is one? Then, we remember: Jesus gave us a *hint w*hen he said, "I am the way." Or, to a young group of cool kids He said, "I am the Link to God and I've already paid for your ticket."

LORD JESUS I
(EVERY KNEE IS GOING TO BOW)

This verse is very clear. Someday every knee is going to bow and every tongue is going to confess that Jesus is Lord. Here is my thinking on this (and I don't make any claims of being a professional clergyman and I have no theological credentials) but I *enjoy* making this confession now! The verse would indicate that someday every knee is going to be *"forced"* to bow; every tongue will be "forced" to confess, etc. So how wonderful it is to gladly and joyfully *want* to confess that Jesus is Lord. To confess on behalf of all humanity that Jesus is the Lord of all humanity, whether and regardless, if anyone and or everyone acknowledges that holy fact. Secondly, I want to confess, i.e. tell any and all, that Jesus is my Lord. In fact, I try to remember on a frequent basis to verbalize this mighty declaration.

Finally, what is most important and most satisfying is that I genuinely want to tell this to Jesus.

"Jesus, you *are* Lord! You are my Lord."

LORD JESUS
(THE PERFECT BLEND)

What a beautiful and precious *blending* of names. And the sincerity by which we pronounce them will indicate any number of thoughts, needs or statements.

a. that Jesus is our Lord.

b. that the Lord is our Supreme Leader and is rightfully, and acknowledged as such.

c. used jointly can show an urgency to contact the Divine in prayer, i.e. dire need.

d. that we are submitting to his "Lordship" over us.

e. describes exactly and precisely who **He** is.

f. that we are calling **Him** "Lord" *now* and willingly so.

g. With the right spiritual attitude, offers immediate access into the Holy of Holies of Almighty God.

h. a wonderful and effective way of prefacing or beginning your prayer time not too unlike " hallowed be thy name."

i. But can also indicate and express your close and comfortable relationship and access with *your* Lord Jesus.

j. a wonderful way of *worshipping* Him.

k. a wonderful way of *praising* Him.

l. a wonderful way of *entering* into His presence.

m. indicates respect, love, adoration and worship, compressed in two words eager to be expressed.

All of the above are merely suggestions, but have been tried and proven by many over the years. In summary, each person needs to develop and use what *feels right* (spiritually) for them.

There is a good possibility that some of these suggestions may enrich one's prayer life and keep the human elements of prayer from becoming too ritualized, stale, etc.

Finally, all of this may be somewhat unnecessary, in that simply repeating (praying) "Lord Jesus   Lord Jesus" over and over may well suffice; all the time thinking or meditating on praise and of prayer needs, remembering that God knows our thoughts from afar off and even *before* we think of them. Our best prayers just about always come when we are in a real *spirit of prayer* and allow the Holy Spirit to make intercession for us.

Finally, brethren (and sisters) pray without ceasing.
I Thessalonians 5:17
Romans 8:27

LORD OF GLORY
(WHO CAME DOWN)

One of the top ten themes of the Bible has to be "praise." Not just in the book of Psalms, which is synonymous with praise, but the theme of praise begins in the book of Genesis, and is still going strong in the book of Revelation. Note that it does not end in Revelation. How can it? For "Day and Night, they never stopped saying Holy, Holy, Holy, Lord God Almighty, which was, and is, and is to come."

God is worthy of our praise. One of the best ways to praise Him is just say the word "Holy, Holy, Holy." Perhaps this is the best way. Holy, Holy, Holy. We mortals certainly do not have the intelligence, nor the vocabulary, nor wherewithal to express adequately our gratitude. Perhaps by repeating key praise expressions of "Praise Him Praise Him" or "Holy, Holy, Holy," or "Glory, Glory, Glory," or "Thank You, Thank You, Thank You," we can *begin* to vent the love and thanksgiving and adoration and acclamation that bubbles over in our mortal beings. One of the better ones I've discovered (and I have no patent on it) is to just repeat over and over, not by rote, but by sincere utterances from our innermost being **Jesus, Jesus, Jesus**.

In this book, I will frequently be telling you what my grandmother said. For this I make no apology, for my grandmother came very close to being an earthly saint. I will not go so far as to declare that, per chance it might reveal my bias. But regardless, my grandmother told me when I was in the third grade that God-had created us so that He could have "fellowship" with us, and we in turn could have fellowship with God. There is a one-line explanation in a gospel song that goes, "He is mine and I am His."

My grandmother further explained "free moral agency" to my little sister and me (pretty heavy stuff for cute little kids) but she could do this in such a way that we understood it and remembered it down through the years. Translated it meant that we "free agents" weren't bound to love God, unless we wanted to and chose to, but, that when God heard us praising Him, or telling Him that we loved Him, it meant so much more to Him—since it was coming from our hearts and He knew we really meant it. Thus, *genuine fellowship* was flowing and

242

being enjoyed by both parties.

It made sense then and it still does, even now.

P.S.   I reckon I could have given you the theological "heavy stuff" version, the way preachers expound it, but then neither of us would have understood it as well.

James 2:1 **".........the Lord of Glory..."**

LORD OF LIFE
(NOW AND FOREVER...THE INVIGORATOR)

How do I ever thank God for all he has done for me? I woke up this morning, started a pot of coffee and then stepped outside into the mountain air. The day had scarcely started, or so I thought. I didn't see the sun. In fact, I did not even know the direction it was coming up. I was in the mountains and because of the previous day's overcast weather when I arrived; I had absolutely no idea where the east or west might be. But I knew it was coming up. I just didn't know *when*.

When my wife awoke, she would think the weather, a misty damp and cool morning was "awful" and dreary. I didn't know any better. I thought it was beautiful. Best of all, it wrapped me in "God." How marvelous. How wonderful. (Perhaps I felt a song coming on?) But that would spoil the day, since I had been endowed with warped vocal cords since birth that never got on key, much less reach a point where then got off key. So I didn't sing. "That was a good thing," to quote a beautiful woman I admire. Nevertheless, this day and this mood didn't actually require singing. This present moment was a time to "*behold*!" Only, not the usually boisterous "**behold**" in bold caps as a preface to..." and see the mighty hand of God." Rather, this was a pondering behold   which meant everything I saw and sensed was God. Spring had evolved almost into summer and had thus introduced new greenery and growth, misty fresh. I gazed at a garden that would produce tasty vegetables in mere weeks. A 50-year-old, black walnut tree that in the vibrancy of the growing season and in the dewy freshness of the morn, now standing before me seemed brand new. I stepped on some stones of slate that were so old that I could not imagine their age. Only that they were already there when any historical character you care-to-name was a small lad. Birds were beginning to sing. These birds had ancestors that were laying eggs and producing off spring when the walnut tree was still contained in a single hull.

My morning meditation totally spontaneous and without planning, could go on and on listing these examples of "God" all around me. Over me, under me, as near as I could see, as far as I could see, God was everywhere in this present moment of wonderment and worship.

Furthermore, He always would be. I looked and looked. I searched and searched. I thought and thought trying to see something that wasn't "God." By now, this wonderful morning of quiet and restful beauty had expanded and allowed my vision to include thousands and thousands of trees on small and large mountains, encircling the lush valley where I stood. Pasture land and meadows, rolling hills, a noisy mountain creek across the road with drops of water that could not be counted, but once had been singular raindrops in the sky over a lake and/or trickles of water moving deep in the ground, but now part of a river stream, on its way to provide a drink to a thirsty cow, power a turbine, or become a participant in a coffee percolator. Only eventually that drop would reach an ocean 1800 miles away and continue in endless cycles. Nothing I saw, sensed or felt, including my humble feet that walked how-many million steps, nothing, absolutely nothing, was not God.

Then suddenly with quiet confidence, I knew that all of my special thoughts and experiences of this wonderful morning time with God had already been experienced and enjoyed many years ago by David when he wrote *my* favorite Psalm.

"Whither shall I go from thy spirit? Or whither shall I flee from thy presence... How precious also are thy thoughts unto me, O God, how great is the sum of them!

Psalm 24
Psalm 19.

LORD OF PEACE
(LIKE A LITTLE LAMB)

History is filled with sad examples of people who sought peace in worldly treasures or fame that vanished like a pinch of salt added to the ocean. Like many that kept after the green grass on the other side of the fence that in another season becomes stubble. Or partners that changed spouses for new misery; or climbers that ascended another mountain, only to find a void of nothingness. Think of the millionaires that stood knee deep in green bills and found their end in suicide, or celebrities who conquered the world in roars of fame, only to kneel to gods of addiction still craving more and more as death took the final round.

The sad examples go marching on and on as thousands of souls "miss the boat" to peace and happiness. They march down the many paths of life. Paths they chose by choice or circumstance. Sadly, and by their own choice, they ignore the path where the Lord of Peace himself stands.

II Thessalonians. 3:16: **Now may the Lord of peace himself give you peace at all times and in every way. The Lord be with all of you.**

LORD OF THE DANCE
(OUR DANCING LORD)

I did <u>not</u> like this hymn. The first several times our church made an attempt at singing it–it was to say the least, unsuccessful and an awkward disaster. Not to mention, embarrassing. It was our "hymn of the month" ordeal. Supposedly a clever way of encouraging us to learn new songs rather than the same old familiar masterpiece classic hymns we all loved. The melody was different and the timing could not be imagined or "numbered." It was beyond strange.

The thing that bothered me most was the words. My rapidly advancing old age and my conservative church-upbringing just did not allow the Lord to dance. Not being a trained musician and being born without a musical vocal chord, I tried to do my usual congregational singing trick and pantomime the words. Pantomime was my specialty. Only this time I failed. The odd-jumping timing did not permit pantomiming.

Then a dear friend/ neighbor died of cancer. She was such a beautiful and gentle spirited woman. And she was too young. Funerals are just about always sad and this particular one was especially difficult for me. In spite of my best macho and stoic efforts, I cried. Wept openly. The sadness was as the hurt and loss of a family member. For me and for others.

When we stood for the final hymn I was totally surprised! The pastor announced that our deceased friend had requested we sing "Lord of the Dance." The shocking thing was that *then,* I *heard* the words of the song for the *first* time. It was vibrant and absolutely beautiful. It was "alive" as she was *alive* and I understood why she chose it.

If you aren't familiar with this song (and most probably aren't) then I urge you to find a copy and <u>read</u> the words. It is joyful and uplifting. Sing, if you dare! It's now one of my favorites and I love everything about it, i.e. its music and words. And I no longer have to lip sync.

The few verses of the song do a masterful job of taking one through the earthly ministry of our Lord, i.e. a capsule of his 32 years, including key disappointments, and ending with a joyful invitation to dance.

Anyone care to dance?

LORD OVER ALL OF ROME
(AND ALL THE REST)

The people living in Jerusalem during and around the time of Jesus had a difficult life under oppressive conditions. Their country was occupied and controlled by the Roman Government and specifically the Roman Army. This control affected, directly or indirectly, almost every facet of their lives, civic, religious and freedom itself. To put it mildly, this coexistence type of life style could not have been pleasant or easy.

What can this mean to us or what can we learn? Jesus had fairly well defined the guidelines in one statement that summarized it so well: render to "Caesar the things that are Caesar's " It was not the mission of Jesus Christ to confront and alleviate all the Caesar-type problems. For, after all, they were insignificant specks on the stage of life at that time. Christ's mission was of soul-importance for all eternity. A little time would take (and has taken) care of Caesar.

Now, back to the main story. Like it or not, we all live or have lived in "Rome." When harsh restrictions or oppressive conditions are a very real part of our lives and virtually enslave us. In these circumstances, whether we like it or not, we must "endure" and coexist. Dictatorial reigns (e.g., Hitler) are the extreme, but there are plenty of other examples, i.e. church denominational bureaucrats, city to federal governments, Supreme Court edicts and employer-employee relationships. Business corporations are classic examples, filled with theory x managers and massive egos.

I have personally lived and worked in several "Romes." There are similarities to being "under occupied control" or even enslaved. Obviously, the big difference is that the employee can always quit. Easier said than done. I also lived in the "Rome" as a draftee in the Army. Draftees do not have the freedom to quit. You live under the *dominion* of a greater "power." And you certainly render unto the myriad of Sergeant Caesar, Captain Caesar, etc. While in the U. S. Army, I was awash in "Caesars" and thought they would do me in. I was suffocated in misery. Now, I can't even remember their names and scarcely recall the grief they smeared and inflicted.

These types of conditions and constraints are not pleasant, to say the least. They vary from inconvenient to unbearable. The one thing that gave me strength-to-endure and some solace, while living and working in "Rome," will sound like overdone simplicity. I got through the "worst of time" by knowing that ultimately my Lord was in control and was indeed the *Lord of all Rome.*

He never failed me.

He brought me through.

In three words: **He is Lord!**

Aren't we fortunate that we don't have to live under such conditions? But perhaps we do. I have lived in a sort of "Rome" on several occasions. Once, for two years in a foreign land as an U. S. Army (draftee) soldier, or another time, when I worked for a major corporation under oppressive conditions. But alas, I survived.

Largely, I survived by knowing (1) that the corporate Caesars were necessary but insignificant in the overall scheme of things, and (2) that their relative importance to what really mattered in life wasn't enough to even count. To put it smugly, I considered them as gnats. Perhaps God did too.

My true allegiance was to my Lord and my God and He never failed me. Best of all, He was *always with me,* through all of the "Romes" in my life.

Just like He said He would be.

LORD <u>YOU</u> ARE SUPREME
(GOD CAN BE A BULLDOZER)

Since all power is given to Him on earth and in heaven I suppose God can be anything he wants to be. In that case, he could be a bulldozer. I got this idea (untraditional, as it may be) from an old southern gospel song entitled "Jesus is a way maker" which goes to say that "he will make a way somehow."

Almost every believer can look back and see where God did exactly this in their lives. Pulled them out of a jam or some impossible mess. Once upon a time in my life as a new manager in a new company (when I wasn't all that confident or sure of myself), I had made a very difficult decision because I genuinely felt it was the right thing to do. Not the proper thing to do, nor the right thing to do, according to "good management practices." And it sure wasn't right according to any company's policy manual. I had set a precedent to end all precedents. And a good personnel manager didn't even set a small tiny precedent. My bosses would hang me. Our corporate lawyers would go berserk. What I had done was WRONG! Not only wrong, it was stupid and absurd and totally unbelievable. And I sure couldn't justify or explain my decision. In brief, it benefited one pathetic individual but it jeopardized dozens of employees and it sure stood every possibility of embarrassing the Company (the unpardonable sin). How could I ever, ever explain that I had wrestled with God for six months and "felt" this was what "He" wanted me to do? Never in my career had I made a decision based on such ridiculous reasoning. When word of my decision became public knowledge the employees did exactly as expected. They went "wild." I had no (zero) good answer for my actions. I waited for the ax to fall. I knew it would fall.

As expected, within minutes of the arrival of the new employee, the various grapevines went berserk. Several employees came literally running into my office. They reported that everyone was upset. One group was getting up a petition to take to the Company president. We had complaint systems in place whereby employees could complain or gripe or question anything and everything! Furthermore, they could do it orally, by telephone, or in writing by a formal complaint system. And furthermore they could do it anonymously, or give their name and/or department. In either case the Company's answer or explanation would be given directly to the person complaining, if he or she gave their name. Otherwise, the answer would be posted on all bulletin boards and printed in the company newspaper. We had made it very simple and easy and quick for complaints of **any** type, major or minor, to be submitted and answered. We frequently answered complaints about lumpy grits, overcooked peas, pay raises, grumpy supervisors, etc.

All systems were in place and in place for 24 hours a day, 365-day usage as employee X arrived. A number of employees marched into my office that morning and confirmed the explosive situation. There was no doubt that my own job and career was about to be in serious jeopardy. I nervously waited for the phone to ring and it would be "the chief," asking *the question* for which I had no good answer. When I could stand the pressure no longer, I quickly (and cowardly) left my office and began walking quickly through the large parking lot. I walked fast so it would appear that I was actually going "somewhere." In truth, I had to get alone so that I could pray. I desperately needed to find a hiding place. There was none. I was frightened. My highly questionable decision had taken me weeks to make. Now it was "high noon" like in a western movie and I had no acceptable answer. My long wrestle with God's spirit was longer than Jacob's. But Jacob did not live in a corporate world.

As I walked my pilgrimage to nowhere I uttered out loud a one sentence prayer: "Lord, you are Supreme! Lord you are Supreme! I did not feel the need to explain that "Lord you are the only one" that can shut these people up Lord y ou are the only one that can stop the petition with all those many signatures L ord you are the only one that can stop the complaints from coming in Lord. You are the only one! No human being can help now, Lord. (I had already called the only two people on the face of the earth who had promised to try and support my highly unusual hiring decision: one was out of town and the other was in the hospital quite ill). I had no one to depend upon except my Lord and today His name was Supreme.

After my brisk stroll through the parking lots, I returned to my office. There is no exciting climax to this scary story for which I praise the Lord. I spent the rest of the day, which was totally uneventful. Not one single written or telephone (or personal) complaint was received on this subject. The much, talked about petition never did arrive. I never received any telephone calls questioning the matter. This was totally unbelievable and can only be explained as divine intervention.

As I drove home that evening, I smiled as I imagined God driving a bulldozer all over the plant that day, rolling merrily along over a lot of obstacles. I admit it is an unusual scene and perhaps not too Biblical. But I have no doubt about it, God can bulldoze through jungles and over our rocky places or over and through impossible mountains.

God is also, most often, a soft quiet voice.

Addendum: There is still no human way to explain what happened that scary day. Or, stated another way, there is still no way to explain what <u>did</u> <u>not</u> happen that day. I learned some hard lessons. And later I could see that I had a front row seat watching the mighty hand of God work in the middle of the business world of a large manufacturing plant in some absolutely miraculous ways. All for the benefit of one single pathetic, ugly individual that did not deserve such Divine attention per our human standards and societal expectations. I am still amazed and stunned (even in retrospect) at the length God went to, showing a designated Divine Love and precise attention and protection to one otherwise undeserving despicable character. Only God could show, illustrate and exemplify such (1) undeserved, (2) amazing love.

As to the hard lesson I learned (when the only two human beings on the face of the earth that could have at least tried to support my unthinkable decision were unavailable), and I walked through that parking lot saying "Lord, you are Supreme!" ("We need a bulldozer, Lord.") The Lord was allowing me to walk through that lonesome valley all alone. Only, I did not know it then, but I was <u>not</u> alone. God can be a "bulldozer" but yet another good name for Him: He is Dependable. Singularly, totally, ultimately, and eternally **Dependable**.

"LORD, JESUS, CHRIST"
(THE HOLY THREE IN ONE)

These three names/titles of our Lord appear together approximately 100 times in the New Testament. This popular triple combination is in frequent usage in our Christian vocabulary. In fact, we hear it so often that there may be a tendency to let these three powerful words evolve into something akin to rote memorization and thus so oft-used that they are uttered in a comfortable fashion rather than being spoken as divine designations. I have known many ministers, whom when speaking/preaching almost always use the trio-term to the exclusion of other words.

Please note that I am not implying that there is necessarily anything "wrong" with the frequency or high usage of these names. What does concern me is that some of us may be in "danger" of having allowed the usage to become more "habit" than divine intent.

There is no doubt that when spoken with sincere thinking/thought there are a myriad of divine applications that can be communicated to God, to our own self and to others. But especially to God!

The term Lord can have multiple meanings when used as a singular title and/or it can be an appropriate preface for the two other names that follow.

Lord, I acknowledge you as Supreme, King, and Master, of All.
Lord, someday every knee will bow and confess.
Lord, I bow and confess NOW willingly, gladly, proudly,
Lord, you are supreme. There is no other.
Lord, I belong to you. And you "belong" to me.
Lord, My Lord and My God.

Jesus, you are the Only Son of God
Jesus, you are my Savior, Shepherd and my Source.
Jesus, you are God's gift to me/us/mankind.
Jesus, you are God's gift to whosoever will.
Jesus, you are the Messiah promised of God.
Jesus, you are the way, the truth, the life and my vine.
Jesus, you are my Redeemer and my Savior.

Jesus, you are my Advocate and my Shepherd.

Jesus, you alone can quieten my storms.

Jesus, you are my peace and my refuge.

Jesus, you are my sacrifice for my sins, my ransom.

Jesus, you are the Risen One.

Jesus, you are the Resurrection and the Life.

Jesus, you did promise us the Comforter. You did send the Comforter.

Jesus, you are my victory; victorious over death and the grave.

Jesus, you are now at the right hand of God.

Christ, "thou art **the** Christ."

Christ, thou are the Chosen One of God.

Christ, you are my Chosen One.

Christ, you have been since the foundations were.

Christ, you are Christ who is King forever.

Christ, you are the Christ who sits at the right hand of God.

Summary statements as affirmation, prayer and worship.

Lord, you are the Christ and Savior, the only way.

Lord, you are Christ Jesus our Savior and Redeemer.

Lord, you are Christ Jesus who became Calvary's Lamb.

Lord, you are my Master and my Lord, Jesus my personal Savior, Redeemer; My Jesus you're my Shepherd and soon-coming King. You are the Christ for every one of all ages and you are **my** Christ that I have accepted and so gladly acknowledge as Jesus, the Lord and Savior and Christ who reigns now and shall reign forevermore.

LORD, MY CUP RUNNETH OVER
(AND I CAN HARDLY STAND IT)

I like the way the Apostle wrote, "of all men I would be most miserable." Many times he would wax poetic, whatever that phrase means. I heard it all my life. My Mother could often "wax that way" and she was not a learned person like the Apostle Paul.

I heard Mother say, several times a year, all the years of her life, when she was telling us about the Hoover days, when Hoover evidently had the entire country in a state of depression she would describe our miserable situation, by saying somewhat poetically, "Many be the times, I cooked the last food in the house, but thank the Lord, we never went hungry."

As a small lad, who didn't yet understand all the facts of life, that statement by my dear Mother, even if it was "waxed," would scare the wits out of me. So, I would usually mumble under my breath and thank the Lord that I didn't starve to death, even though it sure sounded like I came close to it. Quite often, in fact.

In retrospect, perhaps I should also thank Roosevelt that things got somewhat better, even though that might be debatable, since I can vividly recall some skimpy meals we had when F.D.R. was "King." Like having to eat cornbread and buttermilk for the evening meal (ugh) and during my early childhood I consumed gallons and gallons (not at one time, mind you) of "milk gravy" that was more water than gravy; seasoned by grease from a small piece of fatback. I am proud to note that a few years later, when we had become "affluent" we had gravy seasoned with sausage or ham grease. Now that's a good thing!

I well know that when I reminisce like this my ramblings, sound totally ridiculous, but such foolish reflections on *days of old* can bring me to tears. I kid you not. For in such moments, I can sense the Spirit of God on my life (and my family) and knowing belatedly how the Lord's hand was upon me at an early age–when I didn't even recognize it. I sometimes try to imagine the fear and pressure my Dad must have felt, having to worry about how in the world he was going to feed his wife and three small children. Especially, on those days when the furniture factory, where he worked, would have to suddenly shut down and my Dad had no choice but to *walk* out into the country and *search* for a day's work. And many be the times (sound like my Ma, don't I?) that that day's work, i.e. $1.00 was the reason we never ran out of food *that day*. That's cutting it pretty close, isn't it?

But, the uncertainty and the sadness contained in this insignificant personal story are **not** the cause of the tears I cry at such moments. The tears come for reasons far removed from such low points. I shed them because I know now that if "something" happened to confine me in my home for weeks, or even months, there is an abundance of food to eat. Neither do I have to worry which relative we will have to move in with–because there is not enough money to make a rent payment, remembering that I lived in 11 houses, before I was in the second grade. Or, I see the hundreds of pathetic little starving children on television, with extended stomachs, hollow eyes filled with pus, dirty and consumed by flies and most are going to die before very many years go by. And those that do survive are going to live lives of misery and seldom ever have a decent meal–and maybe few little children who will never have a full meal. And as I try to quickly turn the channel, I think there, but by the grace of God, sits me. Why was I born in this country? Why not, in Bangladesh or India or Africa or Mexico? And the list of dismal possibilities goes on and on–except for the grace of God–and certainly not because I deserve the luxury and convenience that have blessed every step of my life.

May I always remember and "hear" these words, *"**Many be the times, I cooked the last food in the house, but Praise God, we never went hungry.**"*

LOVE IN ACTION
(BUT NEVER HOLDS A GRUDGE)

As they say way up in the mountains, "I reckon this" or "I reckon that." This phase is kind of a shortcut way of saying, that I don't have a scientific survey and I don't feel, that based on my experience and my humble opinion and based on my gut feeling that a survey is really needed, but " I reckon that the 13th Chapter of I Corinthians is at the top of the list in fav-o-rite chapters of the Bible. They just don't come much better in content, i.e. containing so many facets of LOVE and in having this subject expressed in such memorable and poetic language. We never, ever get tired of hearing these hallowed words.

One of my grandfathers, with not enough classroom education to even count, and even that piddling amount came from a one-room schoolhouse, known then (turn-of-the-previous century, 1901) and now as *the* Rock Creek School, loved to write. He, Arthur, was in fact the only writer either side of my family ever had in about 100 years. Arthur could write essays, poems, songs, sermons and stories. I reckon he spent half his life writing stuff and the other half chasing down anyone that he could corral as an audience. "Anyone" included family, neighbors, church brethren and sisters and even traveling salesmen. I kid you not.

All of his prolific words were not typed nor penned. Rather, they were scribbled by pencil on cheap tablet paper, so common at that time. Only Arthur could decipher them, which he was most willing to do out loud, if he could find an audience of one or more. Fact is, if you had known Arthur you would have liked him a lot. But one habit of his that would perhaps have gotten on your nerves a mite.

My grandfather was always going around "exuding joy" which was all right, but he had a high volume, distant sounding way of whistling and he pretty near whistled all the time. Know what I mean?

Now, having set the "stage" with this long introduction, let me give you an as best-I-can-recall, a rendition of the Love Chapter re-written in Georgia mountaineer language excuse the errors, if any. And recall, mind you, this was years before the Living Bible paraphrase. Even though we *laughed* at "Arthur" then, it is quite easy to see that he may

257

have been ahead of his time. Plus, he had a lot of ZEAL!

I might be one of the world's best talkers and have a long wagging tongue and one that is constantly chewing like a cow on its cud, so that I talk more than most men and even angels, but however, if I don't have love, and I'm a-talking about pure and genuine beneficial love from my heart's honest bottom, then all I say is for naught and not worth a gnat's eyelash and all my talking is like a clanging cow bell. Even if I have half-a-dozen gifts and can dance on a dime and even do miracles and push mountains into the ocean and I still don't have love, I still don't add up to zero. (Do I "sound" (read) sorta like Arthur?)

If I give everything I have away and offer my body as a sacrifice but still don't do it in love, then none of this amounts to a hill of beans.

Genuine love will go through anything and march over ice covered hills and hot burning deserts and still stay gentle and kind and never want to be a show-off and stuffed up with pride and inflated ego. Love, it don't really have no ego!

Love never does anything bad or rude and never tries to get put in the limelight. Fact is, Love can stay back stage and still keep on "a-loving."

Love, if it's the "real thang" (sic) does not clap and rejoice ever, when bad people do wrong and get caught. Love never gets even irked or upset. Fact is, love don't even have ugly thoughts, or wish bad on others. On the other hand, Love only gets satisfaction when good things happen to people whether they deserve it or not.

Love can take on any situation and still keep calm. It will believe the best and hope for the best for others and pray for others to benefit from the Love of God and Love from others. Fact is, love from God is really what causes love to get started and to spread.

Most about everything else may eventually fade away and be gone but what will always still be around in the end and we will always be bumping into is faith, trust, belief, stubborn hang-on to the end hope, and genuine, **never-goes-away** Love. These three things you cannot always have. But, I reckon, no, I don't reckon, I know the greatest of all the three is Love. Love is God and comes from God. Love *is* God and meant to be given to others.

Fact is, it is hard to keep love penned in.

Grandson's footnote: Please excuse Arthur's grammar and spelling. If he had ever seen any of your mistakes, he would have still loved you. And kept on loving you.

Arthur would certainly have agreed with the following as a conclusion to this subject. It is also a fitting conclusion to his life.

> Love never fails; Love will not disappoint you–not if it is the true genuine kind of love, like God's love. The sermons and speeches are going to stop. Even knowledge and all the special gifts will someday be gone. Even at our very best, we only know a little bit. Even the best sermons only skim the surface and our predictions about the future are cloudy at best. But when the day finally comes that we have perfect Love, nothing else will matter.

Arthur lived with a sparkle in his eyes, a unique happy tone to his whistling, a spry step even in old age, a happy voice when he spoke, a joy from the Lord, and love that spread to everyone he met.

I Corinthians 13:8   **Love will not let you down.**

LOVE OF ALL
(EFFERVESCENTLY EFFORTLESSLY)

I get a "kick" out of being a Christian. OOPS! Let me begin again. That did not sound dignified or sanctimonious enough for someone of my advanced age. Forgive me, dear readers and allow me the opportunity to begin anew on a more sanctified tone; yet, without resorting to extreme stuffiness as though I had once been *seminaryized* in an esteemed place for hallowed learners.

I get great satisfaction in being a Christian. Translated another way, I get a lot of joy in my daily walk with the Lord. In other words, these are "happenings" that are above and beyond the norm.

Allow me to illustrate with an illustration, which is similar to an example. (Only an illustration sounds more important, than merely listing an example.) When we depart this mortal earthly life and go to Heaven, we expect, having been taught down through the years, that we will have a harp, a crown and other such heavenly paraphernalia. Right? Well, what I'm telling about are more like little, but nice, little *fringe benefits*. This page might better be entitled "Fringe Benefits of the Loving God."

Now, I can give you a real-life example: some days when I'm walking quickly down the street, with my mind on a lot of things, and one of the things "on my mind" is how good God has been to me and how I sensed his love in me and all about me and at times it is like Jesus himself is right there beside me, and even though I've got many other things-on-my-mind, i.e. errands, bills to pay, letters to mail, cleaning to pick up, and OOPS, I almost forgot I need to get the oil changed, and I need to not forget to stop by the store for the margarine she needs and all of these lots-of-things and "cares of life" are doing an invisible juggling act, just inches above the top of the head, trying to get inside said head and hopefully arrive inside in some sort of arrangement that might resemble a priority ranking, so that I don't pass by the supermarket and then try to buy the margarine at the Dry Cleaners. I am describing how a somewhat logical, semi-organized mind *tries* to operate. But the key thing, and this is wonderful, is that inside of all these lots-of-things is the *joy* and activated love that, thankfully, will *not* go away. These bubbling emotions in expression are overflowing. They need to be released.

Immediately, there are options: I could stop and preach in a loud voice and tell everyone, within hollering distance, of the wonders of my wonderful Lord. I could mention that He can be with you and in you, not just on Sunday morning in a holy dedicated House of Worship, but He can be with you on a busy street in a busy mind. A lot of people don't know this, sadly.

Then, I come to my earthly senses and remember that "street preachers" are obsolete like the dodo birds, and besides, I'd probably need a permit to preach on the street.

Anyway, I'm not a preacher so that leaves option number two which means I could just quietly walk up to one single person, one individual and tell him or her, how wonderful the Lord is to me. Sometimes I actually do this option number two, and do you know, I have yet to have a single person be rude, offended or faint or slap me. They pretty much let me do the talking. But, to be honest, most of the time my earthly senses jump in and caution me to be cautious, reminding me that I might embarrass and/or violate a civil right. Perish the thought.

Now, finally and in conclusion, let me tell you what I do at times and this will sound so non-profound that you will be flabbergasted: I watch all the people walking toward me (and I could choose someone at random) but I try to follow the "leading of the Spirit" (but this sounds too fancy), so what I do is just receive these little intangible "nudges" which are easy to confirm by multi-indicators carried in their posture, demeanor, facial expression, or eyes. Especially, the eyes. Having selected my "target" which only took a gnat's second, I speak to them in a voice that is a mite on the loud side, but with a "smile" in my voice, warmly, friendly with 100% genuine sincerity; as though the person is an old friend. All the time maintaining eye to eye contact, but never slowing my walking pace.

As I stated in the opening paragraph, I get a kick out of this! The initial "kick" or "satisfaction" comes from the expression I experience from their reaction, which contains in quick-sequence:

(1)　Surprise, who is this?

(2)　Why would he speak to me?

(3)　A delayed but returned greeting, often with a smile.

Didn't I tell you it was so simple? But the reason it works is that it is filled with Love — God's Love. Most of my targets (but not all) are poor or plain people; down and out, non-successful looking and I especially try to target people that are unattractive. It doesn't take a lot of rocket science stuff and educated learning to know that this "category of humanity" seldom, if ever, has anyone (especially a total stranger) speak to them in such a positive and friendly manner.

My greatest "satisfaction" is not the initial "kick" but rather knowing that we serve the God of all compassion and his unlimited compassion never discriminates. Never! Jesus would most likely do something similar to this, if he walked our sidewalks today.

Perhaps he does.

P.S.　Or perhaps, he delegates the task to us?

LOVE THAT SPREADS
(EASILY)

In this country we "typical-average Americans" live such routine, same-old-stuff ordinary lives. Day after day, week after week, until the first thing we know another year has *routined* by. Most of us don't visit and socialize like our parents and grandparents did. We don't have to. We don't need to. We have television. Who needs friends?

Reflecting back on some of the better experiences that I have enjoyed, a common thread seemed to unravel in most of them. In these cases, I found myself involved in *something new* (which turned out to be enjoyable or even a lifetime memory was formed). Usually nothing spectacular but indeed significant and long lasting for me. But one other note in this preamble before I give a real example. Along with the common thread, which simply involved me having to take the initiative to instigate or "spark" the event, most involved plucking "something" from the ordinary and causing the spark. After all, initiating by definition has to be self-instigated.

Let me set the scene. A very hot July day in the small downtown where I worked and managed a small retail store, I heard music outside and there was no mistaking about the instrument where the notes originated. You can never mistake the sound of a bagpipe or an accordion. Fortunately, this was a nicely dressed lady probably in her early sixties, playing and singing to her own accompaniment on an accordion. Her music was "nice." When she walked slowly passed the door, it immediately became apparent that she was blind. And alone. She could easily have been my, or your, grandmother. She was a blind beggar. Only a few coins were dropped in the tin cup attached to the front of her accordion.

Throughout the long hot morning, with the temperature in the high nineties, she continued to walk back and forth the two-block area that made up the main street of Toccoa, Georgia.

Along with dozens of other people, I watched her carry out her routine, with all of us trying to be inconspicuous (as though it mattered with her sightless eyes), with mixed emotions of sadness, pity, sympathy, sorrow and curiosity. A lot of curiosity made up of many unasked questions. Who was she? Where did she come from? Did she have family? How did she lose her sight? Where would she sleep tonight? How did she stand the heat? How did she learn to play all the many keys and buttons without seeing? How did she get here? Who was she?

Now, I have set the "stage" of a non-spectacular event, rather ordinary and even though not frequently seen today. So what is the thing that sparks, so as to turn this scene into a lifetime memory? Regrettably this is written in the first person. I say that because I am about to tell "what I did" and what I did took almost no effort, cost me nothing and was certainly no big deal. Any other person could have done what I did. It was so simple.

I stepped outside and offered her a cup of cool water, and asked if she would like to step inside the store and cool-off while she rested and drank the water.

THE LIGHT
(DO <u>NOT</u> HIDE IT)

There are several ways of presenting yourself as "Christian" in today's society. Please let me list one of the more common approaches.

Politically correct–never mind scriptually correct, it is based on the non-biblical position that one's personal belief is a personal matter. This is one that is very popular. It does not offend anyone, regardless of their own belief or their lack of a particular belief. It is also very "safe." By that, I mean you don't ruffle anyone's feathers or put someone (or yourself) in an embarrassing position. And it is also quite simple to implement. In fact, you don't really have to do or say anything. Amazingly, it is even better if you just remain quiet, passive and non-committed. Certainly, you don't tell them that you are a Christian. You certainly don't ask them, if they are a Christian! You must assume that their "faith" is a personal matter. Their belief is absolutely none of your business. In other words, it doesn't matter to you and neither do you care if they go to hell.

On the other hand, if you don't let your "light shine" think of the horrible consequences!

THE MAN CHRIST JESUS
(VERY GOD <u>AND</u> MAN: HURT, CRIED,
THIRSTED, BLED, ETC.)

I usually think of Jesus as gentle, kind, caring, and compassionate. Words like that. "Shepherd" is one of many terms that depict the Son of Man so well, at least in my mind. But on a few occasions He steps out of that role and we see another side of the usual Gentle One. Like the time in the temple when He really got *upset* and actually used a whip on the money changers. Some would say that He lost his temper. He certainly showed some "righteous indignation," which seemed justified (in my opinion). And there were a number of times when his language or verbal responses were somewhat surprising, maybe even shocking. Calling people "vipers," or like the inside of dirty dishes. He once gave a response that seemed a little unkind when He was told that His own family was waiting to see him.

However, as I ponder on this, it is apparent that I personally need these "glimpses" of other facets of my Lord. These "revealings" pointedly show me the *humanity* of the Son of God, which I tend to forget about. In my hampered mind, the *divine* keeps overshadowing the man Jesus. I keep forgetting that the Christ that could turn water into wine, could actually get thirsty after a long day's journey, and needed to stop by a well for a drink of water. Or that the Jesus that walked on water could actually become exhausted, while walking between villages. I just keep forgetting. I keep forgetting how he could be very God and very man—at the same time. On rare occasions, I do think of when Jesus, as a young boy, beginning to learn the basics of becoming a carpenter, might have hit his thumb with a hammer—and it hurt. Or, when a chisel slipped and cut the palm of his hand, the tender young hand of a teenager—it bled.

I also wonder a lot if the Lord Jesus Christ in all of His holiness and majesty, could still revert to his basic human nature and worry or be concerned about the horrible sufferings that lay ahead. I think He did, for after all He was very God and very Man.

Perhaps, it would be a good "practice" if we, the followers of Christ, made a list of the "basics" of what the Man Jesus had to *undergo* mentally and physically on His way to the cross. And then, refer to the list regularly and meditate on it.

And not put the list away and pull it out on Easter morning.

THE MERCY GIVER
(MY SAUCER RUNNETH OVER TOO)

What I am about to attempt is both easy and difficult. "Easy" because there is so much to write down. The scope is certainly as long as my life and the depth is as deep as God's love. Much of the subject I am fully aware: after all, I am the beneficiary. "Difficult" because I cannot possibly capture it all. Difficult and even impossible because I do not know, or am not aware of many of the mercies and goodness' and thanksgiving and protection and favors that have followed me all the days of my life.

It is similar to what I experienced late one afternoon at the office when I sat at the typewriter and decided that my writing assignment for that day would be something both familiar and pleasant. Therefore, I would just write a brief chapter of two or three paragraphs. I needed to be home in thirty minutes sometimes writers need to push themselves and muster up the discipline and just do it! Forget moods and inclinations: just put forth the effort and the results will come, albeit somewhat reluctantly. After all, haven't I always prided myself as one of those individuals who works best under pressure, even though in one of my rare saner moments I realize such is theoretical nonsense. My topic so I thought would erupt from my fingertips. I was raring to go and write about "the love of God." Then, I would rush home.

I learned several lessons that night and incidentally, arrived home quite late. Point: for me the most difficult things I commit to paper are the Biblical "classics," i.e. God's Love, Grace, the Cross, and other cornerstones of our faith. And all because there is so much to describe and this indescribable is "divine" and mortal minds, dare I say puny mortal minds, can never, never come close to describing such love, majesty, power and on and on. Didn't the gospel writer say it best (and he was a great writer) that "the world could not contain the books..."?

This started out being a chapter on the 'Mercies of God to me, or some such similar title. But time out!!

Before you read any further let me humbly suggest that you try this same "assignment." Just list and tell how God has been merciful to you and your family. Don't write for anyone except God and yourself. It is probably best that you write your own "epistle" before reading mine. But that choice is certainly yours. I will just make one suggestion, let's start out "Dear God."

Dear God,

Two words and I'm already crying. Lord you made me, not me myself, but you made me. And for whatever the reason or reasons, you made it so that I weep easily. I always have. But I didn't cry a lot as a baby or small child. It seemed to start when I was about 18, which was about the time my relationship, became so close to you, even though I've known you since around the time I was 4 or 5. A thousand times over, I've been embarrassed about my "crying problem" in public or in front of another person. But now, for the first time ever, I thank you for allowing me to weep so easily. I sense your love best when I cry and I cry because I sense your love. Moses had to pull off his shoes. I reckon I begin crying before I can even remove my shoes. What mercy you show me.

First, thank you for allowing your Spirit to call me early in life–and allowing me to become your child.
Secondly, thank you for allowing our close relationship to continue. It is the most precious thing I have. I know you! I really know you. And you're real to me.
Thank you for your mercy that has followed me. And thank you for mercies that continue to overflow my cup and my life.
Thank you for the mercies that bless me with good health. There is no value that can be placed on my health. It is due to your mercy and goodness.
These next items are mostly what has made me as I am–and I had absolutely nothing to do with it. My mother and daddy were gifts from you. I did not choose them, you in your tender mercy did.
And I thank you for a large number of other wonderful people that your mercies have crossed my path. Most are dead now, but their

love and influence are still in operation and a viable part of me.

Your direct mercies have allowed me to survive cancer (twice). I have on one occasion even been "mercified" with a heaven-sent instant of Divine healing. Lord, I deliberately put the first two items as number one and number two. They were rightfully placed. But all the rest are difficult to place. They seem worthy of placing near the top of the list. For now I am just listing them as quickly as they come to mind.

Thank you for your goodness and mercy that allowed me (in high school) to find my "Christian Philosophy" in Matthew 6:33.

I need to quickly insert that I do not feel deserving of any of these mercies.

And one of the better examples of your mercy is that even when I was at my worst and failed or disgraced you or ignored you–when I have sinned and I expected (and fully deserved) for your divine carpet and divine canopy to be snatched away from me, it was not. Thank you for your longsuffering, patience and tender loving mercies.

Thank you, thank you, thank you, thank you, thank you for giving me such a wife.

When I run out of words, or I can't find the right words or enough words to express how it feels when my "saucer" keeps overflowing: please note my tears, which flow, especially when words cannot express my gratitude to you.

Oh God, Oh God, my Merciful Loving God, you have been so good to me. And I can't repay you. I can't repay you. I can't repay you.

Note: the above words and examples are not at all the way I intended to express and describe the mercy and mercies God has bestowed on me. How can I do better? Nevertheless

Lord, there is so much that still needs to be said. It is like the song says: "If the world was made of parchment I still wouldn't have enough paper.

Thank you for my being able to walk, to see, to work. Thank you for my being able to see in color. Thank you for friends, for my church, for my beautiful memories. Thank you for the sweet lasting memories of my Mother. And my Daddy, my Grandmother, of Ray, of countless others. And of Roy who once gave me five dollars (when I didn't know that he knew I needed it).

Thank you for the mercies of having so many books, so much food, closets full of clothes, and so many things I don't even need. Lord, in my entire life I have never gone without food, water, clothing or a place to sleep.

Lord, thank you for all of nature. I love trees. I love flowers and birds and the Grand Canyon and the Big Sur and the redwoods. Your goodness and mercy touch me every way I turn; every way I look. I cannot name them all...and my examples seem so inadequate. Your mercy keeps on touching me. Your mercies are so many and so real. I thank you for allowing me to live in love, joy and peace for being born in this country, for the excitement I find in life and in your kingdom. Thank you because I have no fear of death.

Lord, because of your mercies I can't remember the last time I've been bored.

The joy of the Lord is my strength.

Not the end (just a place to pause).

To be continued, for your goodness and mercy shall follow me always...

MORNING STAR
(JOY COMES IN THE MORNING)

I have often made a statement that sounds harsh and may even be stupid:

"Every person needs to go through *depression* once."

Until you do, you will never, never understand what it is all about. Not even trained psychologists with all their esoteric book knowledge. Counselors come closest to understanding those with depression, but that usually comes only after years and years of second-hand experience. Even a short period of clinical depression will surpass vicarious suffering.

It's a little similar to the fantastic job I use to do when I worked in Human Resources (it was called "Personnel" then) I did quite a bit of pre-retirement counseling for employees. Later on, I retired. It should have been the other way around, i.e. retire first; then tell others how. Mostly what I was doing was hypothetical or theoretically whatever the difference. A kin to mumbo jumbo.

The number one "sin" in dealing with depressed individuals is to tell them to "snap-out-of-it." It is commonly handed out freely to close friends and close family members and is similar to telling a dear one to "stop bleeding." If only it was that simple. Let's pause, in parenthesis and promise ourselves, and God, that we will never again be so foolish to give someone the "snap-out-of-it-stupid" advice ever again.

This same sound and wise advice (smile) especially needs to be directed to spiritual or religious "counselors" who advise that overcoming depression is as simple as praying about it and expecting instantaneous miraculous improvement. Of course, God can do this, and sometimes does and most often it does not happen so easily. All the wonderful and wise religious advice, only causes the poor suffering soul to sink deeper into depression, wondering why and what is wrong with them, feeling added guilt because they could not snap-out-of-it and/or have overcoming joy rather than depression.

A whole lot of depression occurs at night. If not at night, then a lot of days seem to turn into long "nights" even during the daytime hours.

Periods of despair and/or nothingness, and/or bewilderment and/or fear and/or dread and/or worries of baseless origin and/or known origin and/or blahs extended into seemingly endless blahs and/or feeling useless and/or tired and worn out and/or uncertainty. The above sentence is a hard and frank attempt to describe "something" that often has no description. Nonetheless, depression is real. Despair and seemingly, hopeless unreal reality reality.

The purpose of this final paragraph is not to tell you how to treat and overcome depression. I wish I could but the possible solutions are many and vary greatly. What would work with one, will not help another. But what I can tell you is that in all the "nights" of depression you are going through, there is a Morning Star. The night is still around you and the Morning Star is miles away, but it is there. And while the Morning Star may seem like a lot of nice symbolism, you can at least *see* the light. You can see the light shining in spite of the darkness; and the star is out there for you to see; and, best of all, it is *ahead* of you.

MY ANCHOR
(...HOLDS...BECAUSE)

It is interesting and wonderful how many ways there are to describe our "faith." One of my favorites is that of an anchor. An anchor is really a rather simple device. It's made of metal, quite heavy, and is designed to hold a cable or rope at one end and the other two or three points are designed to grab or cling to the bottom. Note that the anchor is not attached to the bottom and is actually rather passive. Also, it is definitely not as large, nor as heavy, as the boat or ship attached at the other end. But all these earthly comparisons are minuscule compared to the vastness of the water and the unharnessable power and continuous pounding of never ending waves. Yet, as the words of an old but familiar hymn testify, " my anchor holds and gr abs the solid rock   that "rock" is Jesus." My "anchor" is (1) dependent upon Jesus and (2) my faith in Him, or better stated, my whimsical mustard seed size faith and the all-powerful, always dependable Jesus who is sufficient to secure me, sustain me and save me through any and all storms of life.

We all have access to *the Anchor* but it would behoove us to not wait until the waves are tossing our boat before we grab onto the rope.

Exercise: Make a list of the earthly "items" that you are (or have been) prone to attach your anchor to, e.g., self-sufficiency, savings accounts, 401k plans, real estate, rich relatives, parents and relatives that have an excellent record of longevity, parents and grandparents that are 2nd and 3rd generation God-fearing respected citizens, a priest who specializes in recovering damned souls, or definite plans to make everything right with "the good Lord" before you demise. ("Demise," sounds so much better, doesn't it?)

MY BELOVED SON
(DID YOU HEAR ABOUT THE ANNOUNCEMENT?)

Often times I am overwhelmed by the mighty power of God's word. I am constantly reminded in my spirit that no word of God ever "returns void." His word goes out many ways and in many places, and, it goes out with full authority, but it never, never returns void, i.e. empty or without results. Never mind that the results do not necessarily come immediately, but they always come.

It does not take a lot of words from the Bible to have an affect. A short verse, e.g., "Jesus wept" or a phrase within a verse, e.g., " My Beloved Son " Other, concise yet beautiful examples:

> " Behold, I come quickly "
> " Blessed is he that watcheth "
> "...Take no thought for tomorrow..."
> " But seek ye firs t ."
> " Ask and it shall be giv en you "

MERCIFUL GOD
(TIME AND TIME AGAIN)

Woke up this morning at 5:00 a.m. Started thinking about what I would write today. Lot of choices. A thru Z. Many are easy. Some are especially enjoyable. But there are surprises, which are refreshing. Like some of the names/ titles sound so "easy" or even simple. Like very common terms or titles about "love" or "mercy" or "grace."

Remember the rules. I go only from memory of things I've learned over the years. I rarely refer to other writers or reference. Except for the Bible. And it is enough.

Today's topic to write is one of the "classics." "Mercy." Simple and profound. Beautiful and familiar, yet unending and indescribable. How do I say anything worthy or new about God's boundless mercy? Everyone has experienced it. Volumes and sermons and books and pamphlets galore fill libraries and homes and churches. You sure can't "exhaust" this glorious subject. Everyone is familiar with God's mercy. Firsthand, by experience, intuitive, empirical and observation of God's world and everything in it. Mercy is everywhere, past, present and future. And yet, at the same time it is unique. Blessedly, unique.

What I plan on trying is going to be basic from the heart and highly personal. Perhaps, if I'm successful it will sound as though I'm talking (writing) to God, trying to tell him how good and kind and merciful he has been to me. Impossible, but let's try. The attempt will begin on the next page but I felt the need to prepare you for this.

Before turning the page (and this may be the most beneficial thing I can do for those who read this book) may I suggest that each of you give a few minutes in quiet thought as to *how you would tackle* such a task? How do you thank God for all He has done for you? Perhaps even write it down on paper. Try to do it in 25 words or less or pretend that the world is made of parchment and see if you have enough paper to tell all that God, in his mercy, has done for you.

MY MERCIFUL GOD
(A MORNING PRAYER)

Oh Lord, you've been so good to me. Oh God, how I do I even begin to try, just *try* to thank you. Oh, my Lord and my God, you have been so good to me. I wish I could write a Psalm to you, like David did. Your mercy overwhelms me. The more I think about it, the more it overwhelms me. Oh, Lord you have been so good to me. All the days of my life. You knew me in my Mother's womb. I was born in a small house; not a hospital. Thank you for your mercy before and after my birth. My mother was so young. She must have been afraid. I would have been. Thank you for Dr. Smith and the midwife I can't remember her name. But she and the doctor and my Aunt Eva spent the entire night waiting for me. Oh Lord, your mercy was so real before I was old enough to recognize it. Oh Lord you've been so good to me. In all my 67 years, I've never thanked you for this. How thoughtless of me. I would not treat a friend the way I've treated you. Forgive me, oh Precious Lord, forgive me. Oh Lord, you've been so good to me. Thank you for all the days of my life. I can name five times I was in bad accidents, and almost killed. Only by your mercy did I survive. Lord, I almost got killed as a young teenager. I was so foolish, so stupid. Oh Lord, only by your mercy did I survive. Bless the Lord, oh my soul and everything in me. I am not worthy to be so blessed. My righteousness is like dirty filthy rags. Oh merciful God, your blessings are more then I can count. I can remember so many. But how many special mercies am I not even recalling? Oh merciful God; my Merciful God you know my downsitting, my uprising, my thoughts from afar off. Nothing Lord, absolutely nothing is hidden from you. And yet you still love me and care for me. You are my Shepherd and I do not want. Oh Lord, you've been so good to me. All the years of my life your hand has been upon me. You have run my cup over the brim time and time again. Over and over again. Your mercy has reached directly to me on occasions, which defied human limits. In a high speed head on collision, I lay in raw gasoline pinned inside a car; I fell 50 feet in a helicopter, falling like a rock only to be "caught" in mid air ten feet above the ground; at the split second of impact, rammed from behind on an interstate, I saw my wife instantly hurled toward the windshield and in the next split second, I saw the seat belt mechanism lock just as her head was about to smash into and beyond the windshield, stopped and all the what-ifs are dispelled and answerable only to your mercy. Oh, my merciful Lord and loving God, you alone have saved us with tender miraculous mercy and we can never repay you. Oh Lord my God, your tender loving mercies have enveloped me in terrifying walks through the valleys of fear and death. Cancers diagnosed and confirmed and announced have become vanishing illusions of your unexplainable mercies. Oh Lord, my God, how wonderful and great thou art. My soul sings gratitude's that cannot be penned and need no musical melodies. Your divine touch suffices. And I can only praise you in inadequate human limitations as pitiful rehearsals, until eternally I can fall down on my knees and worship you and praise you "while the ages roll."

Obviously, the above prayer was not written for publication. It is intended as a suggestion. Are there wonderful things that have happened in your life; wonderful mercies bestowed on you that you've never taken the time to thank God for giving you? Certainly you can't name them all. I couldn't. But we need to keep trying.

MY QUIETNESS
(IN A NOISY WORLD)

In the hectic rushed lives, most of us live; we often *starve* for some peace and quiet. Very few things can substitute for peace and quiet.

We do try! We go on vacation. We occasionally read a book. At times we even try to "obey the Sabbath." Some people meditate or become weary in repeating mantras. Acquiring leisure and relaxation is a multibillion-dollar business but we have to *fight* for our peace of the pie. We work hard to save for a vacation, since we desperately thirst for some peace and rest. Otherwise, we work hard <u>after</u> a relaxing vacation to pay for it. We may get ulcers as a souvenir of our "restful" vacation. We strive and plan and exhaust ourselves in the quest for peace.

We missed the boat that sailed. We failed to rest with him in green pastures or to follow him beside still waters; not enough time spent in restoring the soul. When we were weary and heavy laden; when we failed to hear his settling voice all the times he spoke to our storms, **"peace be still."**

MY RANSOM
(ALREADY PAID)

It was usually impossible, by definition and by action, for any person to pay his or her own ransom. We owed a debt to our Creator. One we could not pay. God sent Jesus to "pay" our ransom.

By mustering up extra strength, extraordinary courage, supreme dedication, and especially, perseverance, we humans can sometimes do special deeds and even earn high recognition. Admittedly, we can do a lot of things.

But paying our ransom is not one of them.

MY SON
(THE SON OF "OUR FATHER")

What a beautiful phrase. How many times do we hear a father refer to "my son" and the tone of his voice in saying those true words needs no adjectives attached. How proud God had to be of Jesus, His only Son.

Without thinking about exactly what we are saying (because we've done it so often), we open our prayer by saying, "Our Father."

On the other hand, do we ever wonder if God refers to us as "My Child?" What a mind boggling and humbling thought.

MY ZEAL
(YOU CAN BE APPEALING AND SHOW SOME ZEALING)

Here is a very simple spiritual – mathematical exercise you might want to try.

(1) Call your local neighborhood actuary (or insurance agent) and ask him, or her, how many more years the "tables" show that you have left to live.

(2) Get out your calculator and multiply the number he gives you by twelve.

(3) Multiply that number by 365.

(4) The answer you arrive at indicates the number of <u>days</u> you have to live. Note: If the number appears too small, you can adjust for leap years and increase it somewhat.

(5) Application: In your daily prayer time begin to show some ZEAL for the days that remain. Thank the Lord for them (or whatever the number may turn out to be). The Lord is your zeal. You can of a certainty know that true and lasting zeal can only come from Him. Any other "zeal" you may have is, at best, just a passing fad.

OUR MAKER
(OR NOT WE OUR SELF)

In our world today, there is a lot said about some of our leaders and heroes being *self-made*. Certainly that definition is understood and appreciated. But something is wrong! What is wrong (and is very prevalent today) occurs largely on a private and individual basis: when we think in our heart that *we don't need God*. Even if we don't say it out loud, our every action indicates that this is certainly how we feel. God plays no obvious nor active role, consciously and most likely subconsciously, in our lives today! Thus, we have a society filled with "self-made" individuals. Just like the rich man of the parable in Luke who talked to himself (who better to talk to if you don't talk to God) about pulling down his barns and building bigger barns.

Is there any possibility that God, sitting in Heaven and looking down upon the puny, lukewarm, self-centered miserable flock of "Christians" (quote marks intentional) watches in divine dismay as we go busily about our "missions" (ha ha) of up-sizing our barns: living out the parable over and over again?

Do you remember the harsh, yet sad response from God to the rich man? Does God still think that way today?

THE MANY SPLENDORED GOD
(HAS A MULTITUDE OF NAMES)

Since we can agree that *God is Love* then perhaps it is appropriate to refer to God, as a many splendid thing. One phrase refers to God as our All in All. One minister says that He is too wonderful to describe. Down through the ages the hymn writers have done their best to describe Him. The 40 writers of the scripture in 66 books have given us a great start with all of the many terms and phrases used. In my own preparation for this book, I have personally collected approximately 1,000 names, titles, attributes, etc. Classic sermons have waxed as great poetic scriptural orators, in attempting to describe His royalty. I don't know of any that have claimed to provide the ultimate description. Regardless, we all need to keep on "trying," all the while knowing that we can never accomplish this impossible task of love and admiration.

The lesson I think we can all take from this is that each of us should always be in a ready position to describe our Lord. Not necessarily in dramatic and flowery literary phrases as the orators and poets can do. Instead use words that come from our hearts and our personal experiences ----- in down-to-earth sentences that speak to the expressive need of the moment. Here are three examples that are the most common.

1. Never forget to tell your Lord what he means to you! Perhaps it's a combination of prayer and thanksgiving, but expressed as though speaking to a close friend. This is definitely not the time to address the Mighty Creator in cathedral tones. Make it *personal*. (If, He is personal to you??)

2. Always be ready to tell others what your Lord means to you. This is the time you "utilize" those "names" or phrase that best describe what you are attempting to explain about your own personal God.

3. In your times of meditation use all the names, titles, phrases and attributes that you can recall. Not as rote memorization but as a type of prayer language that issues from your heart

and soul ---- as you try ever so hard, but still never quite attaining, trying to tell God what He means to you.

Doesn't it just about bowl you over that God (Almighty, Creator, Supreme Father of All) wants to hear from you??
WOW!

NEVER FAILING GOD
(AND ALWAYS ON TIME)

I don't have any information to prove this, but at some point in almost every Christian's life, there will come a time when you will feel that: (1) everyone has let you down and/or (2) there is absolutely no one that you can turn to, and (3) there is no one on whom you can depend.

I can certainly recall 31 years and exactly when this crisis experience confronted me. Actually, I did have two (just two) people that could possibly have helped me. Only neither of these two people were available. One was in the hospital. And the other was out of town. In my terrifying situation they both might as well have been on another planet, or dead. And frankly, I didn't have enough faith to trust "just God." The stark reality of it hit me. I had no other choice. I *had* to trust Him!

I now know the never failing God. And I know His Son too.

NO HOPE, BUT…THEN CAME GRACE
(NEVER, NEVER, NEVER GIVE UP!)

When hope had stopped being a word; when sins piled up and couldn't be unpiled; when shame was spread like burnt motor oil; when guilt was growing, slowly, but surely, like rust; a layer of guilt and a layer of shame; the pile kept growing higher and all around like toothpaste out of a tube, with re-entry denied, circling and circling prior to doom, waiting for it to happen.

And hoping it wouldn't.

No way to go

But down, down, down, down.

Why me Lord? Why me Lord? Why not me?

I've only had bad luck and I don't believe in luck.

Bet all my stuff on yesterday's lotteries.

When self-esteem is powered by a cold boiler.

When pride could already hear the falls.

When ego is a known failure and it don't matter and nobody cares   *THEN COMES GRACE!*

NON-SEPARABLE CHRIST
(ANSWER: NOBODY)

Here is a list of four "bad words" I found in the Bible. See if you can see what they have in common and how such unpleasant circumstances can perhaps be of value to you.

A *sword* - can cut you, hurt you and "end" you. It can cut asunder or stab you in the back. It can also help you to be on guard and alert to destruction by evil forces.

A *peril* is not something you put on a string and hang around your neck. It is definitely not a fun thing to experience. Going through a peril can damage you or destroy you. Or, it can develop you; make you into a better, stronger person. It can also make you appreciate the good times.

Distress is similar to a peril. There may not be as much danger involved, but distress can sure dampen, destroy or depress your spirits. When you are in distress, it will get you a lot of pep talks from friends and advice (like Job got from his three friends). If you are not careful distress can destroy you emotionally even if you survive physically.

Persecution has pretty much gone out of "style" in our country and in this modern time. We still read about it happening in other countries. Few of life's cruelties inflicted by humans could ever exceed the pain and evil suffered by persecution. History books record (and sometimes fail to record) millions and millions of deaths. And all because a particular nation or race or religion thought they were superior to an underling group. Sounds rather simplistic and animalistic. It was, but more of the latter. In simple terms, persecution will kill ("wipe-out") the unwanted.

Once upon a time, I conducted supervisory training programs and "people skills" for several major corporations. One introductory session involved having the class participants to list characteristics of (1) the best supervisor they ever had and (2) the worst supervisor they ever had. These easy-to-do exercises caused the groups to loosen up, begin to talk and share among themselves and stimulate. One key point that came out of these discussions was that we learn by watching the behavior and results of others, even our boss. But why, some questioned, do we even care about what misery our worst boss caused? Answer: *You learn the things that you never want to do.*

This classroom exercise also is similar to our own life experiences when we face adversity or are thrown into tough situations. Hardly ever would you volunteer to be placed into circumstances that produced such stress and hardships: Being nipped by a sharp sword, facing a peril on one of life's tough mountain climbs, caught in severe distress of a boggy swamp filled with mud and alligators, or being persecuted by evil forces that relish seeing you ooze misery (even at times when you have done no wrong) and certainly don't deserve such unfair, unjust treatment.

Obvious Point: But when you survive any and all of the above trials and tribulations (and most often you do survive) the adversity of tough times has the unique benefit of strengthening you and making you better equipped, more experienced, toughened and empirically self-assured and inner confident, prepared for whatever future battles you may encounter. And the real spiritual beauty is knowing that your faith and trust made the difference! That quite often, the Lord never lifted you out of the mire, even though you begged Him too, but you learned some real-life experiences, such as where your real help came from: that inner strength from God meant more than tanks and battleships; that knowing God was close-by made the difference, because you had the assurances that He would never leave you or forsake you. And perhaps most of all, how absolutely precious it was to experience the peace of God where there was no earthly or logical reason for you to *feel* peace. In fact, quite often we describe "it" as beyond human understanding.

THE FIRST NOEL
(AREN'T YOU GLAD?)

There were only a small number of individuals who saw and experienced the "First Noel." They can almost be counted on our ten fingers. I'm talking about those precious few that were around when Jesus first arrived on earth.

Mary and Joseph
There was an innkeeper and perhaps his wife.
A small group of shepherds who were fortunate to be working the night shift.
A trio (perhaps 3) of foreign visitors who were rewarded for (1) being alert and studying, and (2) their willingness to undergo the hardships of a long journey.
An old man, who was devout and trusting and who must have had almost as much patience as Job. One thing we do know: the Holy Ghost was upon him!
A very old (but very devout) widow woman who had spent most of her life fasting and praying. (Fasting and praying must have been important and worthwhile back then.)

These, I believe are the only persons we know that are recorded as having seen and experienced firsthand the First Noel.

So, if we suppose that six shepherds came in from the field that night and if we suppose that there were three wise men and add Mary and Joseph and the two senior citizens in the temple, we have a grand total of 13 individuals. These individuals knew there was something indeed special about this child of such lowly birth. These "thirteen" were certainly a very lucky number. (However, I really don't think we, as Christians, should even have the word "luck" in our vocabulary.)

This calculation obviously does not include the innkeeper (and his wife??) because he probably had one room "saved" should per chance an unexpected VIP arrive and need a room. Most motels and hotels still have this hidden practice today. Therefore my assumption is that had he known just who Jesus was, and then Jesus would not have been born in a stable. But let us not be too hard on this innkeeper, because according to prophecy Jesus **had** to be born in a stable.

Interestingly, there are a few others who *almost* knew first hand the tiny first Noel Messiah. King Herald had the rare opportunity. Only, he was too lazy or too proud to get involved, so he delegated his royal privilege. And he certainly delegated to the "wrong" group, when he asked the wise men to locate the First Noel for his evil purposes.

Finally, did you know that it is possible to be **"very religious"** and still miss out on "Heaven" or something heavenly in the form of a small baby from Heaven???

Addendum: A few years later another group of "religious people" working in the temple also missed out by not recognizing "the First Noel," but by then He was about twelve years old. John the Baptist did recognize and acknowledge "the First Noel" as a grown man.

AFTER THOUGHT: Isn't it sad to think of all the people, down through the ages and even to this day that have "missed-out" on seeing or meeting Jesus. And think of all those that were *almost persuaded.*

THE NEW COVENANT
(A LONG-AWAITED REVISION)

The Old Testament didn't work. My minister friends and Bible scholars might disagree with my opening statement, or certainly might think I had expressed the point a bit too blunt. Perhaps they are right. It was a fascinating plan. Or, more correctly stated, it *is* a fascinating plan (because Jesus said he did not come to destroy it, but to fulfill it).

In very simple words, (because I am a simple minded, non-trained, lay person) allow me to make some points as to the major difference between the Old Covenant and the New Covenant. And I will try to cover this complex/complicated subject with a practical easy-to-understand explanation in words, more or less.

First, it involved a multitude of people that were to be governed by a multitude of laws, rules and regulations. Secondly, the leadership of this group usually involved a human being, i.e. a designated leader, Priest, Judge, King, etc., encompassing worship, via a group association, e.g., national tribal, family, versus individual worship. Thirdly, much of the spiritual relation of the people (actually the relationship between the people and God was "religious," rather than spiritual) was dependent upon whether their leader was a good King, or a bad King and the example the King set and furthermore, to the extent they were motivated to follow God and to what extent group dynamics interacted. It became apparent early on that "morality" could not be effectively legislated. Nor, could it be passed on in the genes from one generation to the next.

There were many other things "wrong" with the Old Covenant. A number of very crucial factors, especially when you are dealing with humans born in sin and prone to sin. "Sin" was difficult to get rid of. In fact, it was impossible to get rid of sin, unless some blood was shed. This involved the complex process of sacrifice and then it was further complicated by the need for a priest, a temple, a holy of holies and an assortment of other paraphernalia, having a perfect (free of defects) sacrifice, wearing the right garments or making sure everything was purified and sanctified. Do you begin to get the picture?

And we have yet to even mention God, and for good reason: He was so far away, too Holy to approach and perhaps the most important thing: Love. It would seem that if one person, per chance, He or She had indeed lived a very good life, <u>but</u> others had not, then the one good and righteous would be punished and smitten along with the rest of the group. Were you ever in a classroom years ago when the teacher punished the entire class for the bad behavior of one or two culprits? Did you feel any love or mercy from that teacher? Whatever happened to forgiveness? And redemption from sin?

The New Covenant was radical and introduced:
   A God who loved
   Who gave His only Son
   Who sacrificed for us
   Suffered and shed His blood
   And sent the Holy Spirit so that our relationship with God was
   personal

God's love could be felt, sensed and shared because of the Holy Spirit making Jesus real and *mine*. Not national, not tribal, not family, not denominational, not church based, but a covenant whereby we are *individualized* and sealed with Almighty God.

   Do you get the picture?
   Do you have the New Covenant?
   His name is Jesus.

THE NAZARENE
(PROVED THEM WRONG)

People from the city of Nazareth evidently weren't too highly regarded. Someone questioned, if anything good could come out of that dump? Think about all the sermons and theological dissertations that could be developed from this thought. Certainly, the Son of God from the golden boulevards of Paradise could have chosen a more suitable hometown. Was this place appropriate and fitting for even someone from the lineage of David, King of the Hebrews golden age? No way.

Jesus didn't just preach and talk about humility. But he lived it. Meekly, he lived it.

I can remember years ago feeling ashamed and humiliated because I lived "on the wrong side of the tracks" and in fact, right next to the railroad tracks. And this was when the train engines burned dirty coal.

Now, years later, I'm proud of where I lived.

P.S.   Maybe the message is: it doesn't matter so much where you've been as where you're going.

THE NON-VOID WORD
(GUARANTEED FOR LIFE...AND BEYOND)

No word or scripture, nor any selection of scripture is unimportant. You can't really prioritize them for one verse that may seem of little importance or value, like a secondary road. But if you suddenly need the "power" in *that* verse, for no word in scripture has been sent out without meaning and power and cannot return void or empty, then that particular verse is the <u>one</u> you need.

There are many classic examples of very short verses (some of which may seem obscure) that are custom-built to fit specific and unique needs. To cite one favorite example of what I mean: *For God has not given us the spirit of fear, but of power, and of love, and of a sound mind.*

Certainly this particular verse is not obscure. On many occasions I have used this verse (typed on an index card) for myself and for others that were having major battles with **fear**. It works especially well with multi cards: one for the pocket, one on the mirror, one on the sun visor, one inside the center desk drawer at work, one on the refrigerator, etc. etc.

Read, reread, and read again, over and over. The power in this verse unleashes power to touch the hidden or neglected.

Such a simple technique and yet so very effective because God's word cannot return void!

II Timothy 1:7

THE NOTHING GOD
(CREATED STARS OUT OF NOTHING!)

What a strange "name" for our Lord and our God. What a strange title for our all powerful and all knowing and All Mighty God. Think about it for a few moments and try to recall where in all of the scriptures is there a basis for thinking of our Lord and our God as "The God who became nothing" (NIV)

As a helpful hint, this particular scripture reference is one of the most beautiful selections in all of the Holy Word. It is certainly one of my personal favorites. The phrasing is nigh onto poetic regardless of which translation you read. Some might term it equal or exceeding the finest classical literature. Certainly the immense and intense content in seven verses is without equal (writer's opinion).

There are many other examples where cases can be made as describing instances where the Nothing God can be arguably assigned as descriptive titles for God. Consider these "partial" versus loosely translated and/or amplified.

In the beginning God created the heaven and the earth...the earth was void, i.e. empty. Genesis 1:1

And the Lord God formed man from the dust of the ground...(which means He made man from virtually nothing). Parenthesis mine. Genesis 1:7

God chose...the despised things–and the things that are not–to nullify (void) the things that are. I Corinthians 1:28

What an interesting "paradox" for God's precious Holy Word, so full of meaning and life and truth, has a lot to say about God, using foolish things to confound the wise and quite often, He used nothing to make something and allows much of the world's best, i.e. wisdom and wealth, to come to "naught." Amazing isn't it? Only our God can make good use of void, naught and nothingness.

OMNIPOTENT GOD
(A BIG WORD FOR MIGHTY GOD)

Read the last three verses in Matthew's gospel. Re-read them! Then one more time read these jammed-packed verses as though you are seeing and hearing them for the **first time**.

Look at these 71 words (KJV) not as a "benediction" to a gospel, but as 71 words of vital importance, which they indeed are. Does not every cell in your body and every spark in your mind and every minuscule thought in your God-given common-sense brain tell you that the very last words Jesus said had to be currently and eternally significant? Our preachers, pastors and Bible scholars have a beautiful word of effectively condensing the last twelve words in Verse 18 into one word, saying, "God is Omnipotent." A "fancy" word but a very valid term we need to describe or define "Power" that cannot be confined defined or refined. These 71 words are certainly not a benediction, but are daily and active content of instruction, empowerment, divine description, parameters with no boundaries, marching orders, procedural steps, policy unctioned by the Spirit, action plans and action steps, establishment of major priorities, delineation of the three God-heads in the Trinity; their identification and their authority, transfer of that divine authority to the followers, now and for ages to come, organizational steps and geographic scope of discipleship, a review and reminder of the followers missions and its highest priority as announced in a commandment as stated and delegated by *the* Commander with all 71 words enveloped in reassurance from that mouth of the Son of God, that He, Jesus, would always be with us, **now** and **forever** more.

And it is the writers opinion that the "AMEN" at the conclusion of this particular gospel does not "benedict" but rather signifies the cooperative agreement and blessing of the Father, the Son, and the holy Spirit, both clarified and amplified this great announcement for all followers of Chirst.

Therefore, the fact that God has **all power** is indeed clearly stated and His Omnipotence has been spoken and declared by the Son; spiritually disbursed by the Holy Spirit, so that there is an inward

297

assurance within the very souls of each believer; thus, God's plan for mankind becomes our plan, so that we as followers of Jesus can bask in the Glory and the wonder and the Love of it all–not just now but for tomorrow and all the eternal tomorrow's that come with no ending.

True, we are no where capable of fully understanding the amazement of it all. But we can bask and bask and bask for ages to come.

ONE REFUGE
(ONE IS ALL WE NEED)

When you reach *the end*.
Where is there to go?
The "end" means just that.
There is no more.
No more rope.
No other routes.
No other options.

There is a point where everything is behind.
And there are no more possibilities
The old hymn "He Giveth More Grace" sums it up.
"When you've reached the end of your earthly resources."
Those highly "blessed" with millions.
Those highly "blessed" with talent and fame.
Those highly "blessed" with something called "luck."
Those highly "blessed" with political connections.
Those highly "blessed" with good looks and popularity.
All eventually discover that it all comes to naught.

The eternal conclusion:

There is only one Refuge.

Only one Redeemer.
Only Jesus.
Period.

ONLY GOD THAT REACHES DOWN
(ALSO KNOWS WHEN A SPARROW FALLS)

As a teenager, I remember the last summer before my senior year when a part-time preacher put up a tent on a vacant lot not far from where we lived. The tent looked out of place and stood rather pathetic, somewhat like a lanky man with trousers that lack several inches reaching the ankles. I'm sorry, but that is the best description I can offer. The canvas sides were not long enough. The scene was further warped by the fact that the tent stood next to a rather nice, white clapboard, medium size church. One of them, the church or the tent, looked out of place. I'll let you guess which. They were both making a "statement" and there wasn't a lot of competition between the two.

A lot of snide or uncomplimentary remarks were offered during the next two weeks the tent meeting lasted. The crowd that attended was not very large. (I never understood why preachers back in those days referred to those that attended as "crowds.") Regardless, the "crowds" in the tent were pitifully small; usually between 12 to 18 people and those were swallowed by the ample seating of almost 100 empty metal folding chairs.

Obviously, this type of arrangement wasn't conducive to acoustics for singing or worship in general. I wish I could tell you that the part-time preacher was "great" or even good. You could tell early on that he had never been to any "Preacher School" and most likely had never gone beyond the 7th grade. He did dress "real nice" in a brown business suit, but even this seemed odd in the hot August heat.

Now, that I think back on it, this part-time preacher didn't have the orator type voice you need under an open-air tent. Back in those days, part-time preachers were unkindly referred to as "jack-legged" preachers. I do recall that this preacher seemed sincere, read a lot of scripture and would often weep as he spoke. That's about as positive as I can recall, but do remember, this was a long time ago.

On several occasions, cars with teenagers would drive by and honk their horns in ugly jest. And on some nights there would be a group of men not too far from the tent that would sit and smoke and talk too loud while the tent meeting was taking place.

Most people in the community who witnessed the two-week spectacle were probably glad when it was over. At best, it might have been a two-week diversion at a slow time in history when TV hadn't yet contaminated our quaint little town. In fact, I seriously doubt if 5 or 6 people are even alive now that could remember it at all.

Oh yes, one final note, which I suppose is what you would call "bad news and good news." As far as I know there was only one single person that "got saved" during the entire two weeks.

That very small number is the "bad" news.

The "good" news: the young thirteen-year-old girl who found Jesus in that pitiful scene would go on to become one of the absolutely most committed dedicated serious-about-the-Lord, prayingest Christians I have ever known in my long life. And I should know. She was my sister. And I am so proud to be her brother.

P.S. Now that Mom and Pop are *gone*, she is the one we call on to pray when there are critical prayer needs.

OUR HOPE
(BE OPTIMISTIC IN GOD)

The absolute amazing thing about this brief-brief experience is that *there* was no difference in age of the three gentlemen, although on earth they had represented three generations over a 60-year span. I cannot explain this, nor would I feel the need to try. It also still confounds me that the explicit and vivid details of this now 50 year old story remains just as current in my mind today as it was on that week day morning at about 7:30 a.m., as I readied for work.

I suppose what happened to me could be described as a "vision" albeit extremely brief and I seldom refer to it as such. To be quite candid, I never deemed myself, spiritual enough or worthy enough, to ever have a "vision." Whatever you call it   it was indeed a beautiful, heavenly experience. Over the intervening years, I have relived this event a thousand times and still praise God for allowing me this glorious insight.

My mini-vision was brief-brief, probably requiring a mere second or two. Three at most.

In the short time, I clearly saw three deceased Christian friends. They had each died at separate times within the last ten years and there was no connection between the three of them except that they all knew each other and attended the same church. This experience occurred, as I was busy with my morning routine and pre-occupied getting ready to go to work. I did have a favorite hymn of mine playing on the living room stereo, "Fairest Lord Jesus," which may or may not have contributed to the "vision."

I quite often played this type of music, but I was definitely not thinking about any subject in particular. The main thing on my mind was being ready when my carpool for work arrived. And I can't recall that I had thought of the three deceased friends any time in the recent past.

As I walked hurriedly, passing in front of the stereo, I "saw" (in my mind, yet distinctly *visible)*, the three men walking together, leisurely down a garden trail in heaven. They were obviously going somewhere together. However, there was no urgency or rush in their steps. The path they walked was in a beautiful wooded area (perhaps a park) with many trees and shrubbery. There were flowers but I don't recall any vivid colors or kind of flowers. The trail they walked sloped gently down. I paid no attention to the nature scene just described, since my main focus was on the three as they walked together. They seemed to be talking but I heard nothing (and they did not "see" me) but I felt quite close to them, perhaps 10 yards to the right of them. I did not have a close up of their faces, but 10 yards is pretty close. There was absolutely no doubt in my mind who they were. They looked basically as they had looked on earth. I recognized them with certainty.

There was only one unusual thing about the entire "scene." They all appeared to be about the same age, but even this observation, at the time, did not strike me as the least bit strange as they walked by me.

At the time of their deaths, they were 19, 34 and 82.

With years of hindsight and pondering, I now have my own humble opinion that Jesus allows the Holy Spirit to occasionally "paint" such scenes with indelible love on the memories of our minds. I still can't find adequate words to describe the experience. It was refreshing, real and wonderful to behold.

I Corinthians 2:9: **Eye hath not seen, nor ear heard, neither have entered into the heart of man, the things, which God hath prepared for them that, love Him.**

OUR LEADER
(AND HE IS FEARLESS)

Jesus Christ, "Our Leader" was everything needed in filling the awesome responsibility His Father, had assigned to Him. Try to think of the magnitude and the scope of the assigned objective; the crucial nature and outcomes that were at stake.

all the souls of humanity
all the times encompassed by eternity
the precious "value" could never be measured,
and yet, it had to be presented as a "gift,"
and accepted or rejected by the recipient.
laws, legalism, edicts were to be replaced by something very real yet intangible: Love
promises had to be illustrated by example
the number one key factor by the recipient involved an unseen substance or "hope" with no visible evidence that it exists—all based on *faith* in the giver by the recipient, for the personalized gift—which if accepted was *worth* eternal life.
the personalized gift had to be illustrated and substantiated by the painful sacrifice of God's divine lamb.

Thus, our Leader, (i.e. Messiah, Christ, Redeemer and Savior), possessed all leadership traits.

lead by example
illustrated unblemished character and integrity
absolutely the best as a communicator
not afraid to take appropriate action
knew how to organize and delegate
knew how to "develop" his followers for long term results
could attract and work effectively with all types and classes. He did not discriminate.
practiced what he preached and illustrated by his own behavior.
Example: taught lessons on "forgiveness" and then went on to

304

forgive those who disappointed Him or those who woefully and cruelly wronged Him.

willing to stake his life on the principles he expounded, and as necessary, **die** for His followers.

The above listings are but mere sketches of Our Leader and His capabilities and dedication and LOVE for us. Our response comes down to a three-part answer that only the **individual** can make.

1. Are we willing to follow?
2. If so, under what circumstances, and
3. How far?

OUR MERCIFUL GOD
(DESERVING HAS NOTHING TO DO WITH IT)

You never know when a moment of spiritual inspiration will be given to you. These valued moments don't always come in solemn cathedrals or stately churches or in your private devotions or when there is soft organ music playing in the background. They can even hit you in unexpected non-sacred moments. Perhaps these surprised inspirational "gems" are illustrative of the Holy Spirit being with us *always*. Even when least expected. This may also illustrate the two-edge sword of the Spirit-Word: in a split second, it can cut asunder, with a slice of "conviction" **OR** an unmistakable unction of "blessing."

Example: Last night I was watching an investigative reporter doing a highly interesting feature on a hard-nosed tough sheriff who had taken a "tough" approach (ultra-tough) toward "crime." His results were very impressive with a significant reduction in statistics. His methods were impressive and scary, in fact, very scary and frightening.

He used a broad brush that painted everyone with intimidation and fear. This included those in jail that lived in extra fear, former inmates, and potential inmates. This sheriff actually carried a long hard circular stick (longer than a baseball bat) and he knew how to swing it. His special equipped sheriff/sports car would go 170 mph. He readily admitted that he enjoyed (immensely) high-speed chases. His deputies had already wrecked over 20 patrol cars. He talked with pride of his tactics and accomplishments. He made **no** apologies. Like him or not; approve of him or not: this sheriff got results as proven by statistical results. Various crimes were **down**. He indeed made society "safer" in his jurisdiction. There was no mistake about this!

There was neither any mistake about his attitude. He was insensitive, non-caring and non-loving. I personally felt an evil spirit about his total demeanor.

The TV-report was both intriguing and downright scary. This individual, who ruled like a dictator, did not appear to possess one *iota* ("tiny little bit") of mercy.

Then, as mentioned in the early part of this writing, came my totally unexpected and all-together surprise moment of spiritual inspiration.

I was so glad that Our God, Our Almighty, God of All Power, Our God, who had every reason to be disappointed and utterly disgusted at His creation; that we of sinful hearts and ugly/evil dispositions were not merely tolerated but <u>loved</u> by Our Merciful God.

Yes, there are so many terms used to describe Our God, but it is wonderful, wonderful, and wonderful, that He is a God of Mercy.

Psalm 139:7   **"Where can I go from your Spirit?"**

OUR PEACE
(CAN'T ALWAYS BE EXPLAINED)

On a number of occasions, Jesus began a subject by prefacing his remarks with:

Do not worry
Let not your hearts be troubled
Peace
Do not worry about what you say
Do not worry about your life
Take no thought for tomorrow

The word "peace" appears in our Bible approximately 300 times. Unfortunately, the word and the concept and the practice aren't all that prevalent in our daily lives. However, the striving and the yearning for *peace* are almost always underneath our emotional surface, trying to coexist in the turmoil. This wonderful word, when it comes *alive* in our heart and becomes a part of us, can make all the difference in how we feel; how we act; how we talk; how we think; how we react; how we relate; how we drive; how we rest; how we handle big problems; how we handle little problems; how we shop; how we handle grief; how we handle success; how others perceive us; how we perceive ourselves; etc. etc. Even how we sleep. How we live. How we die?

Our problem is that we try to grasp peace, even fight or argue for peace. We would buy peace if it were for sale. We climb mountains for peace. And in all our struggles for peace, we ignore or forget the Lord, who gives peace.

The Lord of peace himself gives you peace at all times and in all ways.
II Thessalonians 3:16

OUR "SAY THE WORD" LORD
(HE IS CONSTANTLY WAITING ON US)

One scripture scares the socks off us and plainly points out that no man can see God and live. Even Moses had to take off his shoes on one occasion and Moses only saw a symbol of God, i.e. burning bush. And later on was privileged to see God's back side.

I certainly have never seen God. But on two separate occasions, very real, powerful and dramatic occasions, when I sensed God's presence, I was afraid. The extreme joy and wonder I experienced on these two mystical occasions could still not override the uncomfortableness I felt at being so close to his Holy presence and mighty power, I felt nakedly exposed, totally inadequate, intimidated. I felt afraid! It may have been a "Holy fear" but I was scared. In the midst of my unspeakable joy, I trembled and was in total awe.

Thinking back on these two beautiful and totally unforgettable moments in my life, I made a strange connection to a Biblical incident. I belatedly related so easily to the centurion who had a sick daughter and didn't want Jesus to go near his daughter. Only to say the word.

Exodus 33:20-23

OUR SOON COMING KING
(BELIEVE IT OR NOT HE IS COMING)

You sure don't hear as many sermons about "the second coming" of the Lord as you use to. Certainly nothing like when I was a child growing up back in the dark ages. (Dark Ages is not necessarily a figure of speech, but refers to the BIG DEPRESSION and the years following).

Seems like a lot of people back then *wanted* Jesus to return. They would actually get excited about it. Maybe the depression influenced their thinking. Preachers were frequently preaching about "His Return." This was not just at summer revival meetings but you would actually hear sermons on "it" on Sunday morning and at Wednesday night prayer meetings. (By the way, what ever happened to "Prayer Meetings?")

Of course, back then the preachers didn't know <u>when</u> He was coming back. They said no man knew the hour or the day or the year, when He would return. I think that included women too. Of course, this was way back when very few preachers went to college, where they learnt (sic) how to preach. But one thing was sure. They sure knew how to get the crowds excited. It amazed me that these people could get so happy and excited about the Lord returning and the sky splitting open and an angel standing at the beach (one foot on the land and the other foot on the water) raised his head and said "time no longer will be."

This, I must admit, would scare me. For you, see, I wasn't at all sure that I was ready to "go." I can remember feeling the need to go to the altar (Whatever happened to altar calls?) but I managed to hold onto the bench in front of me so I wouldn't have to go down to the altar. And the preacher seemed to be talking to me and worse yet, looking and pointing directly at me and having the organ player playing "Just As I Am" one more final time just for me. But I escaped the "altar" one more time. Only my relief was short lived. Because I still had to go home and face my thoughts and fears in the dark of night. Back then summer revivals (where they specialized in altar calls) usually occurred during hot, hot, weather. I mean Hot weather.

Back then we didn't have air conditioning. (Yes, I was born and reared underprivileged) so I had developed my own method for surviving the midsummer night's heat. I would take my pillow and flip around in bed and put my head where my feet usually went. Placing my pillow on the windowsill, my head could now be closer to the air (if there was any) and possibly sleep a mite cooler. I can still recall how I enjoyed looking up into the night sky and beholding the night's matchless splendor of a zillion stars. All of them, sparkling and twinkling. Lots of times, the moon was there too. The stars were enough amazement for a small boy. And the moon itself was enough amazement, too. But to have them both in the same sky at the same time was better than anything you can imagine at night. I didn't have enough vocabulary back then to describe such wonder. Such beauty. Such amazement.

But then it happened! All of a sudden in the midst of enjoying my own private show (better than anything on TV, which hadn't even been invented or even thought of) of the Heavenly Sky in all its' splendor. But the unspeakable beauty, matchless to behold, could all vanish when I suddenly, for no good reason, so I thought, when I remembered the angel and suddenly wondered where he (or she) was? What if the angel was over at the beach   and about to declare that time was no longer to be and the sky that an instant before ha d held me mesmerized, what if suddenly it split   and I wasn't ready???

Whatever happened to sermons on "conviction."? I don't hear much about conviction any more.

Epilogue: I never learned the day or the hour or the year the Lord would return. But this one thing I do know with a certainty: it is 54 years sooner than it was back then.

P.S.   And now I'm ready. Are you?

Revelation 10:6   **And swear by him that liveth for ever and ever, who created heaven, and the things that therein are, and the earth, and the things that therein are, and the sea, and the things which are therein, that there should be time no longer;**

OUR SOURCE
(NON-ENDING)

We need a certain depth in our relationship with the Lord before this name, i.e., "Source" becomes meaningful. If your relationship is superficial with little or no commitment, then your level of trust is equally shallow. Conversely, if Christ is truly your *source*, then a surrendering has taken place so that the one who has surrendered knows full well that his/her confidence is placed in God. Of a certainty, it is not placed in personal abilities, accomplishments, people, resources or any other worldly assets.

This includes probably the most recognized yardstick of success: financial wealth. The believer who has surrendered to Christ, even one with great wealth, knows and has long since acknowledged that all of his money could vanish tomorrow. Therefore, there must be another source. And that other source and plural sources cannot be talent, reputation or family connection, social status or political pinnacle. We can all cite example, after example, in each of the above categories where these sources were flop failures.

Question: Have you made Jesus your sole reliable source?

There is no other totally reliable source. Even your best friend or favorite relative will at some point most likely disappoint you. Even the human most dear to you cannot sub for God as *the* source.

THE ONLY WAY
(PAY ATTENTION)

Not an occasional way
Not "for convenience only" way
Not for use in emergencies only (firehouse religion)
Not for social benefits. I can make better social contacts at First Church. (Join a prestigious church.)
Not an optional way (like Buddha)
Not an inherited way (cause mother and pop were Baptist)
Not the politically correct way
Not the popular way
Not the seasonal way (for Christmas and Easter)

Jesus is the (one and only) way

OUR ADVOCATE
(WE NEED SOMEONE WHO LOVES US)

When we deliberately make ourselves pause and dwell on God, the primary thoughts we normally have is that of a HOLY GOD! CREATOR OF ALL THINGS: HAVING ALL POWER, ALL WISDOM, and ALL KNOWLEDGE. But especially, we think in wonder and fear of his complete ultimate HOLINESS; this AWESOME HOLY GOD. We can remember that in heaven there is the constant cry from angels around the throne: HOLY, HOLY, HOLY without ceasing.

Even the most saintly Christian among us has difficulty even imagining standing before this HOLY GOD. How can we possibly stand before this AWESOME GOD, much less relate to him; or talk (pray) to such MAJESTY. How could there ever be rapport between this IMMORTAL, HOLY GOD and my own puny, mortal, sinful, ant like, insignificant sinful being? If by some remote chance, I have even a smidgen of "righteousness," it would to such a Holy God appear, at best, as filthy rags.

The very best I can hope to do, or imagine myself doing, is that I lose all strength and fall utterly hopeless and helpless flat on my face at His holy feet and *try, just try,* to speak, "Holy, Holy, Holy."

The obvious point to this dreadful and profound question is how on earth, or in heaven, can we relate and speak to such a HIGH AND LOFTY GOD, so very HOLY? Yes, you can believe that the answer to this frightening and dreadful question is easy and simple, yet completely unique: **"We have an advocate with the Father."**

Spiritual Footnote: " speaking about how do you spell RELIEF and I mean long lasting ("eternal") relief, I spell it A-D-V-O-C-A-T-E.

OUR FATHER
(ONLY GOD AND "ABBA" TOO)

One of the most "helpful" things Jesus did for His followers was to leave "instructions" as to how-we-should-pray. One of the disciples, unnamed, had just made a request for Jesus to teach them to pray. Think about it. Without the response to "teach to pray," we may not have had the "salutation" to God. We would not have the perfect and most appropriate opening line: "Our Father..." We certainly needed some name, title or designation rather than Dear Sir or Dear Lord. We needed the "right" word (preferable <u>one</u> word), to set the tone for our prayers to the Majestic and Holy God, who also, very much wanted to be *approachable*.

We indeed do have **many** that can be used, e.g.
> Most Holy God
> Creator of All
> God of Abraham, Isaac and Jacob
> Great Jehovah
> Omnipotent God
> Almighty God of All Creation
> Lord God Almighty
> Eternal and Everlasting God

There is nothing wrong with any and all of the above. I would suppose all of us have used them from time to time. I once had a well-trained and highly schooled pastor, who seemed to use **all** of them in his Sunday address to Our Supreme God. Nothing wrong with that, I quickly add. If we use every one in this book we still can't adequately and fully do Him justice. He is worthy of all honor and all of our praise. As a child, I got the impression this dear man was "performing" rather than offering up a sincere prayer (from his heart) to someone he knew. Beware!

Really, don't you think what Jesus wanted to do is to "teach us to pray" and He knew we needed to be respectful in our attitude and in our language but at the same time not to be overly intimidated, (it is

O.K. to be awed) but not fearful of coming into His Holy Presence with a loving and respectful "Our Father." Remember Paul told us we could "approach the throne boldly!" Not because of our own righteousness, but because we had met and knew the Father's Son.

OUR MYSTICAL GOD
(GOD DOES EVERYTHING WELL)

Barkley, world-renowned Bible scholar, writes that very few Christians ever have a mystical experience. We all would love to have one. Or, **if** we all had *one*, would we then want two, three, four or more??

Why didn't God plan it where everyone had at least one real genuine no-doubt-about-it mystical experience? Why not see or touch something intangible or at least would not such an experience bring more converts in God's Kingdom? Or if seasoned believers could see a miracle occur before their very eyes, would that not deepen their relationship with the Lord? Why not?

Why not? Think back to the ministry of Jesus, when he lived and walked on this earth. Quite a few "mystical" events occurred then. Examples: Water turned into wine, feeding crowds with a few loaves of bread and several fish, opening blind eyes and putting fresh life in a withered arm. Best of all putting new life into a dead daughter, or a dead for several days Lazarus, walking briskly out of a smelly tomb. Wow!!

Sounds wonderful and great! So why didn't God design it that way? Why not?

The answer I feel is quite obvious and it doesn't require a Ph.D. in preacherology to figure it out, *faith*! Without faith, it is impossible to please God. The just shall live by faith and not by gifts, goodies and free food. Not even for marvelous miracles or guarantees that a deformed body part will be recalled and replaced. As nice and wonderful as these "wonders" are, they do not compare with what God intends as the ultimate outcome: Eternal Life!

It became quite apparent that many people were attracted to Jesus, not for reasons of love and devotion, **but** because of what they could get from Him. Perhaps, they were looking for an "easy life" and not one that required *commitment*.

Thus, one of the answers boils down to this: With the "gift" He gave each of us, i.e. free moral agency, we are free **and** responsible for our personal decision to come to Him, if we choose, by faith and through faith—and nothing else. We then give Him our Trust (another word for faith) and forego any promises for tangible gifts or mystical happenings. As wonderful as these might seem, they are nothing compared to what we shall one day behold and experience; none of which has yet entered into our minds as to what God has really prepared for us.

On the other hand, could it be that we self-limit the **divine**, for a number of dumb reasons. After all, many have been taught that "the days of miracles are over" having ended when the last of the twelve apostles died. (I need to find a Bible verse to substantiate that popular held bias, don't I?) Especially, if we expect to keep God in that *box*.

Remember the blind man in the Bible...let me rephrase that: remember the ex-blind man in the Bible (John 9:25) that was being hounded and harassed because of the scientifically unexplainable arrival of his 20-20 vision (Could it have been the placebo effect??) or could he perhaps have rubbed both of his eyes (in his sleep) too hard and thus knocked off both cataracts, etc. etc. In apparent desperation he concisely explained, not what he did not know, but rather, explained what he did know.

Now I will explain what I do know: One Sunday morning at 9:03 a.m. under bright fluorescent lights, I (1) saw and (2) experienced before my very eyes a miracle of instantaneous healing on my body and in a split second all pain ceased.

1 Corinthians 2:9

OUR VERY PRESENT HELP
(OUR VERY PRESENT HOPE ON THE "911" DAY)

It was so bad that we came real close to losing one of the last things a human loses. We almost lost "hope." Hope is one of the last things to *die*. Therefore, Hope is as vital as "life" itself. Almost. However and thank God for the "however." Lifesaving howevers can last until they are like the last straw in a drowning pool. However, there was a *refuge*. And what had generally been theoretical (perhaps spiritually theoretical) became the **only** thing we had to call on. But it was enough. The deep-rooted believers had always (deep down) believed it, but few had ever had to put it to the ultimate test. The rest of us, including casual semi-serious, i.e. we lukewarm believers had enjoyed having it somewhere in our comfort zone fringe, much like knowing we had an "insurance policy" just-in-case or we could always call the "fire department" just-in-case. But we never let reality thoughts disturb us   however, now the disturbing day arrived and blasted our routine days into splattered memories. Beautiful words that sounded so comforting and reassuring when read or heard when they were lifted from a nice page of God's word. "God is my refuge and strength a very present help in time of trouble." And then like a *blessing* that can only be *divine*, we immediately knew that in the very turmoil midst of our nightmare day we desperately needed God and absolutely had to have him. It might even have crossed our mind early on, that in the tornadoed hurricane that hit so swiftly and in the midst of a very bad thing happening to good and bad people, we were about to experience Roman 8:28 in action and before our very eyes was an experience, we did not want to experience, but God was going to show us not just "beauty," but divine beauty in action, as we beheld *beauty in ashes*.

And our Almost Forgotten God could again be prayed to and our Hidden God could once again appear in classrooms and ball games and even in real nice restaurants and dirty truck stops as we said "grace" unashamedly over our meals.

The next day and the many next days that followed were still bad days and still days that we waited and yearned to "wake up" and hopefully discover that we had been sleeping, and yes, it "was only a bad dream."

Only it wasn't.

And we were no longer sure about many things. And we knew we were going to live in days and months of saturated sadness, fears, anxieties, whatevers, what-ifs and on and on.

THE OMNISCIENT GOD
(HARD TO PIN DOWN: HE'S EVERYWHERE)

The message in Matthew's final chapter and the last three verses are all-important scriptures during Jesus' final earth moment, leaving crucial information for all believers both now and forever. The name and the term "All Power" encompasses the power of God to both now create oceans and rivers and streams, and tiny droplets. It certainly includes the power to make a tiny creature that has not yet seen the light of a single day grow restless after 270 days and begin to twist and turn and kick–ready to become his or her own person. The statement includes energy in water and sunlight and electromagnetic fields in moons and ocean tides and tiny cells needed to start the beat of a heart. The listings of God's power goes on and on without ending. All Power encompasses the Big T in theology, i.e. Trinity.

Our God cannot be fathomed; cannot be explained; cannot be described; cannot be aged; cannot be fully defined; and cannot be tried, treated or tempted. The energy He has made is in many ways the essence of God himself. But man in his entire splendor can neither make nor destroy energy.

This all power includes not just creator-power but all the power to know all things. In one word from theologians, He is Omni. He has all wisdom and possesses all knowledge, including complete knowledge of the future. To what extent, our God "uses" this power, is **not** known to us. This magnificent all-knowing God that we can only begin to know in bits and glimpses has a "range of knowing" that encompasses both past and future. He fully knows far beyond our pitiful range of knowledge.

I would suppose God easily knows the number of stars in all of the galaxies because He created them. In spite of all of these vast, massive, uncountable, beyond our numbering (or even making a good guess) examples just used: is not the knowledge that God has which bothers me. What does give me great concern (and comfort also) are the zillion of small, tiny, minuscule seemingly insignificant things that our Omni God knows. David, in writing my favorite Psalm (you, dear reader, *find it*) says very clearly that God knows my thoughts from afar off, and more remarkably, even before I think them.

Now, for one other "remarkable thing" and this, believe it or not, concerns **me**. I can not understand, explain or comprehend why, God, so all-knowing and certainly knows everything there is to know about me, and yet, He still loves me.

One of the most frequently used "terms" in *trying* to describe God is the beautiful adjective-noun "Amazing." Could it be that the thought just mentioned in the previous paragraph could be the most amazing? There is an apt line, in and old hymn:

"...How could He love me so" to which I add
????

PARADOXICAL LOVE
(OUR MANY FACETED GOD)

Consider our magnificent and wonder of wonders God who is beyond description. All terms of grandeur still cannot encompass the One who cannot be encompassed. When all terms and titles and adjectives of splendor have been exhausted, He is the eternal and everlasting, Alpha to Omega, Omnipotent God, Omnipresent God, and Omniscient God, far beyond the extremes of our most vivid imaginations and highest intellects. The best name we have and ever will have is to quote God himself who said, "I Am." And no number is great enough to quantify all the nouns and adjectives that can be placed after those two words.

Having "settled" that, we can now add to the wonder of wonders by including yet another aspect of our unfathomable God: in many ways He is a "Paradox." The working definition (stated earlier) describes it as two things that don't seem to go together and yet they do. Perhaps few things illustrate the Love of our God and the extent of His *caring* any better than some of these paradoxical features of the God we admire, love and serve.

That the Most Holy and His Sinless Son could love such lowly and sinful creatures.

That he, the Mighty Creator God, who spoke worlds into existence, would use such a worthless substance (dust) to make his first living creatures.

That at one moment in time and place, He would reduce his "plan" to save all human kind to an infant that probably only weighed 6 or 7 pounds.

That he, the King of all Kings, would entrust the greatest royal birth of all times to an unknown teenage girl.

That he, the Holiest of the Holy, would allow His Son to be born into questionable circumstances that would lead to gossip about the mother and concerns about, "who is the father?"

That he, the God of All Integrity, would create a somewhat controversial, small race of people to provide earthly lineage for the earthly arrival of his son on earth. And thirty-three years later this lowly-birthed "nothing" would be declared the King of Kings and King-of-the-Ages...only to then die a shameful death normally reserved for the lowest of criminal.

That he, the All Perfect Heavenly Father, would permit his chosen people to be "founded" by a liar and a cheat, to wander in the wilderness, go without a trained leader for many years, go without a King to lead them, allow his people to use poor judgment, in choosing their own king and have one King with only shepherd experience and even that beloved King would eventually commit an awful disgraceful sin.

Finally, think about this: That the royal lineage that *should* only be listing righteous individuals, certainly the best of the best and read, not just like the Hall of Fame but the Holy Hall of Fame. Never should it include several questionable/blemished characters (and even four women!!). Perhaps, in this "thought" we discover the greatest (and strongest) paradox of all: In everything that was happening, God chose this unusual and extraordinary paradoxical method, i.e. mixing events and questionable people that should not, by earthly standards, be blended together, and by so doing, He foretold by the early lineage of the Messiah that the mission and love of Jesus Christ could never be explained except by grace!

Now that, dear reader, is a paradox!

GOD OF PEACE
(PEACE SCRIPTURES YOU CAN USE)

The verses printed below need no introduction, nor explanation. Read them aloud!

Matt 11:28   **Come unto me all ye that labor and are loaded down, and I will give you peace.**

John 14:27   **Peace I leave with you.**

John 14:27   **Let not your heart be troubled**
My peace I leave with you.

John 14:27   **Let not your heart be afraid**
My peace I leave with you

Lu. 17:21   **The Kingdom of God is within you and that is** <u>**why His Peace is within you at your very**</u> <u>**fingertips.**</u>

John 10:10   **Jesus said I have come that you may have life and that you may have it more abundantly which includes my peace, which** <u>**satisfies and makes you whole**</u>**.**

II Timothy 1:7   **For God has not given you a spirit of fear, but of power, and of love, and of** <u>**a peaceful mind**</u>**.**

Psalms 46:1   **God is our refuge and our strength** <u>**and our peace**</u>**.**

Ephesians 6:13   **Take upon yourself the whole armor of God (which includes His peace).**

Ephesians. 3:20	**He is able to do above and beyond all that we ask or think, according to the power and peace that is active and working in us.**
Matthew 7:7	**Ask, and it shall be given you** **Ask and seek His peace and you will find it.**
Psalms 62:5	**My soul, wait on God; wait only on God, for my expectation <u>for peace can only come from Him</u>.**
Romans 12:2	**Be ye transformed by the renewing of your mind with his peace.**
John 7:37	**If any man thirst (for peace) let him come to me and drink of my peace.**
Philipians 4:13	**I can do all things through Christ who strengthens me (with his peace).**
Mark 11:23	**Whosoever ... shall believe that those things which he saith shall come to pass (<u>including the peace of God</u>).**
Isaiah 40:31	**They that wait upon the Lord shall renew their strength (<u>and their peace</u>).**
Psalms 55-22	**Cast thy burden upon the Lord, and he shall sustain you <u>with</u> His Peace.**
Isaiah 26:3	**Thou will keep him in perfect peace whose mind is stayed on thee.**
Isaiah 28:12	**This is the refreshing.** **His peace renews and soothes me.**

Philipians 4:7 **And the peace of God, which passes all understanding, shall keep your hearts and minds thru Christ Jesus.**

Ephesians 2:14 **For He is our peace.**

Psalms 4:8 **I will lay me down in peace, and sleep, for you alone God, only you God, make it where I can live in safety.**

In my experiences and contacts of having worked with all sorts of people in all walks of life and with all manners of problems, the need for "PEACE" is of paramount importance. Therefore, these specific scriptures on this *much-needed* subject are being included in this book for necessity and for convenience. After all, it is indeed the "God of Peace" himself speaking through these scriptures. Read them aloud and soak them in; let the words become a part of you; let them become etched in your memory by the "Spirit of Peace."

EXERCISE: Stare at the verse. Try to quickly memorize it. Then, close your eyes and say them aloud (softly) as though Jesus was speaking the words to you. Listen as you recite.

PERFECT EVERYTHING
(A VERY APT NAME/DESCRIPTION)

One of my very favorite books is probably unknown to most people. In fact, it is number three on my list of my own Top Ten. You will have a hard time finding it, but you will never regret whatever effort it requires for you to acquire your own copy.

"Perfect Everything" by Rufus Mosely is unique, unique, unique. He says that Jesus is **the perfect everything**. He is an Advocate, Author, Alpha, Anointed one, Abba, Always-with-us, Almighty, Awesome, God, Beautiful Savior, Bread of Life, Babe of Bethlehem, Balm, Bountiful Father, Beloved Son, Bleeding Savior, Blessed Trinity, Christ, Jesus, Our Lord, Crucified One, Creator, Calvary's Lamb, Son, Counselor, Chosen One, Risen Savior, Everlasting God and on and on the listing goes. In fact, the listing never, never ends.

That is the crux and the center of what this book is all about. The names and the titles and the attributes and the "glories" never run out. They are unending. Most of all Rufus was a man who exuded love!

Perfect Everything! Can you think of a more all-encompassing title for our Lord?

Author's note: Mr. Mosley was an unusual and fascinating character. Years ago his little book intrigued me. I have made a "hobby" of trying to learn more about him. The Lord blessed me by allowing me to actually meet and talk with two elderly people (one 94 years old, with a very clear mind) that had actually met and known Rufus. How I envy them.

P.S. Rufus sure didn't stay in a box. But one of my contacts told me that Rufus, who traveled a <u>lot</u>, often carried his belongings in a cardboard box rather than a suitcase.

PERFECT PEACE
(FOR TURMOILED MINDS)

Time and time again, I've seen it happen in my own life. And I've seen it happen with others in their own struggles. You've seen it happen. When your world was coming apart at the seam, (or is it at the equator?) When you were exploding inside and about to explode outside. When there were no good answers. Only bad answers. When above all else, including the solution itself, what you needed most was *peace*. I've been there! Suddenly, the peace that passes beyond understanding is there with you. Inside you and/or around you. Invisible, yet almost touchable. And as soft and soothing, as a warm blanket of low tumbling fog moving across the Golden Gate Bridge at 4 o'clock in the afternoon, it rolls between, around, and straight through all obstacles.

This soothing sweet comforting peace can arrive in many beautiful ways; on various "vehicles." A chariot from Heaven that arrives without a sight or sound; an angel that may have brushed you with wings you never felt; the beautiful and ever present Holy Spirit made the delivery; or Christ Himself was there and without knowing exactly how, you touched the hem of His garment. And probably most often, *the peace* didn't so much as come or arrive; it was just *there* and it was *yours*. Most often the "vehicle" that effected the delivery was one of the many *unique* peace scriptures. (Never mind grammar correctness; all God's verses are unique.) All you had to do was read it or hear it; and receive it. Perfect Peace. Wonderful Peace.

THE POTTER
(SOME TIME IT HURTS)

Scripture verses describe in detail how the Master is our Potter and how he takes a crude hunk of ugly drab colored clay to use as the raw material from which to make us. A rather humbling experience if you mentally walk through the thought process and visualize our lowly beginning. A substance, so plentiful that it has little value, nothing outwardly attractive. What possible use or application would or could a piece of clay have?

Skip quickly through the purification, mixing, molding, manufacturing, heat-treating, and so on. Skip even beyond the delicate artistic finishing processes, and finally to the beautiful end product. How relieved we are that we have a refined, polished, painted, glazed and glorified vessel. Fit for service by the Master, we proudly await our time of service. We are honored to be of use to our Master. And to others!

Now comes the crucial test. Are we going to be an active ready-to-be-used, which may well require our going out into a tough world, getting dirty and being thrown around and maybe even suffering a few cracks and chips?

Or, are we going to sit up on the top shelf and look pretty and collect dust?

QUICKENER
(GOOD Rx FOR LUKEWARMITIS)

Behold!! There is no great chasm between man and God. No insurmountable distance between us and our Lord. No impenetrable barrier than divides the Creator from His creation. Certainly there is no longer a guarded Holy of Holies that does not welcome us. Amazing!! So how do we get from here to there? There is no great chasm; only a brief "synapse."

The Holy Spirit provides the spiritual force that crosses the "synapse" between God and us. Until that spiritual action occurs, we are nothing but potential in filthy rags, standing still, null and void. To be quickened is to be kindled by God's fire, enlivened by the very breath of God so that a smoldering fire can burst into searing intense flames. Our very spirit cannot be connected to God's spirit until we are quickened. Until then, we are worthless, useless and lacking. Not all unlike the dust God once held in his hand   until quickened by his breath and molded into His image.

The Holy Spirit *kindles* fires in cold-hearted believers, and enlivens lukewarm "wouldabees." He enlivens those on back row pews and fringe arctic outposts. The Holy Spirit is within us and at the same time all-around us. The Holy Spirit is the *Quickener*. And the Holy Spirit is *the always*.

SUGGESTIONS: Make a list of the top areas in your life that need to be quickened.

THINK: "God cannot use <u>lukewarm</u> because it does not get rid of dirt and filth.
And it's not very refreshing to drink either."

THE LORD IS MY QUIETNER
(AND HE SPEAKS IN THE SILENCE)

When nothing else has worked and I have done all the usual things to calm the storms around me and nothing seems to work. When I've prayed and prayed, until I felt dry of any more prayers. When I've walked through worldly resources and considerable assets and spoken aloud, but to myself, "none of this is worth eight cents to me right now." When those closest and dearest can't even help me. When disappointments, uncertainties and fears have ganged up on me and formed an overwhelming all consuming knot of emotionally and physical impenetrably barriers. When I've thought of all alternatives except the unspoken self-induced end. And then, in some unexplainable way "that passeth understanding" a miracle of peace settles exactly inside the midst of the turmoil and while I don't yet have the answers and don't know when the storms will end, if ever, an assurance has come and I surely know that both mind and soul *will* survive. The Quietner has come, not early, but in time. And God is in control. The quietness touches me. Soothing quietness. I begin to breathe again. And God is in control.

THE QUESTIONER
(HAVE YOUR ANSWER READY...JUST IN CASE)

Nothing seems so stark, so definite as a digital clock when it "announces" the time to you. Especially when you first see it. Especially when you awaken in the darkness of a night, and not really knowing if it is about 2:00 a.m., or about 4:00 a.m., or 6:00 a.m. You begin, in a half-awake attempt to search for the clock. Finally, when you see it, the clock doesn't tell you: "somewhere around 2:00 a.m." or "approximately 4:00 a.m." Instead, it tells you with definite preciseness, that the time is 4:41 a.m.

Once Jesus held a discussion with his disciples about whom the people were saying he was. The disciples replied by telling him the three most common responses that were being tossed around among the people in the villages. But then he ask the same question, but with an entirely different slant: a **direct** question that demanded an individual answer, i.e. "But who do you say that I am?"

Imagine for a moment: Jesus walks up to you, looks at you directly, his questioning eyes fixed unmistakably upon your eyes and with the question mark at the end of the sentence, waits for your answer.

REST IN A WEARY LAND
("I WILL NEVER LEAVE YOU OR FORSAKE YOU")

To put it mildly, we live in a weary land: rush, rush, rush, noise, clamor and racket. NOISE, NOISE, NOISE! Radios blaring in the car, the office, the home and on the beach. Twenty-four hour places to shop. Twenty-four hour television and remotes that go around and around.

Personal problems, financial problems, family problems, job problems, crime, evil, deceit, hypocrisy, sickness, accidents, illness, uncertainties, wars, depression, recession, inflation and on it goes. Disappointment, failures, fatal diseases, near death, and death. Woes, fear and you-name-it. Fires, tornadoes, hurricanes and hailstorms. No rest for the weary is putting it mildly.

I personally try very hard to put my "faith" to practical use, and not just pull it out when my time comes to cross-chilly jerdun. (sic)

Very few of the problems listed above are within our control. Some we may even have brought upon ourselves, such as financial problems (e.g., if we gamble) or some health problems (e.g., if we smoke or over eat) or accidents (e.g., if we DUI). But most befall us and we have no choice in the matter. Since the "worrying" we do is an exercise in human nature that is (1) natural and (2) non-productive, what can we do that can be of practical use. So, keep reading.

Since God spoke the world into existence.

Since God can fling stars into space and set them into precise orbits.

Since God could part seas and smooth out rough roaring waves.

Since God can make ears hear that have never heard.

Since God can keep a running count of the number of hairs on your head.

Since God can make worthless, dead eyes come alive and see

Even able to see in living color.

Since God can make trillions of people and each one of them still be unique.

Even identical twins and triplets.

Since God cares about small, petty things that seem so unimportant.

Like small already plentiful drab-colored sparrows.

Since God showed and proved his love by giving His Only Son.
Since God said that He would never leave us or forsake us.
And the list could go on and on.

Why do we worry and fret about so many things great and small?
Can we even grow *one* hair? Should we perhaps compile a list of all
the problems we have solved and all the worries we have erased by
worrying about them?

Don't we sometimes get so overwhelmed with the problems and
concerns of life that we would like to "give up" and start all over
again? Easier said than done! But here is a suggestion that is certainly
worth trying: A return to the *basics* and keeping it simple and
biblically based.

Let's pretend for a moment that you have just finished praying. You
open your eyes and Jesus is standing before you. You do not know
what to say, but He smiles at you and a tremendous peace comes over
you. Then, He speaks "Peace. Peace be still "

Listen to the words of Jesus and imagine that He is talking just to
you.

> Come unto me all you that labor and are loaded down with a
> heavy load.
> Look at the flowers of the fields. They aren't even spinning or
> working at all.
> Take time to walk in green pastures and take a sip of cool water.
> Let my words and my peace and my love quieten the turmoil in
> your inner-being.
> Don't be afraid!
> I (alone) am the Bread of Life.
> Drink of my water and never thirst again.
> Could Jesus not speak to you and calmly say, "Some day all of
> these matters that weigh so heavily on you will seem as nothing?
> If my Father created something out of nothing, can He not turn
> all of these things that trouble you back into nothing¾and
> *nothing* cannot even be a memory?"

RISEN LORD
(THE ONLY GOD THAT EVER DID)

Here is a question for you. And I really don't know if any of us *mortals* can ever (as a mortal) give the correct answer. Maybe there is no one correct answer. And now for the question: What is the title, or term, or phrase, which most appropriately describes our Lord Jesus Christ??

Just scanning this book refreshes our memories of the dozens, or hundreds of choices, we have. Time after time, any grouping of "names" can run the gamut from one, A to Z, or Alpha to Omega, or Shepherd to Master, or King to Servant of All, or Servant to Ruler, or All-consuming Fire to Meek Lamb, or Anointed One to Rejected One, or King over all, Babe of Bethlehem to Eternal God, Only Begotten Son to King of Ten Thousand, or Prince of Peace to Mighty Thunder, or No-place-to-lay-his-head to Owner-of-a-Thousand-Hills!!! Wow! (Which is a "mod" way of saying, "Praise our Almighty God.")

Indeed they run the gamut, but none or all can fully describe our God, who is both Creator God and Personal God, i.e. Jesus!

Having written all of this, and now back to the question posed in the opening paragraph, I offer an answer. If Jesus had not risen, everything including our lives, past, present and future, would have been for naught, zilch nothing. But he indeed did arise; he did arise after being cruelly killed and, having his body handled by close friends, was prepared for burial and buried in a tomb, a tomb that was sealed and guarded.

Nevertheless   nevertheless (read it aloud; no, shout it aloud) A.R.O.S.E. from the dead, victorious, over death, hell and the grave.

He arose. He arose. Christ Jesus arose from the dead.

And by a faith that comes as clear as it ever can to being *tangible*, **we know it!**

ROCK OF AGES
(OLDER THAN ADAM)

Never having been very knowledgeable about any of the *sciences;* having spent most of my working life in "management" and "people" areas, I definitely do not have anything close to a *scientific* mind. In fact, when I am around those who are trained in any of the sciences, my multi-complexes begin to surface a saply. ("Asaply" is a word I just coined, so get with it Spellcheck.)

Therefore, being somewhat retarded in the sciences, imagine my stunned amazement to learn fairly recent that **everything** has a unique frequency or resonance. For example, and this is a perfect example to make my point: even a rock or stone will have its own "number." A rock of quartz, granite or coal will each have a specific frequency. In my mind, from long ago, and now, there is nothing any more dead, any more lifeless, any more *fixed* than a stone. Have you ever heard the phrase, "stone dead"? So when I sat before a computer that could actually read frequencies in all sort of substances, e.g., chemicals, animal, viruses, etc., I was highly flabbergasted and utterly amazed. Not necessarily at the wonders of science and technology, but divinely amazed and awed at God! The God of Nature, the God of Creation, the God of anything that was made and without Him nothing was made. Furthermore, our God can make something out of nothing. Isn't this exciting?

I have been awed by God before. Many times. In fact, it continues to amaze me how many times God can awe us. Perhaps that is why, we and many of our hymns and praise choruses sometimes call Him the Awesome God.

Now that I think back on it and remember, when some critics wanted Jesus to shut the people up, who were getting excited, Jesus told them that if they did shut up, God could allow the stones to cry out. Therefore, Jesus was **not** just speaking figuratively as pastors learned to do in Preacher College, but He really meant it. Hence, and therefore, God could have formed a choir from a pile of ugly, dead rocks and had them sing in any *key* of "K" using sharps or flats or triangles. Note the symbolism of these musical terms just cited. And don't forget about the Key of "J."

Who would have thought we could get excited over a rock? The excitement continues. He built His church on one. He told us we should best build our foundation on 'em. He is *the* Solid Rock. And the listing goes on and on, forever, because God rolled the stone away and Jesus walked out and can be accurately called the Rock of Ages. Didn't I tell you, the list goes on and on? Hallelujah!

ROCKS AND STONES
(ONE DID "HARM" THE GIANT)

Can you fill in the blanks:

Jesus built his church on a ____ and David used a small ____ to end a reign of tyranny and we can use a ____ to find a shade or tie a ____ around our neck.

We shouldn't make the mistake to fully see the many ways that God tells us, or reminds us, of his ever-presence (the peace word is omnipresent). Did you ever think about the many ways the Bible uses rocks or stones in real and symbolic ways.

David used a small rock (pebble) to end the tyranny of a giant that was threatening God's people. A large rock can be used to provide a shade for us, while in a hot and dry land. Or a rock becomes a millstone to hang around the neck.

THE REAL KINGDOM KING
(WHERE DID HE SAY IT WAS??)

The "Kingdom of God," is mentioned a lot in the scripture. Almost 400 times.

The term also gets a lot of mention in the Christian vocabulary of today, especially in recent years. The subject seems to be *in vogue* in a number of preaching ministries and many appear to have a special "calling" to expound a particular brand of "Kingdom doctrine or Kingdom belief/practice."

Certainly I am not qualified to jump into the melee and attempt to separate the goats from the sheep or begin pulling out the weeds growing amongst the multitude of followers. Neither can I identify the foxes that need to be disintegrated from the politically correct wheat. I must leave this to the brave-hearted and/or esoteric experts. Or, I'll even leave this to the pseudo-experts who swallow at gnats and camels while millions starve and elaborate headquarters and shinny temples are constructed.

What I do know and therefore feel well qualified to take a position on is my own favorite verse on this subject, Luke 17:21. For the entire verse is summarized succinctly, when Jesus said, **"The Kingdom of God is *within* you."** This startling verse to me is very brief, very powerful, and very encouraging.

And <u>all</u> that Jesus meant by "the Kingdom" (and He should know) *is within me*, and since it is *within me* I can use it, share it, show it, and be strengthened by it. What a wonderful gift and what an awesome responsibility, and what a comfort for God's spirit to be so close and personal to me and my innermost being. Wow!

P.S. Historically, what an odd place to find a Kingdom. But can you name a better place?

THE REDEEMER
(THIS IS THE ONLY ONE, YOU KNOW)

There are several ways to define "redemption." We can speak of "redemption of a nation" or "redemption of a person."

But to get technically specific, there can only be one kind of spiritual redemption in the *disposition of grace*. Personal redemption! Therefore, the rest of this subject will be written in the first person, the only way that, in the end, redemption is measured.

I needed a "Redeemer." Not my sister, not my brother, not Peter or Paul, but it was me needing a redeemer. Certainly, I was born in a "Christian family" and right in the buckle of the Bible Belt. That certainly didn't hurt my case, but it didn't redeem me either. I had a fairly decent "Christian genealogy" with 3 or 4 of my grandparents professing Christ in varying degrees. I never saw one of my granddad's inside a church, until he was funeralized in the same church where he was baptized about 60 years earlier. My other grandfather varied greatly in different periods of his life, as to his commitment. So I couldn't count on them, even if they could have helped my personal redemption, which, of course, they couldn't.

Then there were my parents: both earthly saints 99% of their mortal lives, as best I could non-objectively judge, who are now serving their non-ending terms as heavenly saints. But they tried to help with my redemption, encourage, teach, pray, discipline, motivate and occasionally lay on a guilt trip or two. But all of their fine efforts could not redeem me. As David DuPlesse put it: "God doesn't have any grandchildren."

I tried several things in lieu of God's redemption living a good and moral life, turning over many new leafs, reading the Bible all the way through, making New Year's spiritual resolutions, doing good deeds, going to church, not swearing or cussing and counting on my dear parents. None of these ever came close to redeeming me. I still needed a redeemer.

God has only "children" and each one has to be redeemed by the only Redeemer (that's not coincidentally) He supplied. In fact, He gave His only Son, Jesus, who in turn gave His life by shedding blood (without such, there is **no** redemption) in order to cover my sins and redeem me.

The "contract" is between me, God and His Son Jesus. And there are no loopholes.

THE REFRESHING
(ARE YOU RUN DOWN, TIRED, WORN OUT??)

The word refreshing only appears twice in the King James Version of the Bible.

I had read the Bible from "cover to cover" several times and never "saw" this verse. At least it never registered with me. I had also studied the book of Isaiah on occasions but still never noticed this unique verse. I found it during a long airplane flight while reading a little booklet by Norman Vincent Peale. This was over 12 years ago and this short verse has been "mine" ever since.

Isn't this type of biblical experience, one of the many things that makes God's word, even His printed word, come alive. *Personally* alive, so that even one brief verse can seem to suddenly appear from some sort of seemingly veiled obscurity, and become activated with a personalized revelation.

This "refreshing" is usually received and experienced as a type of spiritual inspiration from God to an individual, (i.e. me) and appears to be customized for very specific, pressing needs. Only the precise knowledge, sensitivity and power of the Holy Spirit can handle such an individualized assignment that lifts a verse or verses and still leave everything intact in God's Holy word, which is always for everyone and whosoever needed a customized "fit." It may erase a concern, provide long-sought insight, envelop an insoluble problem, fill a void, calm an internal storm, or address any number of innumerable impossibilities.

Or, this much needed refreshing may not do a tangible thing to resolve your immediate onrushing, unstoppable quandary, except *refresh* you with a peace not understood or explained; but let you know that God is where He has been all the time: *there* (ever- present) and still in control!

Do you need a refreshing? We need to dissect and digest each word in this impactful verse.

This is the refreshing.

This is the place of repose

This is the resting place.
Let the weary rest.

Do you need a refreshing? I love this short little verse. It's mine. And it's yours, too. But we have to pay attention to the last four words.

Acts 3:19
Isaiah 28:12

THE RESTORER
(THE SOUL'S CONSTANT REFILL)

This is the refreshing. Isa. 28:12b

We all need to be restored from time to time. Even Christ needed to get away from time to time. There is a difference in "restored" and "refreshed." Common sense and spiritual insight both tell us that normally we first need to be refreshed, in order to be restored.

This is the refreshing.	**He restores my soul!**
This is the resting-place.	**He restores my soul!**
Let the weary rest.	**He restores my soul!**
This is the place of repose.	**He restores my soul!**

This is another one of those remarkable verses. Almost obscure, I (shamefully) had overlooked it for many years. So beautiful, so simple, and so touching. I found it (when I was desperate for a refreshing) not on a desert, but in an airplane at 30,000 feet, returning from a tough business meeting that had, among other things, left me physically and emotionally drained. In a major reorganization study, my position had been eliminated. I was flying home to tell my family that I no longer had a job. Beyond that I had no answers or plans. I needed a refreshing. I discovered this verse in a small booklet written by Norman Vincent Peale, entitled "Thought Conditioners, Forty Powerful Spiritual Phrases   "

Dr. Peale suggested that the phrase "This is the Refreshing" should be repeated slowly saying the words softly, and emphasizing their soft quiet melody

At the same time, conceive of peace, rest and renewal, coming to you. I would personally add: say them (softly) aloud. The spiritual process of being renewed brings the much needed restoring. On a number of occasions, I have witnessed severe cases of depression or an "almost" nervous breakdown "cured" when the desperate one was able to "get alone" and have some (even a day or two) of quiet time. But in my own limit of experience the "quiet time" was effective when the individual was the beneficiary of concentrated prayer and divine refreshing.

These words were my spiritual lifeline for several weeks and aided me in my career upheaval. End result: Romans 8:28 in action.

There are seventy dozen (approximately) ways to aid in "restoration" of troubled minds and pathetic individuals stressed almost to bursting points. Most of these techniques are capable of bringing varying degrees of relief and rest. Perhaps, temporary rest. They include counseling, group therapy, retreats, seminars, reading self-help books, listening to tapes, mediation, hospitalization, pastoral counseling, supportive friends and more self-help tapes. Many find their best resource to be in self-realization, forgiveness and acceptance, and in the final analysis, agreeing with the Psalmist David who said that it is God that restores the soul.

Thou will keep him in perfect peace whose mind is stayed on thee... Isaiah 26:3a

He restores my soul. Psalms 23:3a

...This is the rest wherewith you causes the weary to rest, and this is the refreshing... Isaiah 28:12b

THE RULER
(A VERY OBVIOUS TITLE, OR IS IT?)

Why should you waste your time reading about such a simple and well-known "title" or "name" as *Ruler*? Of course, Christ is our Ruler. Just about everyone knows this. Even those that don't accept Him as Lord, King, Savior, Messiah, and Master still know in their heart-of-heart that He is Supreme and Divine and they should acknowledge Him as Ruler. And even if they don't accept Him *now* as their Lord and Ruler never mind, someday they indeed will, on that day when every knee bows and every tongue confesses that He is "Ruler" and Lord.

Many of us are fortunate enough to know that He can even be a loving and kind ruler, as a gentle shepherd that guides and rules his flock, protecting lambs and sheep for their own best interest.

Now, having said all of this, which we already knew, let me suggest another application for the term "ruler." A "rule" is also a *standard* by which others are measured. Thus, Jesus Christ has established standards for His followers/disciples. Best of all He has presented these standards by examples of His own life. Jesus not only explained and expounded via His words, teachings and sermons (of which the Sermon on the Mount is the classic), but by the real life examples our Lord illustrated: love, tenderness, caring, commitment, faith-results, prayer and His willingness to sacrifice His own life. This listing is not all inclusive because others can still be listed, such as empathy, tears, patience, loyalty, forgiveness, humility, suffering, obedience. And the list goes on and on

How long since you and I washed any feet??

EXERCISE: Compile your own list of the "examples" Jesus left us. This list becomes
(1) Your objectives (and standards) to accomplish in your own walk with the Lord, and
(2) Your own checklist for which you can measure your "walk" to the standards we have been given.

P.S. Is it any "accident" we call "it" the **Golden Rule**?

A SOUND SLEEPER
(SWEET DREAMS)

Based on a few scriptures, you could possibly make a case that Jesus was a sound sleeper. Anyone that can sleep through a storm has to be a sound sleeper. Especially if it is in a small boat being tossed about on a raging sea.

Let's list some reasons why Jesus was sleeping while the others were frightened.

1. Perhaps he was tired and needed sleep.
2. He had prayed before going to sleep and
3. Knew his Father was watching over him.
4. Perhaps he quoted some scriptures (which some people do in order to fall asleep and/or just to sleep better).
5. He decided not to worry about things, knowing his Father was in control.
6. Maybe he knew he could always walk away from the problem.
7. Having created all things, he knew everything there was to know about the boat he was on and probably knew it could outlast the storm.
8. Wanted an opportunity to teach the disciples a faith lesson.
9. Knew that the winds and the waves would obey his will if He said, "Peace, be still." (Sounds kind of like a hymn in the making, doesn't it?)
10. Perhaps he remembered things his mother, Mary, had told him, when he was very young.

Some of the above items are written with a bit of jest. But I'm hoping they will serve as a type of "checklist" so some of you dear readers can reduce your worrying time.

I have several wonderful friends, who are otherwise dedicated conscientious God-fearing exemplary Christians. You could model your life after them. At least you can until a routine thunderstorm starts developing. Then they go into a panic and are overcome with

348

trembling fear. And with good reason. When they were growing up their saintly Mother would take all three small children and together they crawled under the bed and hid until the storm passed. Today, years later, their fears are still deeply imbedded. Sad and pitiful. And yet today, they trust the Lord fully to do everything, including taking them to Heaven when they die. But He evidently doesn't "qualify" to take care of them in a summer storm. Sad.

Do we trust Almighty God except...?

Now I lay me down to sleep

"For God has not given me a spirit a fear, but of power and love and a sound mind."

Isaiah 29:9
Psalms 4:8
Psalms 129:2
Jeremiah 31:26
Proverbs 3:24

SHEPHERD OF LOVE
(LOVE UNTO OTHERS AS YOU WOULD...)

It is an unfortunate occurrence that all of us experience. Subjects that are of vital importance to us can become "commonplace." This includes special people and special events. In spite of their original and long standing significance, even these with personal emotional attachments can slowly erode, due to such factors as familiarity, simplicity itself, preoccupation with other matters and other cares of life are gradually lumped together, until their mass becomes an immovable force that absorbed you without your ever knowing it has happened. Much akin to a creeping buildup of immunity, carelessness, or plaque. We can probably all cite examples that other people are guilty of, e.g., another birthday, another anniversary already, another dear old friend ignored. And the list of omissions goes on. Resolutions are made and remade. And still the list goes on.

A return to the basics: when you have something important to:
> review, think through, re-think
> tell someone
> communicate clearly
> express appreciation
> apologize for
> have a written record
> go on record with a statement
> make a commitment
> restate a promise
> get someone's attention
> re-emphasize an important fact
> express an emotion
> try to describe an intangible
> untie a tongue
> ???

If any or all of these are important, then you need to keep a written record and write-it-down. Keep your written items super-brief and keep your system simple. As one example, keep one list of the people you need to visit with the next month. Look at it daily and check on your faithfulness at the end of the month. After all, we have some "shepherding" duties of our own **the** Shepherd of Love expects us to do.

Jesus has always been the Shepherd of our Love and He constantly touches us with His Love in ways too numerous to count. But here is a switch in the way it is normally done: How about a letter to your Lord? How long since you really said thanks; expressed appreciation, or just re-told Him how much he means to you; or tried to describe the depth and breadth and innermost feelings of your love for Him?

SOOTHING PEACE
(BE STILL...AND WAIT...AND SEE WHAT HAPPENS)

There is nothing that can surpass the peace of Jesus that passes beyond understanding. It is precious peace. It is sweet peace. It is calming peace.

Occasionally, it just settles softly upon you. Without asking for it or even expecting it, so soothing and out of the blue.

Like this morning while driving back home after running several errands and buying some groceries   I don't even recall what I was thinking about at the time, but quietly and suddenly, without any known reason, the peace came in the car onto me and all around me. I didn't see it. I didn't need to. Still, it was very *real*. Touchable real. With no effort, my eyes began to cry and I could only marvel at this special and unexpected anointing of His Peace.

I almost pulled off the road. But it wasn't necessary. I wept and wept in joy and felt as if God's arms were around me. Perhaps they were.

SPIRIT OF GRACE
(FALL ON ME)

There are approximately 165 references in the Bible about "grace," with 30 of them directly associated with God or Jesus. Just to list a few. The grace of God

The grace that is Christ
The gift of grace
The grace of our Lord
The grace of the Lord Jesus Christ
With Christ by grace are you saved
Of the father, full of grace
The Lord will give grace and glory
The grace of our God
Grace and truth come by Jesus Christ
Grace of God was given

Hundreds of books have been written on this beautiful subject and thousands of sermons. As Christians, new or old, we can all give touching examples of grace being exercised in our individual lives.

THE SPOKEN WORD
(BECOMES_____)

Now they call them "sound bites." Very brief, usually one-sentence statements that are spoken primarily for the benefit of the media. Concise statements that are appealing to the ear and contain (hopefully) thought provoking content. Thus, these brief little "verbal packages" have a better chance of lodging in the brain's memory rather than passing quickly in and out with all the other "stuff."

While sitting inside a fast food restaurant, I gazed outside the large plate glass window, where I was seated and there, less than five feet away was a sign on the front of a pickup truck that immediately caught my attention with a "sound bite." You will find it listed below in a collection of spiritual sound bites. At that very moment I was in the process finalizing my own list of sound bites. After you read them, I highly recommend that you collect your own list of spiritual sound bites.

Matthew 4:19 "Follow me and I will make you fishers of men."
Comment: We greatly prefer to follow fads and style, and our favorite ball team and   a demanding supervisor or   one of the many enticing pleasures of life.

Matthew 8:26a "Why are you afraid, O ye of little faith?"
Comment: One reply, when the Holy Spirit causes you to "hear" this verse, "I know in whom I have believed and He is able."

Matthew 4:4 "Man shall not live by bread alone."
Comment: An effective sound bite that reminds you to readjust your priorities.

Matthew 14:31b O thou of little faith."
Comment: This five-word sentence has the ability to grab your attention, (perhaps shame you) and snap you back to your "source."

Matthew. 15:34a How many loaves do you have?
Comment: How long since you have taken inventory? Sometimes a little bit is a lot, if God is in it.

Matthew 22:29 "You do err, not knowing the scriptures, nor the power of God."
Comment: Note the sequence. Knowledge of scriptures, then "power of God" follows.

John 4:26b   "I that speak unto thee am He."
Comment: If you know what you are talking about, and, if you have God's anointing on your life, it really doesn't require a lot of words to make your point.

John 2:19b "Destroy this temple and in three days I will raise it up."
Comment: Often times, it takes a little while for our feeble minds to understand.

Matthew 26:11 The poor you have with you always but I'll only be with you for a few days."
Comment: Pay attention and get your priorities in order.

Luke 24:49b "... but tarry ye in the City of Jerusalem until you be endued with power from on high."
Comment: Tarry time is now in short supply. Besides, we now have TV. But most of us appear to also have a "shortage" of power. Do you suppose there is a correlation between tarrying and power from on high?

Revelation 2:7 "He that has an ear, let him hear what the Spirit saith..."
Comment: And we have two ears!

John 3:3 "Verily, verily, I say unto you, except a man be born again, he cannot see the Kingdom of God."

Comment: The sound bite of the ages–to whosoever.

Luke 7:50 "Your faith has saved you; go in peace."

Comment: It would appear that it is our **own** faith that "activates" our salvation. And once "done" we can have peace. Such simplicity for such complex and profound needs!!

John 9:25 "All I know is that once I was blind and now I can see."

Comment: He might have added: "I rest my case."

And finally, from a homemade 6 x 16 sign I saw attached to the front bumper of a pickup truck:
>   **WISE MEN**
>   **STILL**
>   **SEEK HIM.**

P.S. Do you reckon angels ever drive pickup trucks?

THE SILENT GOD
(HUSH LITTLE CHILDREN)

Who says that God can't be silent? His Holy Spirit, which indeed *is* God and *is with us*, doesn't have to be always busy and actively involved in rearranging a zillion stars. Guess what?? Neither do we. Why isn't it all right to just be quiet! If silence is bliss as all the poets seem to imply, then why is it that we haven't been "blissed" in a long time.

These thoughts came to me while I was watching a marriage counselor on television (which my dear wife **told** me to watch). The points were being made about the necessity of a husband and wife not just communicating better, but going so far as to have a *sacred* time together. One husband had been caught with his beeper hidden in his socks. This was a no-no. As a parenthetical note, let me say (that this one thing I will never be guilty of, because I don't own a beeper). A key point was then made about the importance of the sacred moments of being together and that during this time, nothing (especially phone calls) should be allowed to interrupt the couple.

Then came the specific thought we seldom hear: that it is perfect if this very special time together *evolves* to the point where absolutely nothing is being said. This period of silence is not necessarily planned, but when it does occur, it is *ideal* and the silence should be enjoyed together.

Why, why, I thought wouldn't it also be appropriate and proper for it to become a part of our time with the Lord. It can be an expected part of our devotions or of our meditations. It could easily become an *unplanned* part of our prayer time, i.e. where we just "become quiet" and do nothing but think, listen, wait, or, whatever seems natural in our spirit.

Is there scripture to back this procedure up? You bet there is! But, rather than me tell you where to find it, why don't you try something a little different:

> just be still,
>> become quiet,
>>> and

THE SOURCE
(WHOM ELSE?)

This title for our Lord is one of my favorites. Of course I have a lot of favorites. We all do.

He is the source of my "*hope*." Even my faith may waiver, but my hope never does.

He is the source of my "*confidence*" which is built on a solid rock.

He is the source of my "*strength*" even when I am at my feeble low point; somewhere below zero.

He is the source of my "*faith*." He alone gives substance to my intangibility.

He is the source of my "*purpose*" in life, and the only one that really matters in the long haul.

He is the source of my "*love*" for others, especially those that may not deserve it.

He is the source of my "*rest*" when I am desperately fatigued and don't think I can go on.

He is the source of my "*quiet*" in a noisy world, when I need to slip away and be alone with him.

He is the source of my "*peace*" when all pseudo peace has failed me, and I often can't explain

His peace–but it is real!

He is the only source of "*Perfect Peace*" because He always understands and has an endless supply of unconditional, all-encompassing love. He knows exactly the right way and the perfect time, can even communicate in a small still voice, is always patiently and lovingly available, and yet none of these beautiful gifts to me are based on whether or not, I deserve them. I doubt if I ever do. Gifts of grace!

And, He is the source of my zeal!!!

THE SUPREME SACRIFICE
(ULTIMATE, ULTIMATE)

During the time that Jesus lived on earth, it would have been somewhat difficult for the early disciples to talk about his death. Especially, to talk specifically about the *way* he died. For during that period in Roman history, the worst mode of death for a convicted "felon" was **crucifixion**. And this method was reserved for the worst of criminals. This cruelest of cruelty was a **disgrace** on top of all the ugliness and horror associated with such a death. The question can then be posed as to who actually "killed" Jesus Christ, the Holy Son of God? Who killed the Savior? Who killed the kind, gentle Shepherd? Who killed the Good Master, the one who loved and taught and spoke in such memorable parables? Who killed the King of the Jews and smirched it with mockery? Who killed the kind hearted Son of God that went around teaching love and feeding the hungry and healing the sick and lame and even leprosy?

Who were those that not only performed the long-suffering Killing Act? All, who were there that endorsed the act, either directly or were in supporting roles. Who were those who would assume guilt by even standing around and watching? And wouldn't this include even good people, who did nothing? Who didn't even oppose or speak out? Weren't they all guilty to one degree, or a lesser degree? These are "good" questions for hard and tough situations and quandaries. Now, they are hypothetical, then they were real life questions. But regardless, they *deserve* answers. Together yet, they *require* answers.

Aren't we glad that we weren't there when the crucifixion actually occurred? It's hard enough to read about the cruelty, pain, suffering and death. I shall never forget, as a teenager reading Jim Bishop's "The Day Christ Died." When I reached those crucial pages that described in painstaking ugly details of what Jesus actually experienced, I began to cry. I could not control myself, nor did I try. I think it took me 30 minutes or longer to get through the vicarious suffering in those pages. And I was in our living room in a safe, comfortable place—while Jesus was on the cross. I wasn't even near.

At the time, and immediately following, I got "upset" because the gospel writers did not give more information and more descriptive detail. After all, this was without any doubt in my mind, one of history's most important moments. What is **the** most important? Perhaps his birth and "arrival" on earth? Perhaps, the all-important victorious instant of his resurrection? But the crucifixion was certainly the saddest and most cruel moment of all times—before or since.

Much later, after a lot of reading and studying; and a lot of time for reflection, I could derive a lot of possible reasons for the brevity of the four gospels to this momentous happening." They may have been ashamed, so why "talk" about it; they and their contemporaries would have understood the "cross" as we understand the electric chair. Hence, explanations weren't necessary. It was "enough" to write... "and when they were come to a place called Golgotha, the place of the skull, there they crucified him"

With all the knowledge and feeling I acquired many years ago from Bishop's book, the mere reading or quoting the above sentences is enough to make me shudder and want to cry. The horror of what Jesus went through has never dimmed or diminished or faded. And it shouldn't ever.

Hardly any sacrifice ever comes easy and no sacrifice can be free or without cost. This one, the supreme sacrifice, sure wasn't easy. And it cost the life of God's Son. His only Son.

TEACHER
(TEACHER'S PET???)

There are several places in the scriptures where Jesus is called teacher, or, referred to as a teacher. This is obviously a very descriptive title. But more than a title, it has a further meaning for us as his followers. Think about some of your special or favorite teachers you enjoyed during school; especially middle school and high school. This is the time when we all began to have role models even though we probably didn't realize what we were doing or even what the word or concept meant at that early point in our life. We did know we liked, really liked, being around these particular teachers. And that we learned more because our interest was high and our heart and minds were really into whatever we were studying. How wonderfully strange, but we did not want to miss their classes. Most amazing, we still enjoyed these times, even and in spite of the subject matter being difficult. We were motivated and wanted to try harder. What really mattered was that we had a strong desire to do well and to please the teacher. The desire to learn was high and the enjoyment pushed us!

Let's use this as a self-evaluation technique and see how many of these examples could apply to our relationship with the Master Teacher:

1. How often do I approach Jesus, in prayer or deliberate meditation saying, "Lord, teach me to pray with right motives," or, "Lord, teach me to be humble as you were humble."
2. Lord, am I anywhere near being a role model or an example for others to follow?
3. Is my eagerness to study and learn the scriptures a burning desire?
4. Am I the "example" I need to be so that others see Christ in me?
5. Do I enjoy my "time with the Lord" and do I seek more and more to commune with him?
6. Does the "joy of the Lord" burn within me?

7. Am I taking specific steps to prepare myself to be a "Teacher" for others?

Luke 6:40:   **The disciple is not above his master; but every one that is perfect shall be as his master.**

THE AVAILABLE GOD
(HE'S NOT IN A BOX)

Thinking, the other day, about "prayer," I had this "notion" that many of us (I know this "chiding" includes me) go about our prayers doing some wrong things or unnecessary things. Another way of putting it: we may use too much effort and/or ritual. (By "ritual" I mean *oral* ritual versus motion ritual.)

Let's list some guidelines that the Psalmist David or the Apostle Paul or the Apostle John might consider for our benefit.

1. God is readily available. We don't have to yield or gnash. We don't have to don our sackcloth or pile on the ashes. POINT: He is readily available and did in fact say, I am with you always. Read the last sentence of Matthew's gospel.

2. God doesn't need nor require a long preamble like the Constitution of the United States. Jesus suggested we merely say "Our Father" and then get on with our prayer request. Jesus also gave us the example or an effective short get-to-the-point prayer (Luke 18:13) "Lord be merciful to me a sinner."

3. God doesn't require a long notice that we are about to approach Him in prayer. Nor do we need an appointment. Nor does He need a formal introduction. However, it surely is an advantage if you know His Son. This immediate availability can be illustrated by the crude/hurried/desperate/urgent/informal/brief exchange of the thief on the cross.

4. God most likely is not overly impressed with long, extended prayers. Surely, if "length" had much merit then the model prayer often called the Lord's prayer; more accurately entitled the Disciples prayer would have required more than four and one-half verses (or 66 words) and required about 23 seconds to *recite* the entire prayer. "Recite" does not sound like the best term for a prayer coming from the heart, does it? Incidentally, 32 of the 66 words are three letters or less, which means about fifty percent of the language in this

beautiful prayer are very small words. This would tend to indicate that God doesn't really need long or difficult or fancy vocabulary words to get His attention or be impressed with our learning. In fact, to overly summarize this point, only hallowed, temptation and trespasses could possibly be considered as "fancy" words due to their length.

5. God does not necessarily need to have a lot of scriptures quoted to Him whenst (sic) we pray. (I will probably get a lot of criticism on this, which is only my humble opinion.) It seems that ministers and lay people alike are prone to using generous amounts of scriptures when communicating with God. Most likely, God enjoys hearing *His* scriptures quoted and knows it is our way of trying to be sanctified and respectful. It may be one of the "cuter" good things that He sees His children doing. It is sure better than listening to serpents.

Let us rejoice and be glad. We serve an accessible God who enjoys fellowship with His creation. He knows us by name and knows the number of hairs on our head (Or in my case, He knows the number I used to have.). We can pray to him any time and anywhere. We don't have to go to the "capitol city" annually or on any other type of pilgrimage. We no longer need to take a sacrifice because His Son became our once and for all sacrifice. We can take tours to the Holy Land (if we prefer to) but such treks are really not necessary. His Son, who used to spend time in the Holy City is, no longer there. We really don't need to burn any incense. Personally, I think some incense smells nice. But some of it smells awful. There is an old spiritual that says, "I can call Jesus anytime." (I almost feel like singing.) But let me continue. We do not have to go to a priest and tell him tales of woe, because we have the High Priest, and He is touched and feels and knows all about us. Yet He still loves us.

Imagine that: Yet He still loves us.

THE CHRIST OF LITTLE ONES
(HE STILL SAYS: LET THEM COME UNTO ME)

At a very early age, I began to learn about Jesus. I can easily remember and pinpoint my very first ("solo") prayer because it occurred when my great-grandmother died.

Shortly thereafter, I remember my first visits to Sunday School classes and the sweet spirit of our teacher about the   stories she told and the beautiful cards with color pictures of Biblical stories that she lovingly handed to each of us as the class time ended. My younger sister and I walked alone to and from the church. It was almost a mile each way. My, how times have changed.

By this time I was beginning to *know* Jesus. I mean, really **know** Him. The person who played the biggest role in this growth experience was my grandmother on my mother's side. I never knew my father's mother. But this grandmother became the most influential person in the early years of my life. She certainly taught by example, as we watched how real and natural the Lord was in her life, not just on Sunday when she made sure we were all in church, but she lived the *love of Christ* in front of us. This was during the days of World War II that Tom Brokaw wrote about. My grandmother spent long hours kneeling before the old fashion trunk (her "altar") in her bedroom praying for her sons, while they were in the midst of heavy fighting in both the Pacific and European theaters. They returned.

The one spiritual talent or gift that Grandmother absolutely excelled in was explaining spiritual issues in such easy to understand ways ("Grandma, where did God come from?") and causing her grandchildren to *grow* (without us even realizing it at the time) in the knowledge and love of God. Her lessons have never left me but have always been a vital part of my own spiritual foundation.

Finally, there is a third person that had a significant and long lasting impact on my life. Long lasting in this case can be pinpointed back to my third grade classroom about 60 years ago.

It really isn't much of a story to have "survived" so very long in my memory. In fact, it is not a "story" as much as it is a one-sentence incident. I can remember my teacher, Miss McBath, telling us that, "as a Christian, if you were standing on a ladder painting, you could talk or pray to God while painting that it was as easy as that."

Not much of a story, you are thinking. Perhaps, but it has out-lasted a lot of stuff and time, in an otherwise not-so-good memory, for over three decades.

The point of sharing these stories is very simple: to show the impact a so-called average run-of-the-mill Christian can have on others, especially little kids, in shaping their lives for eternity.

After thought: Do you suppose Miss McBath grossly and illegally violated the civil rights of a cute little innocent vulnerable boy and cruelly overstepped the line between church and state, thereby causing the cute little fellow to grow up amiss and become a Bible toting villain that would eventually turn him into a (perish the thought) religious fanatic???

THE GOOD HUMOR GOD
(EVEN PIOUS PEOPLE SHOULD LAUGH QUARTERLY)

How many times have you heard someone making a half-serious remark, pondering and wondering: Does God have a sense of humor?

Well, I will not even pretend to answer the question, even though I personally think he does. Once and only once, I asked Him for a unique and direct response to a special make no mistake-about-it "event." And He instantly did.

If, and I emphasize the if, I were to attempt to answer the above question, I did not particularly like His answer, but I got an instant easy-to-understand about whether or not, God has a sense of humor, the "con" position would point out that since there is so much sorrow and evil in the world, and, to continue on this line of reasoning, that God, being an all knowing God which, to explain, means that God knows everything since He is all knowing. And since He knows all, it stands to reason that He surely knows about all the sorrow and the evil, and, since He knows this, it stands to reason that He knows how *much* sorrow and evil there is. Translated, this means He has it, i.e. all the sorrow and evil, quantified, which is a fancy CPA word which means all the sorrow and evil have not only been counted, but have furthermore been added up. Thus, since God has the information before Him, how in heaven's name could He think there could be on all of God's green earth, plus the non-green sections, the Sahara desert as one example; how could anyone, including God, who incidentally knows all, even begin to think there could be anything funny enough to even smile aloud, much less laugh about?

And another point in support of naysayers that God "could not have a sense of humor" is the fact that what makes any of us laugh at a joke is the scientifically known fact that what makes a "joke" funny to the "hearee" is that the punch line is in effect a surprise, i.e. surprise is what causes us to laugh. Therefore, since God already knows everything including the future and none of our thoughts are hidden from him (Ps. 139) then nothing (including the punch line) in a good joke, or event could make him laugh.

Now that is a very good, logical and sound argument on my part and is exactly convincing and difficult to refute, debate or argue. However, all of this non-weighty subject does have one large   tremendous faulty flaw. What I failed to consider, in my brilliant deduction is that you can't put God in a Box like I tried to do. I was wrong. Very wrong. God can laugh if and when and where He wants to.

Amen and Ha, Ha.

One last thought for icing. Oh, yes, what did Solomon say about all those merry hearts God made?

I rest my case.

Amen and Ha, Ha.

THE HIGH PRIEST
(THE TOUCHABLE HIGH PRIEST)

Almost all religions and "belief organizations" have some figurehead or leadership position or positions. Quite often they are referred to as "priests."

The person in this position is highly revered and held in great respect. The followers normally focus tremendous attention and respect to the individual in such a position. This attention borders on worship and adoration, even love of a high order.

However, in spite of all the focus on the priest, and even on the High Priest, the real purpose and intent of this lofty position is **not** the Priest, but rather the Divine Being the priest represents and serves. The followers need a priest that can approach this Holy God for them and on their behalf. In other words, it is normally understood that the lowly followers are no where close to worthy of approaching or even communicating with God.

The High Priest then holds our fate in his hands and we are far removed from "our" God. This is a brief summary of how the priesthood normally works.

Not so, for we Christians! How beautiful and how precious that Paul gives us this one beautiful verse-description (even if we had no other similar references), that we do have a high priest who is easily accessible and one who is *touched*, i.e. understands us and all our infirmities. Infirmities is a broad word that means our hurts, pains, fears and anything else that concerns us.

Another verse puts the icing on the cake by clearly stating that nothing else, not height or depth or creatures or whatever can separate us from our Lord and our God and to put icing on top of the icing, we can boldly approach the throne ourselves. Me and God. You and God. Face to face. Wow! Imagine that!

370

THE LORD THAT FILLS MY SAUCER TOO?
(WHAT HAPPENS WHEN MY CUP RUNS OVER)

Driving down the highway one morning, I heard a country and western artist singing about "drinking out of my saucer, cause God keeps overflowing my cup."

If I'm not mistaken, that beautiful thought comes out of one of the Psalms. It's not beyond my imagination to think that the young shepherd, David, sang these words first, only he probably used a lyre instead of an amplified guitar.

If this "down home" way of describing God's abundant blessings is somewhat unsettling to your sophisticated upbringing, do not despair. Perhaps I can handle it better than most, being that when I was a very small boy I often saw my grandfather drinking his coffee from the saucer. I later learned that this was uncouth and broke several rules of etiquette. Imagine if Martha Stewart's grandfather did this! My grandfather died never knowing how crude he was. Later on my grandmother told me that he drank the coffee from the saucer because it was hot and he needed to hurry and to get out in the field and start plowing. Common sense had taught my grandfather a basic rule of physics, i.e. that a hot liquid will cool faster if you increase the surface area to be cooled and decrease the depth of the liquid. I have no idea where he ever learned physics. He obviously did not relish the idea of burning his tongue.

Perhaps, the songwriter could have explained the saucer-drinking better by saying "Lord I can't possibly begin to count all my blessings unless you stop overflowing my cup long enough for me to try counting the blessings I've already got "

THE REVELATION
(WHAT A BOOK!! READ IT)

Many, many Christians avoid the final book of the Bible for a myriad of reasons and excuses. Mostly excuses. You've heard many of them and hopefully never used them, such as:

It's too hard to understand.
God didn't mean for us to understand it.
My pastor said he couldn't understand it, so why should I try.
It was written in symbolism because God didn't want us to understand it.

Over the years I usually managed to stay away from this book. Even during my high school years, except on a couple of rare occasions, when I took it upon myself to read the Bible from Genesis to Revelations. This meant that I was obligated to read Revelations, if I were to complete my assignment. I read and reread this challenging book. I must admit that on these occasions reading Revelations was something to look forward to, since it meant I was about to complete my literary marathon.

Once when I was a young lad, I was fortunate (or unfortunate??) to have a visiting evangelical-teacher visit our church and spend several weeks (nightly) explaining in great detail the book of Revelation. Evidently the Lord had bestowed upon this very nice gentleman (1) an unusual zeal for this book and (2) a large colorful banner-chart that hung over the pulpit area, reaching from one side of the church all the way over to the other side. We are talking about a wall-to-wall colorful chart on the mind-boggling book of Revelation. It was large? To a young child it was helpful (and difficult) to behold since the large colorful chart was filled with a multitude of drawings, time lines and symbols including dragons and horns and fire. A devil and a few angels were also present. It was absolutely fascinating to look at (for the first week or so) and certainly more time absorbing than filling in the O's in the church hymnal.

Leaving the explanation and theological interpretation up to the experts, I would like to point out three interesting observations for your consideration and as enticement for your study of this book.

1. There are quite a number of classical verses that are beautiful to read, *especially aloud.*

2. For a book that is admittedly difficult to understand/comprehend there are a surprising number of "Mark Twain" type verses, i.e. the few verses he could understand bothered him a lot more than the ones he couldn't understand. Perhaps too easy to understand, some verses speak with amazing clarity to your consciousness. In other words: they *convict* you at your core! Case in point: When I was a mere teen, after reading Revelations for the very first time, this impossible-to-understand strange book, I immediately and clearly knew how God felt about any and all Christians (me too) being lukewarm in my Christian life. I also understood what he meant by being lukewarm. I recognized that fortunately I was not a "cold" Christian, for after all I had a minimum of faith and works in operation (several days a week). But at the other extreme, I fully and totally knew I was also <u>not</u> a "Hot" Christian, i.e. always on fire for the Lord (seven or more days a week). Therefore, I knew by the process of elimination that I indeed was (perish the thought) *lukewarm.* But to make matters worse, this supposedly impossible to understand book did a fantastic job of describing how allergic even the Almighty God was to lukewarm. He would *spew* the group out of his mouth. Spew is, to say the least, a vividly descriptive of distaste.

3. Finally and appropriately, since our theme is "names and titles" of our Lord, the final chapter of Revelations is so illustrative. I counted approximately 40 terms (including 12 implied titles) and repeated words. I doubt if there is another place in the scriptures where so many divine terms are to be found.

SUMMARY: Regardless of what your opinion may be or regardless of how well you understand the book of Revelation, it is an absolutely amazing intriguing masterpiece. There are enough understandable scriptures to make it worth capturing and memorizing. There may even be a few verses that you will wish you did not understand or wish that you could interpret with less clarity. And all those many puzzling esoteric verses that remain, we can all pray for understanding and with eager anticipation look forward to the day (which will come) when our minds will be opened and Revelation is fully ours.

"Every word of God is pure."

Be prepared to be delightfully surprised **if** you read this book with a sincere searching, earnest heart and **expect** to be blessed, because God's word will **not** return void or empty. In fact, I know some people (myself included) that have received a mystical "reward" while reading this fantastic, glorious Book of the Revelation.

Revelation 3:14-22: "To the angel of the church in Laodicea write: These are the words of the Amen, the faithful and true witness, the ruler of God's creation. I know your deeds, that you are neither cold nor hot. I wish you were either one or the other! So, because you are lukewarm—neither hot nor cold—I am about to spit you out of my mouth. You say, 'I am rich, I have acquired wealth and do not need a thing.' But you do not realize that you are wretched, pitiful, poor, blind and naked. I counsel you to buy from me gold refined in the fire, so you can become rich; and white clothes to wear, so you can cover your shameful nakedness; and salve to put on your eyes, so you can see.

Those whom I love I rebuke and discipline. So be earnest and repent. Here I am! I stand at the door and knock. If anyone hears my voice and opens the door, I will come in and eat with him, and he with me.

To him who overcomes, I will give the right to sit with me on my throne, just as I overcame and sat down with my Father on

his throne. He who has an ear, let him hear what the Spirit says
to the churches."

THE SHEPHERD
(ALWAYS ON DUTY)

There is something both beautiful and comforting about the word and the concept shepherd. At times, all of us have experienced fear and felt total helplessness. Not at all unlike a small lamb confronted by a mountain lion. No self-resources to escape the peril. The only hope is a shepherd to thwart the lion. Or many times the "lions" in our lives would not have come if only we had stayed near the Shepherd in the first place. "The Lord is my Shepherd" is memorized early in our lives, but we can become immune to the strength of the verse by rote words without benefit of thought. The next time you are faced with a lion (or even think one is creeping up on you) do not walk, but run to the Shepherd. It can likely be as easy as thinking and verbalizing (out loud) **the Lord is my Shepherd**.

Some translators tell us that Abba Father can be translated Papa or Papa God. To some of us this almost sounds irreligious or disrespectful. Certainly presumptions to think that we can refer to the Holy God as Papa. Maybe its because as a child I wasn't allowed to call my Daddy, "Papa", nor my mother, "Ma" or "Mama." It was always Daddy and Mother. And I had no problem accepting that rule in our home. Only in my Dad's later years did I sometime and with deep affection call him Pop or Papa. Evidently, there has to first be a special and loving relationship with one's father. And so it is with Abba Father or Papa God. This may well amount to one of the better examples of "communion" between a child and our Heavenly Father. And the added beauty to this thought is that you will know when it feels right to call him "Papa God."

THE TEAR WIPER
(THE LAST BOX OF KLEENEX)

The prophet Isaiah gives us a beautiful promise, " God will wipe away all tears " every since I was a child, I have heard this comforting verse. Usually, I visualized this scene as one belonging in the book of Revelation, where the Sovereign God would at some magnificent event wipe away all the tears from all of humanity in some sort of tear-wiping ceremony. I evidently heard sermons as a child that painted this lasting portrait in my mind. And I can recall my Mother reinforcing this heavenly event.

As I grew older and acquired learning and wisdom (smile) I decided this might be symbolic, whereby the Lord would erase all unpleasant memories from our minds and we could then live happily ever after in heaven. This type of thinking (I call it "heavenly pondering") can lead to a myriad of divine options. Such as, will God even allow anything sad to enter our minds in a perfect paradise? Or, is there to be a one-time event whereby we all have a final opportunity to vent our sadness and then enter into the joys of heaven? There are no ends to all the possibilities that can enter into our minds. Howsoever, there is also a verse that states that our minds cannot conceive all that may occur, so *these* cannot enter into our earthly (feeble) minds.

Who says we aren't allowed to speculate and keep trying? One scenario that I personally like (maybe because "I thought it up") is that perhaps Jesus will take us aside *individually*, and allow full and ultimate disclosures of unhappy, tragic sad events we experienced and explain them.

Some of you are thinking: Wow that will take a lot of time. Well, you stand respectfully corrected, because *time* will not be a factor.

Remember the old hymn our grandmothers used to sing: "We will understand it in the sweet bye and bye?"

One final thought on the subject of God wiping tears. I really don't think this verse is symbolic in any sense, and if you doubt me, read the last part of the verse in Isaiah 25:8.

"...The Lord has spoken–he will surely do it."

THE TIE THAT BINDS
(AND BINDS AND BINDS AND BINDS)

We sing about the "tie" that binds us together with God and causes us to be in unity.

There is a divine presence because God is Divine and bestows this special blessing on us as *His* children. Unfortunately, we have a tendency to take this "marriage" for granted, just as we are often proned to do with our "husband-wife" wedding. Brethren, this ought not to be.

Our relationship with God is certainly of supreme importance. However, our "tie" or connection with God is only the beginning. The 1782 words of the author, John Fawcett, Page 87, in the "Cokesbury Hymnal," "Blest Be The Tie That Binds" speaks of the further binding with our fellow believers in Christian love.

Where this has been a great benefit to me is when I have met a total stranger, e.g., business meeting, airplane flight, happenstance encounter, once in a lifetime meeting, etc. Once we learn that we are both believers, the rapport we establish is immediate, warm and genuine. Obviously, one or both of the individuals meeting have to be alert or tuned to the Spirit so that the kinship is recognizable and can thus be developed. Speaking from personal experience, I do know this spiritual connection is unique and can be enjoyable and lasting. After all, it is kinship based on blood. Our, Savior's blood.

Recently, some friends of ours relocated to another city and I learned that their eight year old son, in adjusting to his new school was being kidded by a number of his classmates and they had nicknamed him "Preacher Boy." It had not yet become a big problem, but since it was somewhat out of the ordinary, his mother casually questioned him as to why he felt he had acquired this nickname? His response to his mother was immediate but matter of factly. "Because I usually ask the kid I am just meeting "where do you go to church?" His mother was a little puzzled, but knew her young son had a personal relationship with Jesus and their church and church programs were enjoyable and important to Timmy. But still keeping the tone of her questions casual and low key she inquired, why do you ask them about church?

Timmy's answer was quite astute for one so young. He explained to his mother:

"I'm trying to get to know other kids since I'm new in school, and I want to make new friends. Whether they go to church or not tells me something about the kind of person they are...and maybe whether I want to become friends with them or not."

Timmy then volunteered to his mother that he was disappointed at how few of them went to church. And he further added; "Besides most of them laugh at me when I ask about church... but I keep on asking."

It would seem to me that Timmy may be several steps ahead of most of us adults in (1) having a deliberate method of trying to select good friends, and (2) already aware that there is a Christian tie that can bond people. Even at a very young age.

Later on in life, Timmy may encounter something I have experienced in recent years. In some ways, it has a lot of merit. In other ways, it somewhat troubles me. I'm referring to Christian Business Telephone Directories that only list businesses owned by Christians and advertised as such. As I say, I don't have my mind completely fixed on this strategy but feel the merits can be debated.

Point to Ponder: If there had been a Jewish Directory or Christian Directory available to Jesus on his travels through the countryside, would He have stopped at the well in Samaria and talked to the non-kosher woman? Or would He have continued on, to a sanctioned water well and dealt with his own kind? Ouch!

How then shall they call on Him in whom they have not believed?
And how shall they believe in Him of whom they have not heard?
And how shall they hear without a preacher...
How beautiful are the feet of those who preach the gospel of peace,
who bring glad tidings of good things!"
Romans 10:14, 15b

THE TIE
(OUR MOST IMPORTANT RELATIONSHIP)

This short title of our Lord may surprise many of you, but it will be quickly obvious as to the origin. Some might even describe it as "cute." It is not meant to be cute or trite. I include it with serious intent and consider it quite descriptive and useful for studying yet another facet of God's love and power. The origin for my purpose is from a familiar hymn we sing in our churches quite often, "Blest Be The Tie That Binds," words going back to John Fawcett in 1782.

The "Tie" should be capitalized because it is **the** Son of God, Jesus the Christ and Our Christ. More specifically the Tie is the Love of God, which loves and connects ("ties") us to God. This connection is <u>initiated</u> by God. In common terminology of this modern hi-tech age in which we live, we can explain the process (and could even design a flow chart to depict the functions, activities, flows and outputs) by saying God initiates the first step by having the Holy Spirit contact us by various and sundry techniques (proddings, nudges etc.) of the Spirit (usually gentle movements and moments) that tend to show love, attention, concern, etc. to gain our personal attention. Let's pause and say wow! Imagine the High and Holy God *contacting us*!

This initial process having been executed, the next equally important step is <u>our</u> responsibility to implement. Note, this divine system is programmed so that God does not force our reply, nor dictate our decision. Please note that there are no stated limits as to the number of times He may or may not call/prod us. However, the process is simple and beautiful from this point on. And if, and only if, our response is affirmative, the connection is immediately made and affirmed. The "Tie" now exists between us and Holy God. We are henceforth connected and bound, heart, mind and soul to God and He to us. Wonderful and Amazing.

A couple of important comments are in order at this point. If our flow chart did in fact exist there would be at least two important sub-systems or paralleled systems showing other vital steps required for the total system: repentance, confession, forgiveness, adoption/new birth declaration of faith, etc. And an important third flow of information known as documentation in systems work indicating that our name has been duly recorded in the Lambs Book of Life. Shame: perhaps a few of you thought the book of Revelation did not apply to our generation.

When we first began this chapter on this title or name of our Lord, many of you dear readers wondered if there was really all that much to say about such a simple, two-word title. Well surprise surprise. There is still another important part of this subject to be discussed and enjoyed.

In the meantime, let us rejoice and be exceedingly glad that we have the wonderful, precious connection with our Lord.

Dare I say that this is **the** most important tie or relationship we will ever, ever have. Of course, I dare say this is the most important and wonderful and precious and lasting relationship connection we will ever have. In fact, it has eternal ramifications.

Amen and well said!

THE TRUE MANNA
(YOU CAN ONLY GET IT FROM ONE SOURCE)

We kid ourselves when we think we can have a gratifying/satisfying life and feed on any and all kinds of worldly foods and beautiful scrumptious meals prepared by seductive chefs of our modern lives. We deceive ourselves trying to make believe that life feeds us a lot of mannas, (plural). When in fact (scriptural fact) there is only *one* "true Manna," (singular).

Some of the pseudo mannas can at best satisfy our appetites for temporary moments. At worst, they become interim diets that lull us and dull our senses and infiltrate our spirit until we arrive (instantly or gradually) in a backslidden condition. In this condition, we can usually see the EXIT door. But the danger of dangers is that the diminished remainder of our spirit-self is usually out-voted two-to-one by the contaminated former self and Satan. Thus, the Exit door stands in red neon readiness but no rush is made for the eternal escape.

LISTING OF FALSE MANNAS.

More time devoted to television (and rental movies) than to reading the Bible.

A beach home or mountain home, (especially on weekends) that precludes being in church on Sunday.

A Sunday morning activity, e.g., golf, tennis, fishing, water-skiing, boating.

An "addiction" that detracted you so that you were tempted away from the True Manna. Surprise: A large number of addictions are non-narcotic.

An "unhealthy" individual that becomes an *addict*, thus, influencing your behavior to sin, evil or naughtiness (or, all of the aforementioned.)

An Unpleasant Exercise: (You, need to take.)

Make a list of the "false mannas" you have experienced or are currently experiencing. To aid in this task make a list of potential problems, pitfalls.

There is no particular significance to the order in which they are listed.

If you do not find your false-mannas in the list then there is space to list a few of the multi-mannas you have faced.

   Note: You are invited to share your own experiences:
         mpactassociates@cs.com

THE TRUTH
(AND NOTHING BUT!)

Truth needs no definition. It does not require defining. Everyone, saint and sinner alike, understands truth. There are no degrees of truth. It is either truth or it is not truth. There are no shades of truth. It is truth in the bright light of the noonday sun and it is truth in the dark of the night without even the light of the moon. Truth needs no defense. Truth does not need explaining or defending or expounding. Truth is truth.

Truth gives us our only true freedom. Truth is uncompromising. Truth is our standard. By this "standard" we can measure any and everything—including our lives.

Jesus said, "I am the truth " As his disciples, do we live in the truth? Do we exhibit (without even trying) truth in our daily lives? As natural as breathing in and out, our lives should *exude* truth!

Some of the early would-be followers told him he asked too much, i.e. his sayings were too hard. But going to the cross wasn't easy either.

THE UNOBTRUSIVE GOD
BUT YOU CAN FIND HIM)

This is another one of those "names" of the Lord that "I made up." At least I think I did, since I cannot recall ever hearing it before. It means God, in spite of His Might, Power, Glory, and Holiness, can choose to be inconspicuous and unobtrusively when the occasion requires.

The scriptures are filled with examples:
God moved a lowly unknown shepherd boy into the position of a great king.
He spoke through the mouth of a donkey.
He used a weird sort of preacher man who ate wild food and often startled people, as the individual to introduce the Lamb of God.
He transferred His only Son (from heaven to earth as a tiny baby) to an unlikely barn in an obscure town.

It gets kind of *touchy* but quite often the Lord allows some of His followers, even today, to move unobtrusively into positions of influence or positions of opportunity, so that, in the midst of the "enemies camp" we can testify and witness for Him. I once found myself in the middle of a country club ballroom with horribly loud music and with extra-horribly loud drums a drumming and several hundred people all talking, at the same time, loudly while I shared with several people, (mostly strangers) about an amazing thing God had done for me. They had little choice, other than being rude, but to listen to my "story" about God's grace and goodness. Incidentally, I was not dancing or drinking. I had not planned or even thought in advance about doing such a bold thing in such unexpected circumstances but I knew the Holy Spirit, unobtrusively had arranged this strange, albeit beautiful, moment of opportunity for witnessing. In fact, had God told me earlier that I was going to be presented with such an opportunity, most likely; I would have tried to talk Him out of it?
Most times God is definitely not meek and mild in His mode of

385

operating. Sometimes He is a loud thundering voice. Occasionally, He is a whirlwind. A few times He sends angels to boldly communicate and make announcements. He can appear in the middle of a whirling wheel. At least once He suddenly appeared in the middle of a stormy sea, walking on the waters. The Holy Spirit visited in the upper room announced by a mighty wind and surrounded by tongues of fire. Another time, He astounded the troops by appearing as the fourth man walking in a fiery furnace. Jesus, Himself, suddenly appeared in the middle of a locked room and offered to let Thomas look and touch his recent wounds that only recently turned into fresh scars.

None of these instances were unobtrusive in appearance or method. But if per chance, you are ever walking along side a road outside of town and a nice stranger joins you in your stroll and begins talking, so that your *heart burns within* you, then you will know that you have shared a glorious and memorable visit with our Unobtrusive Lord.

Luke 24: 31,32

Point to Ponder: Obviously, God delegates a lot of the unobtrusive assignments to the wonderful Holy Spirit who is a master at tip-toeing and speaking in a small, still, gentle, voice. On the other hand, if a dramatic unforgettable earth-shaking entrance is needed where people need to be stirred up a bit, what with flaming tongues of fire and mighty rushing winds and strange speaking so that bashful, fearful introverts are instantaneously transformed into extroverted soldiers-of-the-cross and raring to go on life changing missions and turning the world upside down   . Well, those types of assignments can be handled just as easy. Piece of cake.

TO GOD BE THE GLORY
(HE IS THE GLORY)

Here is a worthwhile spiritual exercise. You might want to try (in private) something that will prove refreshingly different. It may grab you as fanatical, elementary or silly. It may grab you as ritualistic. Whatever, that's OK. Just try it. Think of any blessings or "nouns" you have to be thankful for and each time you have the thought immediately say aloud one of the following:

To God Be the Glory!
Thanks Be unto God!

God Is Good!

His Mercy Extends to Me!

His Mercy Is So Real!

His Mercy and Love Wraps Me

In His Everlasting Arms!
He Knows My Name!
His Is the Glory!
His Is the Kingdom!
His Mercy Endures Forever!
He Speaks to the Storms and

His Peace Is Beyond
Understanding!

He Has Loved Me!
He Has Died for Me!
He Has Saved Me!

He Has Redeemed Me!
He Has Prepared a Place for Me!
He Will Never, Never, Leave Me!
His Mercies Are Too Many to Count!
He Promised to Send the Comforter!
He Did Indeed Send the Comforter!
He Is with Me Always!
He Has Made this Glorious Day!
He Runs My Cup Over!
He Is External!
He Is Steadfast!
He Loves Me with Everlasting Love!
He Is My Rock!

He Is My Tower!
He Is My Joy!
He Is Lord and Savior!
He Is God!

TOUGH TASKMASTER
(WE WEREN'T PROMISED A ROSE GARDEN)

A strong argument can be made that Jesus is a "tough taskmaster." This is not necessarily one of our most favorite titles to bestow upon our Lord. We would much prefer to call him our Gentle Shepherd, Everlasting Arms, Loving Savior, Prince of Peace or Spirit of Grace or Forgiving Love.

Indeed, he is all of these loving titles. Scriptural evidence supports such terminology, as does the Holy Spirit that administers these and other beautiful gifts to us and for us.

On the other hand, when you read in the scriptures, i.e. *hear him speak* such commands to his followers as
"love your enemies"
"if someone hates you   love them"
"if someone abuses you, then you must pray for them"
"compel them to come in"
"when someone strikes you, turn the other cheek"
"when someone takes your coat; give them your shirt"
"forgive seven times 70!"
"If someone steals from you don't ask for it back"
"Except you eat the flesh of the Son of Man and drink his blood, you have no life in you"
"if your right eye offends you, pluck it out"

Questions: How many times do we stand in church and sing those wonderful old hymns   without actually realizing what the words are saying: take up the cross and follow me or Onward Christian Soldiers marching on to war?

Doesn't sound like a picnic does it?

Another hymn asks, "have you counted the costs?"

TOWER
(EVERYBODY NEEDS ONE)

The name of the Lord is like a strong tower. The righteous run to it and are safe.

This verse is a real and practical confidence builder – not in yourself but in your God. How reassuring to <u>know</u> that <u>the</u> <u>tower</u> is *there!*

There are several advantages to having a tower versus a shelter. A shelter is nice to have. But having a tower is better. A shelter is nice to ward off the elements of rain, hot sun and cold winds. But in a tower you are safe behind thick impenetrable walls; you are high enough to see the enemy and you are in a better position to fight back. A tower affords defense and offense!

But perhaps, the best thing about having a tower is you have somewhere to run when trouble is about to hit. You <u>know</u> it is there, better yet, you can see your tower from a distance. You just need to use it, get there in time and not depend on your own strength. Best of all, this is an *oral* Tower. You can get there quickly by *speaking* the name of Jesus.

Isn't it sad how many people get in trouble because they've never used it? And it was there all the while.

TRINITY
(EXPLAINED FOR LITTLE KIDS)

Perhaps the most difficult theological subject to explain is that of the Trinity or "the Godhead." As a small inquiring child I never seemed to have a lot of success in getting very good answers to some of life's greater mysteries. Come to think of it, I never did get an acceptable answer to the "birds and bees" question either. And the explanation of God being three persons, (or, maybe it was two persons and a ghost) and yet all three of "them" were actually just one, well, now that was a pretty tough concept to comprehend correctly, or just to barely grasp, at best. The discussion usually ended by my being told "to wait until I was an adult" and then I could understand it. Seeming to have no other recourse, I decided to wait, even though I'm sure I continued to bring the subject up once or twice a week. That may be what gave some of my family members (those that knew me least) the idea that I would "grow up and be a preacher." It did cross my mind that probably the only way I was ever going to learn about the Divine Triune would be to go to "preacher school."

You can imagine my dismay, when I finally became an adult, and I still didn't understand it. Worse, even the preachers who had been to preacher school didn't seem to understand it either. Or, for certain, they didn't seem to have the understanding (or misunderstanding") of the mystery subject.

So at this point, I did what I should have done years ago. I went to my special person, who also happened to be a spiritual guru: My Grandmother! She could answer any question, or if she couldn't answer it, she could handle the question so that I left satisfied with her explanation. Like for example: the time at age 7 or 8 when I asked her, "where did God come from?"

To my question about the Trinity, she explained in one sentence: "God, who is our Heavenly Father is so powerful, so wise and so Holy, that he knew we would never be able to feel comfortable or at ease with him, but He loved us so much that he wanted to show us how much he loved us and also how much he wanted to have fellowship so he sent his only son, Jesus, to earth in the form of a little baby boy, (so

Jesus was both God <u>and</u> man) to grow up and live on earth but then die for our sins but after three days he arose from the dead, which proved he really was God's Son and then he left our earth and rose up into clouds until he was back in Heaven with his Father and then they, God, his Father, sent the Holy Ghost, which really wasn't like a ghost, but was a "spirit" and since it was a *spirit*, it could be anywhere and everywhere at the same time, which was a good thing, because since Jesus was also a man, he could only be in one place at a time, but the spirit, which was really the "presence" of Jesus and God and so all of this about God and Jesus' other spirit, which sounds like a complicated thing and kind of scary at times is really a very good thing for "them" and us, because we can have Jesus with us at all times because the Holy Ghost or Spirit of God is always around us and we can pray to God (which is really "talking" to God) and this allows God to have the fellowship with his people which is the only thing God ever needed from us and we do this by thanking him and telling him how much we love him."

Didn't I tell you I had a smart grandmother? And all of that knowledge in just one sentence.

THE UNNAMEABLE GOD
(HAS A SON NAMED JESUS)

Once while reading a "spiritual" type book, the author, an obviously brilliant and highly educated man with splendid credentials, explained why it was not plausible or appropriate to call God or the Supreme Being, by any other name, or even one or more of several names Father, Almighty God, or Supreme Being etc.

The author went on to explain that no mere mortal, or human creature, had come anywhere close to having the ability to "name" the Supreme Being or develop a title that could encompass all his greatness. He went on to suggest that if we insisted on using a "name," something like "Higher Light" might be the more appropriate term. He also explained that his suggested title had the added advantage of avoiding *gende*r and alleviated this impossible quandary for us.

To a certain extent, I can agree with a number of this author's points. After all, our "God" is so lofty, so totally wise, so holy, holy, holy, so untouchable, that we cannot get close enough to him so that we fully know or even partially understand all of his greatness and goodness and grace.

But as to ascribing to this Mighty Being as an appropriate name, I personally don't have a problem. Why? Because I met his son Jesus!

THE UNSEEN HAND
(ALWAYS AROUND...ATTACHED TO
THE EVERLASTING ARM)

We hardly ever see the hand of God. There is a good reason for that. Most of the time it is unseen. Quite often that is because we are so busy we fail to see it, or the "movement" happens so quickly we aren't able to comprehend the Divine in action. Later the occurrence is belatedly obvious to our dull vision and we can fully acknowledge that the hand of God intervened and His mercy saved us.

Unfortunately, this delayed analysis (especially when the emergency is past tense) can explain away the divine assistance and give the credit to coincidence or maybe even luck.

My grandmother, now deceased, told me once, that when a person who claims to be a Christian is living a godly life, there is no such thing as luck!

My own pet peeve is when so-called Christians (permit me to judge) explain away the reality of their life being saved by saying the "man upstairs must have been looking after me."

I think my grandmother would also say that there ain't no man upstairs. It is the Most High and Holy God of Heaven and Earth (and the same one who owns all the cattle on a thousand hills) that saved my hide from an otherwise horrendous death. Coincidence and luck don't cut it.

P.S.   I'm not a theological professional so you might want to ask your preacher, if my grandmother was wrong. I can't imagine anyone thinking my grandmother could have been wrong.

UNSPEAKABLE GIFT
(AN OLD, OLD STORY THAT NEVER GROWS OLD)

The NIV translates this term as the *indescribable* gift, in other words, there aren't enough words, nouns or adjectives to fully and completely describe our Lord and all that he means to us, or all that he does for us, past, present and future. Thus, He is "unspeakable."

Have you ever had the experience of having to prove this point? I have had a couple of opportunities. Once, while driving on an interstate highway with a captive audience of a young Chinese couple. They had just arrived in America and were eager to "learn everything," including about our religious philosophies, our church system and about our God. They seemed genuine and sincere, so I gave it my best shot for the next three hours.

Wow! But did I ever learn some lessons myself. As a born-in-America, raised in the Bible Belt, long time Christian, I had been so accustomed to our Christian's vocabulary and terminology that I had grown *immune* to their significance and their value. Therefore, it seemed that almost every other word I used had to be defined and explained to my audience, both highly educated and fresh out of the Beijing uprising. Have you perhaps developed the "immunity" to all the power and glory and vitality?

To describe and explain the greatest story ever told involved a holy divine being, who possessed all power and knowledge so that he could create everything and at the same time He was totally and completely holy. And then something went awry (sin), so that he needed to communicate and reach mankind but this human creation wasn't able to relate to such a supreme and holy being. So He devised a plan to send His Son in the form of a small baby, so that we would be able to "relate." But sadly, this His only Son was killed and though He sacrificed His life   and so on. We all know how the story goes. But they didn't! I needed words like Shepherd, baby Jesus, King, Advocate, sacrifice, eternal, friend, Holy Spirit, grace, resurrection, bread of life, etc. etc. I needed them defined in order to desperately tell the story of such love and why such a high and holy and mighty immortal God could desire fellowship with such mere mortals that were so undeserving.

Jesus became **all** and answered all questions and has been the light, the life, the way, the solution, shown love, proved love and a **personal** God for whosoever.

Do we begin to see why the "Gift" was unspeakable abov e and beyond words?

Wow!!

II Cor. 9:15

THE UNITY OF GOD
(INTIMACY MESHED WITH DIVINITY)

We have been married nearly 50 years. One of the many times I cherish my wife is at night when we first go to bed and the noises and activities of the day have been given silence. There may be some brief conversation or there may be none. The peace and the cherishness of being together suffice. No, it more than suffices; it satisfies and envelops the two of us into one cocoon of God's love and unity.

Sometimes when I'm just on the verge of falling softly asleep, I make an attempt to repeat some of my wedding vows, but my conscious state is now incapable of words.

Fortunately, out-loud words aren't required and if I attempt them they are customarily blended with unspoken thoughts of cour se, "I *take this woman...*" you gave her to me I can't remember " *the worse;*" only "*the better*" and this bliss is your tangible touch on our lives and your spirit melted us into your Unity of One. And then and I don't even remember when, I am asleep.

There is no substitute there is nothing that ever comes close to the touch of God's *Unity*.

THE VICTORY
(RAH, RAH, RAH!!)

Remember the cheerleading yell, we all used in High School, that started out, "Give me a V" etc. etc. and eventually spelled VICTORY!!

THE VICTORY CHEER (for believers).
- V   Attach me to the Vine
- I   Want-a-be part of the Great I Am
- C   Christ is the Only One
- T   Run to the Tower, Truth, and Truest Friend
- O   Only Son, Only God, Only Way Jesus
- R   Righteous, Redeemer, Resurrected Rock of Ages
- Y   You Lord, You Lord, Yea, You Lord Jesus.

"O sing unto the Lord a new song; for he has done marvelous things: his right hand and his holy arm have gotten him the Victory."
Psalms 98:2

There are a number of soul-stirring verses in the Bible on "VICTORY." In fact one can become excited just reading about "Victory," so just think of the fever produced by reading (or yelling) them out loud.

And here are several verses to add icing to the cake.

"But thanks be to God which giveth us the Victory through our Lord Jesus Christ. I Corinthians. 15:57

"... That through death he might destroy him that had the power of death, that is, the devil. Hebrews 2:14b

And deliver them who through fear of death were all their lifetime subject to bondage. Hebrews 2:14b, 15

For whatsoever is born of God overcometh the world: and this is the Victory that overcometh the world, even our faith. I John 5:4

THE VISIBLE LIKENESS
(WE BECOME LIKE HIM)

Jesus was the "person" the early disciples could see. They might even touch him or watch him eat or get thirsty and drink. They saw him get irked, perturbed and even angry a few times. They even saw him walk on water. Maybe a few saw him turn water into wine. And they saw him perform miracles. They saw him use a whip once. They saw him hold kids on his lap. They saw him wash feet. They saw him cry. They saw him sweat. They saw him sweat drops of blood (if they were awake). They even saw him die, but probably only *one* witnessed the horror up close. The others probably watched from a safe distance. And wow, they even saw him after he was resurrected. And, how about the ascension into the clouds?

What they actually saw *was God*! Certainly, God's Son. Watching this marvelous variety of human and divine deeds, they actually saw the visible likeness of God. Therefore, this eyewitnesses account that we have means that we too *know* what the visible likeness of God is like.

Now comes the point I am trying to make. It may sound somewhat strange, but I feel it is valid: The "life," we live as believers, e.g., our words and our deeds; our attitudes and our fruits become the only visible likeness of Christ that those around us will probably ever see!

Think about it. An awesome responsibility, isn't it?
"Love one another as I have loved you "
"Greater love hath no man ."
"Love your enemies   ".
"Love one another "
"For love is of God "
"For God is love "

Acts 11:26: **...and when he found him, he brought him to Antioch. So for a whole year Barnabas and Saul met with the church and taught great numbers of people. The disciples were called Christians first at Antioch.**

399

VICTORIOUS LORD
(OUR OVERCOMING LORD)

"Death is swallowed up in victory.
O Death, where is thy sting?
O Grave, where is thy victim?" I Corinthians 15: 54, 55

This is one of my favorite (ah, yet **another** favorite) verses in the Bible. This one makes the Top Ten because it is jammed-packed with fantastic, wonderful, spirit-lifting, knock-the-devil-back-in his-hole-again spiritual dynamite! In fact this may be Number 32 on my supposed "Top Ten" list.

To expound and extrapolate (sic) and explain on a verse that certainly needs *nothing* in the way of explanation or clarification. Absolutely nothing! All it needs is to be read. Better yet, to read out loud, i.e. aloud, and orally. Best of all, is to memorize it once and for all and keep it on the front row of your memory bank. Jesus Christ is our victory and Jesus Christ is indeed victorious.

Having memorized and committed to this, you can forthwith and henceforth and forever more have at your fingertips immediate access to the Power of Almighty God. To state it another way, you have at your tongue tip, with a quick flip of the tongue, the ability to release quick-as-a-lightning-bolt a spiritual-verbal vim and vigor packed victorious Satan-conquering victory over the very worse things a mortal human being can ever confront anywhere in an entire lifetime, including the scariest cruelest time of all which obviously is the end or near end of a lifetime when the "Big Fears" are facing you in the eyeballs. Quick math makes those six eyeballs facing your two eyeballs! Overwhelming, despair evoking odds, would you not agree? I am of course talking about DEATH, HELL AND THE GRAVE!

I ask you point-blankly, **can you name** anything or any things more frightening than death and/or hell and/or the grave and/or any combination thereof, that can mentally, physically and spiritually "wipe you out." If so, I double-de-dare you to name it.

Now, after having scared you (and myself) half out of our wits, let's take a deep sigh of relief. For, we indeed do know, on a first name basis, (he knows ours and we know his), the One who is the Victory and has already (past tense) won it (The Victory) and is therefore fully and duly qualified (by God) to announce now and forevermore that He is Victorious over Death, Hell and the Grave.

P.S.   And anything else, including the demons of Hell, one cares to add to the list.

And printed above is a classic "victory" verse to summarize this wonderful power given to us as our very own victory and bestowed upon us by **our** Victorious Lord. A verse for every "Christian Soldier" to memorize.

THE MAIN VINE
(SECONDARY VINES WILL <u>NOT</u> BE)

I was once involved with an adult Sunday school class that spent months and months studying the Fifteenth Chapter of John. This chapter must be one of the most jammed-pack chapters in the entire Bible. The very first verse lets you know in no uncertainty who is the main vine and who is the Keeper of the vineyard.

The next verse tells right away what happens to any and all branches that do not produce any grapes. They are the bad or poor branches that get whacked off and hauled off. But this verse doesn't stop there. Even the good branches get purged or pruned (and I bet either one hurts) so that they produce more fruit.

Think about it. Just *two* verses into this jammed-packed thirty-three verses, you get the distinct impression that the "boss" of this vineyard can be tough; that he expects a lot!

Perhaps this is the real reason that our class took so long. We probably decided that a couple of verses were enough at one time and that we best take it slowly, so as to have time to "heal up" before the next tough step was explained and discussed.

But didn't someone once say that if you've got to amputate something, you probably don't want to do it an inch at a time.

Well, at least we had a week to wonder about what "He" was going to do with all the dead branches He cut off.

VINE
(HOW SIMPLE; HOW CRUCIAL)

Some things are easy to understand. Very easy! The "True Vine" is a prime example.

He is the vine, make no mistake about that. I would not have it any other way. I get my strength from the vine. The vine is my source. If I get cut off from the vine, the conclusion is obvious. The conclusion is also quick. It's succinct. I die.

He didn't *suggest* I bear fruit. But he told me what would happen if I did not bear fruit. The only way I can bear fruit is if I stay attached to the vine. He told me that I absolutely could not produce fruit by myself that I had to stay attached to him. He is the vine. The life is in him. It is definitely not in me. That I understand.

He went on to explain what happens if I don't bear fruit. I get purged, which simply means I get cut off from the vine. Not only do I get "cut off" but he went on to explain what happens to branches that are no longer attached. I wither. After I wither there is nothing left except I'll be gathered up with other dried up withered useless branches and thrown in the fire. Ouch! I get burned.

I can't remember if it was Will Rogers *or* Mark Twain that said it so well. He had heard someone complaining about not being able to understand the Bible that some verses were just too difficult to grasp. To which he replied that it was those sections that he *did* understand that bothered him! Me too!

THE WAY
(AND IT IS ONE-WAY)

Jesus did not say, I am the way you should follow when you find it convenient to do so, nor did he say I am the way you can follow in times of stress, or when you have a life threatening emergency (my grandmother called this "firehouse religion"). Jesus did not say I am the way you can use, when you need to establish social contact or build your customer base.

Jesus did not say that he was the way to be followed when time was available, so as to not interfere with golf, fishing, or sleeping late, after a tough week at work.

Jesus did not say, I am the seasonal way to especially be followed on Easter Sunday and during the Christmas season. Jesus did not say, I am the way to follow when the mood strikes you, or, I am the way to follow whenever a religious mood happens to hit. And Jesus did not say that if we followed him "X" number of miles within a certain period that we would probably be O.K.

Jesus did not suggest we follow him on good weather days and when there seemed to be no threat of rain or thunderstorms. Neither did He say we could follow him whilst He was walking nice smooth trails that tended to be on level ground, or down slight inclines and that we shouldn't concern ourselves when He had to climb steep hills; especially if the weather was hot and humid or cold with bitter winds blowing in our face.

Jesus did not say we should follow Him when there was no one around to see us together, per chance the word got out that we were a religious fanatic. Jesus did not say we should consider our walks with Him to be similar to a hobby that we occasionally pulled out from a dusty closet shelf.

Jesus may or may not have said it, but He probably does not like lukewarm trail walkers. Jesus probably prefers walkers that will walk with Him not only through the nice sections of villages, but also when He walks through the ghettos and slums sections.

I don't think Jesus planned His walks very well for quite often He seemed to find Himself low on food, or, maybe even out of food. And

I doubt if He made reservations in advance for He once mentioned that He didn't have a place to lay his head.

In fact, walking with Jesus might have some anxious moments. Who knows when He might call someone a hypocrite or a viper or even a whitewashed tomb? On occasion, he might cause a local farmer to lose a herd of hogs. Or, who would care to be around when he upset the esteemed religious leaders of the day. That could be embarrassing.

But on the positive side, I imagine a walk with Jesus would be one that you would never forget.

Or, never regret.

THE WEEPER
(ONE VERSE, TWO WORDS)

The shortest verse in the Bible receives only scant attention. Quite often it reminds us of early days in Sunday School when very young Bible "scholars" trying desperately to recall a Bible verse often quoted it in frightened and timid voices. And we are amazed by this "cute little verse." But perhaps nowhere else in the Bible are there two words that give as much insight into Jesus. We easily see him (and are in fear) i.e. Lord, Master, Holy God, Creator, Awesome God, and on and on. But God weeping! Think of what we would be missing if we did not know that our God once wept.

Tears can and do tell a lot about a person, because they go *beyond words* in expressing deep emotions. Tears can especially be helpful in portraying the depth of a man's emotional hurt, for; after all, a lot of men think they aren't supposed to cry. This brief and telling scene of Jesus crying is much akin to the oriental proverb of a picture being worth a thousand words. Here we have an unforgettable "portrait" of our God who once flung stars into their magnificent orbits, being touched so deeply that He actually wept.

Can you ever erase this "scene" from your mind??

THE WINGS OF GOD'S LOVE
(A FUNNY STORY WITH TEARS)

Someone once asked me if the Bible, or my faith in God, had anything to do with building self-esteem. This was shortly after I had spoken to a group of young people and had shared some of the problems I had not enjoyed as a teenager, e.g. pimples (acne had not yet been invented), two long skinny arms (neither of which could barely hold a wristwatch) and two very long skinny legs, interrupted by two knobby knees (neither of which matched), all of which was capped off with a somewhat oversized head. I eventually would be forced to try and wear the largest sized headgear the U.S. Army stocked. (The Army gave me a lot of headaches.)

Not a bad list of *starters* for producing a bunch of complex inferiority complexes that would cooperatively form an introverted, shy, bashful, backward, timid, skinny boy from the hills of North Georgia. Oh, pardon me! I almost left out two other conspicuous features that I certainly did not need, especially at this embarrassing time when I was a teenager (for what seemed like 15 years in duration) and certainly (the Lord should have known) at a time when the last thing I needed was anything else (much less two things) to make me look even more conspicuous, but low and behold, on the top, as already stated, of my oversized head was some curly white hair. No self-respecting macho (grin) boy wanted curly hair, much less white (not blonde, but gravestone white) hair. And my otherwise perfect mother did not help matters by mentioning at least twice daily (and more often, if we had company, "visitors") that, "Oh, if only she or just one of her daughters had been blessed with curly hair." Can you believe she said, "blessed?" The only "blessing" I got from my white head was not needing a reflector, on the rear fender of my bicycle. Plus, the fact that the white sissy-looking stuff forced me to become a pretty feisty fighter, as I got a lot of "practice" (almost daily) because the other boys made fun of my white curly oversized head, which caused them to call me a "sissy." Henceforth, I was forced to fight daily (at least 5 days a week) to prove I weren't (sic) no sissy. Years of this type of persecution will eventually make even a skinny funny looking kid a fairly good fighter. Certainly many were amazed (including the coach) that none of my skinny arms ever broke off in the fast fought fraying of flying limbs. Finally, and I'm glad this is the last conspicuous feature that doesn't need mentioning. At the other end of my non-magnificent body was a "foundation" (smile again) of two non-massive tiny feet ("footzies" they were called). In fact, I kept the ridicule of having tiny undersized feet through many of my adult years by having to wear size 7 shoes. At age 50, I bought me some super thick socks and just arbitrarily started wearing size 8 shoes, which had the added advantage of moving me out of the "Boys" department.

All of the above is a deliberate way to take a humorous look at some obstacles I faced. Most everyone does–of one type or another. Still, I know that I was truly blessed with a lot of love and always under a spiritual umbrella of love and divine orientation. The key thing is that, not just individuals (which is a must) but as a family we "knew God" and walked and lived with Him. He was never a Sunday morning tradition. He was *real* in our lives. He never became commonplace in our home, but it was "normal and usual" to expect and experience his presence.

Looking back on my many complexes and feelings of inferiority, I can see how these "negatives" taught me to rely on my faith. I always knew everything would work out okay, and it most often did. The Bible verses we lived and breathed were not some theory, but they were truth and life–as real as bread and gravy. A scripture verse was not just some words to tickle our ears. Nor, was it some future comfort to be quoted when we finally had to cross over chilly "Jordan." These words **meant** what they said. I really did know early-on that "I could do all things through Christ ." and I did know that "the joy of the Lord was my strength " and I really did know that the most important thing in life was to "be right with the Lord" and I really did know that I should never, never put my trust in earthly things, be they gold, or money or job or education or stocks and bonds, nor fame, nor popularity–buy the only thing I could really count on was not people (including my own Mother and Dad), to repeat the only thing I could count on was my Lord–and his name was Jesus!

The Bible is packed with vital lessons. I learned (without having to try very hard) like "consider the lilies of the field   they toil not, neither do they spin" and "it is in Him that we live and move and have our being" and, " seek ye first the Kingdom of Heaven and all these things " and "the Kingdom of G od is within."

Later in life, I would be able to look back (like a lot of people) and see that I had lived, so much of my life beneath God's wings and that much of what I had become was a *direct product* of God's grace and as simple to explain in retrospect as Romans 8:28; as the Lord had taken so much of the misery, (complexes and pimples), and used *them* to eventually make a person that could be caring and sensitive (with some overdeveloped "ever flow" tear glands) and have a God-given talent of being able to relate to any and all kinds of people, and with a minimum of effort, be able to show his love. The same tender and marvelous and touching love He had shown and shared with me.

Don't get me wrong. All of these beautiful verses did not transfer my life to float on a nice bed of roses. But they did go a long way in allowing me to keep things in perspective and know who was in control (and that I did not have to be). Most of my complexes eventually "got better" but a few are still hanging around in the shadowed fringes. Almost all of my personal image problems got vanished or certainly got "altered." My arms and legs have basically remained sort of skinny but midway between the skinny arms and the skinny legs, I grew a "beer belly" (and have never even tasted beer). My troublesome head of white curly hair developed a difference of opinion, with one half of it deciding to turn gray, and the other half deciding to just fall out, desert and just fall out. But .

P.S.   My feet haven't changed.

P.S.   My feet never did make it out of the "sevens."

P.S.   For a number of years, I've been the happiest person I know.

THE WORD MADE FLESH
(GOOD NEWS...AND THEN COMES THE GREAT NEWS)

This is perhaps one of the more telling terms to describe the **mission** of God's plan for his son, Jesus. An extensive/amplified translation of this verse might read:

> God wanted us, his children, to know and understand his ultimate plan for mankind, but he knew that first we needed to be able to relate to him and that he (God) must be able to relate to us. There had to be rapport and understanding. And this would certainly not come easily. In some way, he must show and prove his love to his lowly, mortal human creation. To do so, He had to overcome gigantic chasms of holiness, power, wisdom, knowledge and communication. Never in all times had a more difficult challenge emerged.
>
> Thus, this seemingly impossible quandary, multi-complicated and multi-complexed was overcome in what turned out to be divinely simple and exhibited his supreme love, in an amazing way.
>
> God sent his son, (even his only son), in the form of a human (i.e. flesh) to bring the message (the word). God is his word, and his word is God.
>
> No human being ever, ever, expressed it better and more succinctly than Oswald Chambers, when he wrote *and condensed* the "Greatest Story Ever Told" into a four-word sentence.

"GOD BECAME A BABY."

THE WORD
(HAVE A BAND-AID HANDY OR A TOURNIQUET)

I love the Bible. That should come as no great surprise. Many of us love and cherish this unique Book of books.

Somewhere in the subconscious mind, we may be "programmed" to think there is a spiritual obligation to cherish this Book. Perhaps. Perhaps not. But there is nothing wrong with that if, in fact, we "inherit" some sort of duty bound obligation toward this Book. Sort of like an eleventh commandment.

Let's do something different. Only we do it *separately together*. Does that make sense? I didn't think so. But humor me. (Writing a book like this is, of necessity, a lonely life.) So at times I sit here writing and can sometimes visualize that you, the reader and I are really face-to-face. (Corny, don't you agree?)

Here is the "exercise" we each do separately together:

We will each list forty-nine (49) reasons why we love the Bible. Why forty-nine? Where did I get that number? Did I pull it out of the air? Not really. I got the idea from the Bible! How often should we forgive someone? Seven times seven. No, seven times seventy is 490, so I took a tithe of that and cleverly arrived at 49. My own list will be "hidden" elsewhere in this book. If I listed them below where they rightfully belong, then you might be tempted to peep and cheat. Far be it from me, to tempt you.

One final note. Some of you are asking in a whinny voice, "can't we just do a top ten list? Answer, NO! Everyone does a top-ten list on everything, under the sun. There is probably a top-ten list somewhere of the Top Ten Lists. To do our best means we must do forty-nine!

The Bible is precious and deserves our best. Don't you agree? Certainly you agree? Otherwise, you would sound lazy or obstinate, or heathenish. Or, all of these. Oh, by the way, I thought of a "cute" sub-title to this ("The Word") chapter. How about, "Be Careful When You Examine a Two-edge Sword. You Might Get Cut."

Matthew 18: 21,22 **Then came Peter to him, and said, Lord, how oft shall my brother sin against me, and I forgive him? till seven** times?" Jesus saith unto him, I say not unto thee, until seven times: but, until seventy times seven.

WORD INCARNATE
(MAJOR THINGS JESUS DID FOR ME)

Let's do another one of those spiritual exercises that many of you enjoy and   many of you groan and start to skip the page, (perish the thought).

Here goes: Make a list of the 'Top Ten' things Jesus did for me, as a "follower" of Christ. Most will be fairly obvious, probably the first five or so. Then, somewhere around number "five" or "six" you will probably *personalize* the list so that it *custom fits* your own thoughts, preferences, priorities, hopes, etc. In developing your list, don't try to get too fancy or "theologically." Express *your* thoughts and opinions. Use common sense. Mentally scan the "red letters" stored in your brain and/or scan the gospels, especially the captions, sub-titles, etc., normally included in most translations. Finally, visually scan the red letters.

I will list mine (elsewhere in this book) so as to not infiltrate your own thinking. This is also a good exercise to use with a family member or family group. Or, Sunday School Class or Bible Study group.

A major benefit is that it should (1) cause you (and others) to re-think or deeper-think a lot of the basics of our precious faith that otherwise we take for granted or sub-consciously ignore (blaze') because it is old or familiar. Isn't it a shame that we, seriously dedicated Christians, can evolve into a "stale state" and actually become *immune* to the beauty, trust and value of our Lord?

Secondly, the exercise is a good way to naturally provoke group (or private) discussion.

Go for it!

WORD OF LIFE
(FORTY-NINE REASONS)

Here are forty-nine reasons that I came up with as to why I love, appreciate and need the Bible. To me, the Word is alive with life and the life is *the* Word.

1. It is the most alive book I've ever read.
2. It is truly the only eternal book–and always will be.
3. It cannot be destroyed (many have tried).
4. It has never needed revising. It never will.
5. It does not need a single word to be added.
6. It does not need a single word to be deleted.
7. It is the only book that states and vouches for its *own* authority (i.e. God's).
8. It can explain (historically) what went wrong in the past.
9. It can provide precise guidance for unknown futures.
10. It is a "map" that I need for planning and direction.
11. It can help me in important goal setting.
12. It can be used to disarm the enemy.
13. It contains good advice for raising children.
14. It provides the only successful way for confronting guilt (and over-coming same).
15. It provides an effective way of "auditing" my progress as a Christian (or lack of).
16. It contains "gems" for dealing with many serious problems, complexes, fears, etc.
17. It allows me to experience the reality of the love of God.
18. It is absolutely the world's best all time "how-to" manual.
19. It provides me with many Biblical positive role models.
20. It provides some negative role models, so I can learn how to avoid evil.
21. It provides me with the "standards" I need, to be wise, productive and ethical.
22. It gives me light to overcome darkness (nothing else combats darkness like light).

23. It provides me with a "mirror."
24. It acts like a spiritual enzyme that causes spiritual growth.
25. It allows me to understand God's plan for the ages (and for all mankind).
26. It provides me with my own personal "taskmaster" (which is something I need).
27. It is the only Book that never becomes "old" or out-of-date.
28. It is the only Book that is inexhaustible.
29. It is the only Book that is *pure* and *holy*.
30. It is the only known book to be completely and totally inspired.
31. It is a book that can charm, chide, correct, chastise, comfort, condemn, compel, conquer, consecrate, console, and convict.
32. It is the book that is concentrated, correct and consistent.
33. It is flawless, faithful and forever.
34. Its words can be *fixed* or *hidden* in my heart.
35. It is an entrance for me; and a light for my path.
36. It can be "eaten" and become my joy and the delight of my heart. (Jer. 15:16)
37. It became "flesh" and lived among us.
38. It still lives in us now (if we allow it).
39. It is the sword of the Spirit.
40. It is best used as an active partner and not a passive, bookshelf filler.
41. It is not just a book; it is and has become a vital part of me.
42. It contains a lot of "begats" and even they contain nourishment.
43. It is able to *wash* me and *feed* me and *warm* me.
44. It is absolutely the *best* book I have for learning/knowing my Lord and my God.
45. It is He that provided the plan of my salvation and eternal life.
46. It has a personalized vitality so that it seems to be written for unique needs.
47. It never gets old.
48. It will not and cannot return void.
49. It will never pass away.

THE WORLD'S OWNER
(AND ALL THE CATTLE)

One of the scriptures that has always been *special* to me for as long as I can remember: "for every animal of the forest is mine, and the cattle on a thousand hills." This particular verse and those immediately before and after verse 10, are both symbolic and factual is defining God as the owner of earth and everything in it, on it, and around it. This is an interesting way of saying God owns everything. Why shouldn't he? After all He created *it,* which in human terms would give him rightful ownership. How wonderful and how awesome.

So, why is this verse special and important to me? Answer: Probably for the same reason it is important to a lot of people. There is just something extremely satisfying and comforting, especially at the very moment in an opening prayer, when I am about to approach my God and ask him for something of crucial importance. With the thoughts encompassed in these verses, I have assurance and reassurance of his ability to deliver.

I do find myself often using part of the tenth verse as an opening statement: "Lord, you own the cattle on a thousand hills." This concise sentence for me is a beautiful way of acknowledging some of the attributes and wonders of the God I serve and states in *part* what I believe. I suppose, for me, it is much like a one sentence Apostle's Creed. Or, it is like a "condensed book" that puts volumes of thoughts and beliefs that express the foundation for faith, hope and confidence. Admittedly, these are vital things that I don't really have to tell God, (he already knows my thoughts) but I feel the need to, in some way to express them.

The other verses, in Psalm 50, contain quite a list of things God states he does not need. But then there are two very descriptive verses, where, in one sentence, God states *what I do want from you.*

The Living Bible prints these key verses (v. 15, 19) in italics. My grandmother told me long ago to always pay particular attention when God writes in Italics. (Just kidding)

Perhaps you have your own favorite verse as a type of one sentence affirmation of faith?

416

WORTHY OF PRAISE
(DON'T LET A ... TAKE YOUR PLACE!)

Once I heard someone say that the emphasis a church places on "praise" can be correlated to the overall success it enjoys; that exciting worship and spiritual enrichment is connected to the *"barometer"* of praise. Could this same premise apply to individuals?

Unfortunately, many traditional churches limit and cloak their expression of praise, per se, to certain anthems or the singing of the doxology. As a general rule, these are the same churches that are not experiencing a lot of growth. In fact, many, if not most, are declining. Some of the large mainline denominations are in serious decline. As a sad example, the United Methodist Church has decreased several million in the last 15 years.

In 1994, a major newsmagazine did a cover story on the growth and decline of all of the larger denominations in America. While the article did not go into a lot of depth in explaining the reasons for the dramatic growth enjoyed by those denominations leading the pack, a quick perusal of the top five, indicated that all but two were denominations that definitely employed, a more "loose" and casual style of worship and at the very center was extensive and orally expressed praise. It can also be noted that one of the two denominations not included in the "praise groups has indeed "loosened up" quite a bit and now expresses (largely via praise choruses) praise to the Lord.

And I dare say that a similar study could be made to ascertain that the non-praise groups are the very ones that are leaving the church or at best *evolving* out of the church once they escape the parental/traditional church and head out-on-their-own, usually when they leave for college. The most commonly heard complaint of this group is that, as teenagers, they have been "bored to death." They quite often complain about the "dead music," and "the same old stuff."

Except for Pentecostal and/or many black churches, "alive-praise" hasn't been a normal part of worship in most churches. Certainly this has been the case until the latter part of the twentieth century and into the 21st century. Like them or not, the sudden appearance of the charismatic movement is synonymous with praise, praise, praise. As someone said, "How in David's name can you have true praise without being oral, joyful and excited   and letting it out?"

Admittedly, the attitude toward praise causes many to feel uncomfortable. But the negativism is outweighed by a lot of pro-praise evidence: praise and synonym-type words are mentioned over 1000 times in the Bible. And, you might as well throw out the book of Psalms if you aren't in favor of praising God and letting your love and joy be known.

Fear not if "alive-praise" disturbs you. God, in his understanding and tender mercies allows the Holy Spirit to provide silent ways to express joy and spiritual communion. I know a few people who are sometimes "blessed" and overwhelmed by the goodness of God and when this occurs they do not jump or leap or run or clap their hands, or even say a word out loud; they simply weep and quietly cry tears of overflowing joy.

There is a summarizing verse that fits this subject so well: "God inhabits the praise of his people." The bottom line is that God can handle whatever method or mode his children might use. God certainly isn't threatened by sanctimonious dignity or traditional style, or even the lack of *outward* praise. For, after all, He's still got the rocks!

A GOD WITH X-RAY VISION?
(BEWARE!! AND BE GLAD)

A young boy asked his father, "Does God have x-ray vision like Superman?" A pretty typical question, for a young lad.

Many years ago, another father, David talking to his son said, "My son, Solomon, acknowledge the God of your father and serve him with wholeheartedly devotion and with a willing mind, for the Lord searches every heart and understands every motive behind the thoughts."

As a young boy when I needed it, for correction or pre-correction my grandmother used to admonish or chide me by singing in her high shrill voice:

> *There is an all-seeing Eye watching you*
> *Every step that you take*
> *Every mile that you make*
> *There's an "Eye watching you.*

Actually, I needed my grandmother's "singing" when I got older. Especially when I was in high school. And especially, especially when I was in the Army. But she made a lasting impression and I can still hear her voice at times.

Shame on me!

THE YOUNG CHILD
(EXTROVERT OR INTROVERT?)

We know so very little of Jesus as a young child. Why is that? We would certainly like to know more. But why? What purpose would it serve? Obviously, it would satisfy our curiosity. We can know of a certainty that the Bible told us enough. Barely enough; but enough.

What we do (1) know and (2) can glean from the scriptures is that:
1.   He was born in meager circumstances.
2.   There were several unusual events of a divine nature surrounding his birth and the period immediately following.
3.   He got lost once and worried his parents.
4.   He astounded the religious leaders by asking profound questions.
5.   He lived for a brief time in Egypt.
6.   He most likely played around his earthly father's carpenter shop. Later on, he probably worked with his father, perhaps for several years.

Beyond these rather skimpy biblical details, there is nothing else we know or that we need to know. We can suppose, assume, or imagine a lot. We can even wonder if John had reference to anything that happened in this early time frame, when he says that even the world itself could not contain the books that should be written. Maybe so. Maybe not.

Here are some interesting points to ponder:
Were his parents neglectful when he got lost?
Did people talk behind his back about his questionable family background, his mother's unusual pregnancy?
Did they share with him the beautiful stories about his birth, the visitors from far away, about the time in Egypt, etc.?
Did he exhibit divine traits early on?

The point in bringing these questions up is of little value. If we had the answers, while interesting to some, they wouldn't make any difference. Eventually, Jesus would say, "It is finished," indicating that everything He was to have done had indeed been completed.

This childhood of the Christ-child isn't really all that different than what routinely happens today. In adulthood, the emphasis is on the person as a man, i.e. what the man has done, accomplished as a man. When an individual becomes a CEO, doctor, attorney, minister, president, few people dwell very much on the early years of childhood or adolescent. Except perhaps the media. Some reporters thrive on minute background trivia and especially any negatives. Can't you just hear a reporter question: how can you, Jesus, the son of a carpenter think you have the right to lead the Jewish people? Do you have the credentials to be a Messiah? Did the philosophers of Egypt influence your thinking, when you lived there as a young child? Don't you think you should stop your followers from calling you Rabbi or Master, until your credentials are thoroughly investigated? Hey Jesus, don't you think you are getting carried away with all this love stuff you preach? Have you cleared it with the synagogue leader? Has Pontius Pilate approved the selection of your 12 apostles? Haven't you stepped out of line by recruiting non-Jewish followers? Have you ever tasted wine or inhaled Turkish tobacco?

With all the acquired wisdom of knowledge or experience of hindsight, what we can say of the young child, Jesus is: that his birth and life fulfilled a number of Old Testament prophesies; that he obviously had the blessings and anointing of God on his childhood and that he faced a very unusual /demanding/controversial/challenging earthly career that, although short-lived, would be blessedly successful, before relocating via a spectacular departure to a "higher position" and a very, very, very, long future.

A glorious, never-to-end, future.

THE LIGHT AND EASY YOKE
(ONLY IF YOU ARE PROPERLY YOKED)

In this day and age, it is kind of hard to relate to a "yoke" much less being hitched up to one. The word has pretty much passed from usage. At least, popular usage. There are several very interesting scriptures that speak on different aspects of being yoked together.

Jesus tells us to take His yoke and learn from Him　(Matthew 11:20)

Galatians speaks to the value of our liberty and freedom and tells us to beware of yokes that entangle us into a yoke of bondage (Galatians 5:1)

Paul told Timothy (and us) about the "tough yoked" i.e., being a *slave* and having to wear a yoke. (I Timothy 6:1)

As I reflect back on my rather long life, I can recall some times when I was "yoked" to some very tough unpleasant circumstances and situations. In fact, I've also been yoked with some pretty bad fellow humans. Like a half way decent coworker that I enjoyed for about the first 3 to 5 minutes of each workday. Then he turned unpleasant, sour, depressing, bitter and dismal. To him, anything, and every subject under the sun became bombarded and poly-pessimistically saturated with negatives. Now, in all fairness to this unhappy, sour individual, he did not necessarily mean to direct all of his misery to me. But since we were yoked together in rather close proximity, I had little choice but, against my best efforts, to become absorbed with his pathetic misery. I soaked up this dismal misery via osmosis during an eight-hour workday, minus the first 3 to 5 minutes, I mentioned earlier.

At times I've been yoked to a not-so-happy neighbor who tended to spread his mental germs on me, even to the point that my nearly-always overly optimist bubbly personality became tainted. Usually, bubbles are nice and pretty. But I've seen big bubbles erupt out of contaminated wastewater. And probably the worst of the worst is that I was once yoked for 3 years, two weeks and 5 ½ hours to a dictatorial, fire-breathing boss. Make that capital "B" Boss who constantly foamed

Theory" X" intimidation and spewed ever present profanity. Therefore, I was yoked with this spewing volcano all day long and in my nightmares from whence I could not escape "it"? This monster, made Louie on the TV "Taxi" program seem like Dale Carnegie. I kid thee not! Talk about a yoke, this was no joke. (Rhyme intentional)

Now I bet all you readers can begin to get the picture and now cite your own real life example of an odious yoking together.

Perhaps by now we are all wondering, what in the world all of this has to do in a so-called "religious book?" What is the point?

The points (plural) are as follows and you already know them but tried not to let them jump so obviously in front of you. But first, let's have a theological agreement: did not Jesus say "take my yoke upon you .   learn of me." Note: "He" has offered to be yoked to these, our fellow yoke-buddies <u>all</u> the time. We at least get some relief and respite.

Finally, here are the points to remember when you are captive and unpleasantly yoked in misery and agony of despair:

1. Become salt and rub off on them. (You are certainly close enough.)

2. Become a light set on; in this case, a nearby hill and shine, shine, shine.

3. Pray for them, as instructed by the Good Book, because this fellow yoke buddy is surely persecuting you, in addition to doing all sort of spitefulness, using and abusing you.

4. After you've done a lot of number 1 through 3, you are closer to being prepared to *influence* them, via semi-preaching, telling them "parables" and doing some pseudo counseling. Look on the positive side: You've got a ready-made captive audience.

5. Pray together. (Yes, you read that correctly). Pray (out loud) for them. But first, sometime when the two of you are private or semi-alone, ask if you "might have a prayer together?" Then, before they can answer (or faint) begin

to pray aloud (softly of course). And by the way, overcome the strong temptation to *preach* to them during the prayer.

6. Perhaps, I should have put this instruction as number one. Throughout this yoking ordeal try very hard to show (1) love and (2) patience, and (3) joy. Every day before you go to work read Galatians 5:22 and then repeat the verse throughout the long day.

7. Think of it this way: God has yoked you to a mission field. Most missionaries must travel half way across the world to work in their assigned field. Piece of cake!

Behold, I have saved the most important point until *last*. However, this is the key point and becomes absolutely vital as your *preparation,* before you even dare think of being yoked as described above, make sure that you have first served your own apprenticeship in Yokeology 101 as described in the verse below.

Jesus said: **"Take my yoke upon you and learn from me, for I am gentle and lowly in heart and you will find rest for your souls. For my yoke is easy and my burden is light."** (Matthew 11:29, 30)